COLLECTED ESSAYS ON 101 ART WORKS

from the permanent collections of
the Wichita Art Museum

by
Howard E. Wooden
Director

Wichita Art Museum
Wichita, Kansas
1988

Published by the Wichita Art Museum
Printed by Rand Publishing Company, Wichita, Kansas

Library of Congress Catalogue Card Number: 88-51543
ISBN: 0-939324-39-3

Cover Photo: Richard Anuszkiewicz, *WAM '77,* acrylic on canvas, 1977.

Back Cover Photo: View of Wichita Art Museum building, Edward Larrabee Barnes Architect, 1976-77.

To my Wife

(Height precedes width for all dimensions.)

Photographs by Henry A. Nelson, staff photographer.

This book consists of a collection of essays dealing with 101 art works acquired for the permanent collection of the Wichita Art Museum during the years since 1975. That was the year when the building program for the new Museum was undertaken and when a special art acquisition project was initiated. Those art works acquired must of course be viewed against the broader content of the Museum's otherwise vast collection of American sculpture and painting. It is only then that relevance in supplying continuity within the total collection will be fully appreciated.

What is of special interest is that at the onset of the program, the objective of widely expanding the collection was conceptualized as an integral aspect of the planning of a new Wichita Art Museum building. And throughout the months of construction and thereafter down to the present, more than 1,600 art works have been acquired, all of which were selected specifically for the purpose of broadening the existing collection and of filling existing voids.

One hundred one of these acquisitions have been chosen for discussion in this publication. Ninety-one of these works are American paintings and sculptures. The remaining ten are among the many British watercolor drawings by major British artists of the 18th and 19th centuries. These were collected in recognition of the enormous debt owed British watercolorists by American painters. Moreover for an American collection of the calibre and magnitude of that in the holding of the Wichita Art Museum, a comparatively small group of carefully chosen British watercolors serves as excellent backdrop material for broadening the museum visitor's understanding of American art and its British heritage. In preparing all of the descriptive essays, an attempt has been made to briefly interpret aspects of the subject where appropriate and, more importantly, to examine certain essentials of compositional dynamics.

It has been a rare privilege and a most rewarding experience for me to have had the opportunity of being on hand throughout this exciting moment in the on-going expansion of the permanent collection of the Wichita Art Museum and I am deeply indebted to all those who have so willingly participated in making such growth possible through their generous donations of time, of purchase funds and of actual art works. There is no question but that the work of the Volunteer Alliance of the Friends of the Wichita Art Museum in generating funding has constituted the principal single force in making this acquisition program so successful. Indeed, it is the Volunteer group that conducts the various supportive activities and directs regular benefits and the annual membership drive, all in behalf of the Museum. And in so doing over the years, the Volunteers have amassed truly significant monetary income for use primarily for the art purchase program. In addition, there are many individuals who have been consistently supportive. And in that connection I most especially cite Mrs. Mildred Graves Weir of Kanahoe, Hawaii; the Trustees of the Paul Ross Charitable Trust of Wichita; Mr. & Mrs. S.O. Beren; Mr. & Mrs. George Ablah; and Mr. Philip Kassebaum and the Trustees of the Price R. and Flora A. Reid Foundation, among many others. I also express deep gratitude to Ms. Dorothy Dehner, Mr. & Mrs. Sam Dorsky, Mr. & Mrs. Sol Fishko, Mr. & Mrs. Lawrence Fleischman, Mr. & Mrs. Kurt Olden, Mr. & Mrs. Harvey Rambach, and Ms. Virginia Zabriskie, all of New York City. Of course, there are hundreds of individual donors who through their participation in Museum projects on a continuing basis have accomplished so very much in making the art acquisition program possible. To all of them I am indebted on behalf of our staff and board.

I am indebted also to the staff members of the Museum and most particularly to Lois Keene who suffered long hours of typing and retyping the various versions of scribbly copy for this publication, and to my former and now recently retired assistant, Mary Lee Archer, who was always on hand to flawlessly assist in every conceivable way. My warmest appreciation of course goes as always to my wife, Virginia Wooden, who with keen and discerning vision has been responsible for many fresh and helpful suggestions and for

selecting many of the most important works added to
this collection since the inauguration of the new
museum program in 1975.

H.E.W.
October, 1988

BENJAMIN WEST (1738-1820)

Abraham and Isaac Proceeding to Mt. Moriah
Oil on canvas, 1799
20¼'' x 29¼''

Various episodes derived from Old Testament as well as ancient Greek and Roman tales were popular themes in art from the late Middle Ages and Renaissance down into the 18th and early 19th centuries. Indeed, by the late 18th century, such themes were chosen largely for the purpose of offering moral instruction, and painting in this manner was generally known by the term History Painting.

The Pennsylvania-born artist, Benjamin West, was among the most prominent History Painters of the period. In this particular work executed by West in 1799 and titled *Abraham and Isaac Proceeding to Mt. Moriah,* a key moment in the Old Testament story is clearly depicted. Abraham, occupying the center of the composition, is shown as an old bearded patriarchal figure who, in answer to the Lord's bidding, leads his beloved son, Isaac, to sacrifice. The handle of the knife which Abraham will use in the sacrifice is revealed beneath his outstretched left arm that points along an upward sweeping path toward Mt. Moriah. Isaac, portrayed as a nude youth, carries on his back the wood for use at the sacrificial altar.

Of course, the story itself, as told in Genesis, 22:1-8, is a tale of God's method of testing Abraham's faith. But what is interesting here is the fact that Isaac, although an Old Testament figure, is actually portrayed as a classical Greek statue of a young Apollo, thus recalling West's enthusiasm for ancient art that he had come to know during his stay in Italy as a young artist. Such usage, of course, points up the Neoclassic interest of the period. Of greater significance, however, is the fact that the Old Testament story itself, as depicted here, contains images which are really in many respects prefigurations of New Testament themes. For example, the wood carried by Isaac is generally read as the prefiguration of the cross which Christ will bear on the road to Calvary. Similarly, Abraham's sacrifice of his son compares with God's sacrifice of His son Jesus through the crucifixion. And, though not depicted here, the climax of the story is the ultimate salvation of Isaac by virtue of the interception of the Lord's angel, thereby prefiguring Christian resurrection as taught in the New Testament. It is through such parallels that the story and the painting teach moral lessons, thus justifying the application of the term History Painting as understood in 18th century thought.

It is likely that this painting was commissioned by William Beckford for Fonthill Abbey, a neo-Gothic structure designed in 1796 and finished in 1807. Beckford's financial reverses in 1823 resulted in the auction of the Fonthill art collection. Included in that sale was this painting by West. Two years later the structurally unsound Fonthill collapsed.

Benjamin West was born in Springfield, Pennsylvania, in 1738. He studied art in America as a youth but left for Italy in 1760 for three years of travel and study. In 1763, he went to England where he stayed for the remainder of his life. In 1765, he was a founding member of the Royal Academy of which Sir Joshua Reynolds was the first President. In 1772, West was appointed Historical Painter to King George III and on the death of Sir Joshua Reynolds in 1792, he was elected President of the Royal Academy. West died in London in 1820.

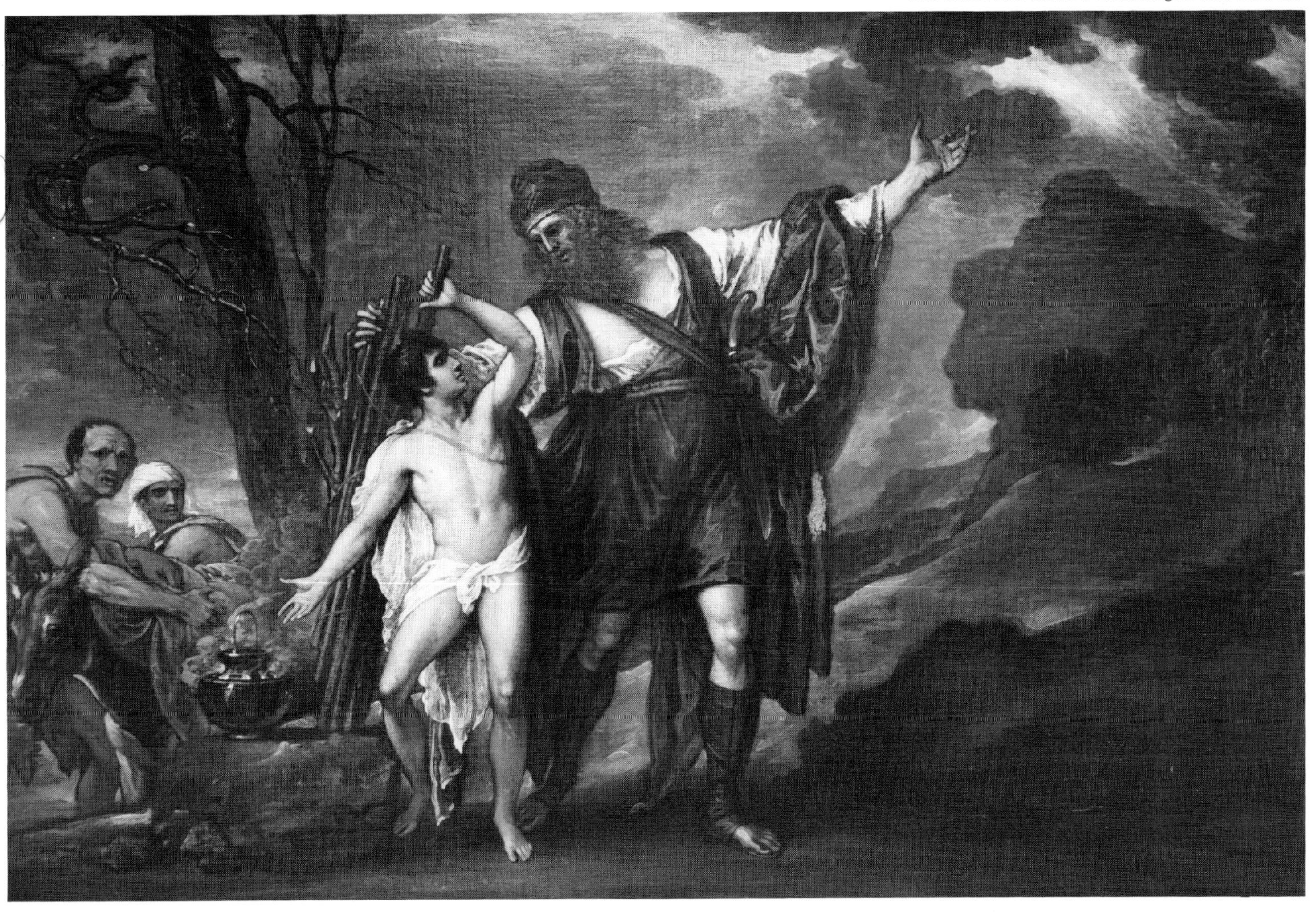

1975 Purchase, Friends of the Wichita Art Museum Art Fund
(1975.14)

THOMAS BIRCH (1779-1851)

Ship at Sea
Oil on canvas, 1802
31¹/₈" x 43¼"

With the growth of foreign commerce following the Revolutionary War and throughout the 19th century, marine views became popular subjects for American painters. Indeed, soon after the adoption of the U.S. Constitution, early Congressional legislation proved especially favorable to American shipping beginning with the Act of July 4, 1789, which allowed tariff duty discounts on foreign merchandise imported in American-owned vessels. And subsequent legislation throughout the late 18th and early 19th centuries offered further economic stimulation of American shipping.

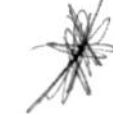

This work executed in 1802 by Thomas Birch and simply titled *Ship at Sea* is a portrait of an unidentified ship sailing across rough seas. In the background, a rocky coast is barely visible through the dense mist. At the far right of the composition, a small vessel can be seen sailing off in the distance. Dark threatening clouds suggest a brewing storm. Of particular interest is the precise treatment of detail and the convincing portrayal of movement, space and fluid water with cresting waves. Indeed, while this is one of Birch's earliest marine paintings, it is also one which clearly demonstrates both the technical control and the keen ability for careful observation which were to characterize his work throughout the mature years of his long and distinguished career.

Birch was born in London in 1779 but emigrated to the United States in 1794. For a time he worked as an engraver with his father, William Birch, whom he actively assisted in producing a well-known series of historical views of the City of Philadelphia. No doubt it was the busy port of Philadelphia which inspired him to paint marine subjects. And buyers of competent marine painting were readily available, for not only American painters but Americans as a whole were now becoming increasingly aware of the sea and of sailing ships with the steady growth of the merchant marine and the expanding prosperity resulting from the ship-building industry and re-expansion of maritime trade, a fact which certainly contributed to Birch's frequent interest in marine subject matter. However, Birch was also an accomplished and widely-recognized landscapist and portraitist and was elected president of the Pennsylvania Academy of Fine Arts. He died in 1851 at the age of 72 years.

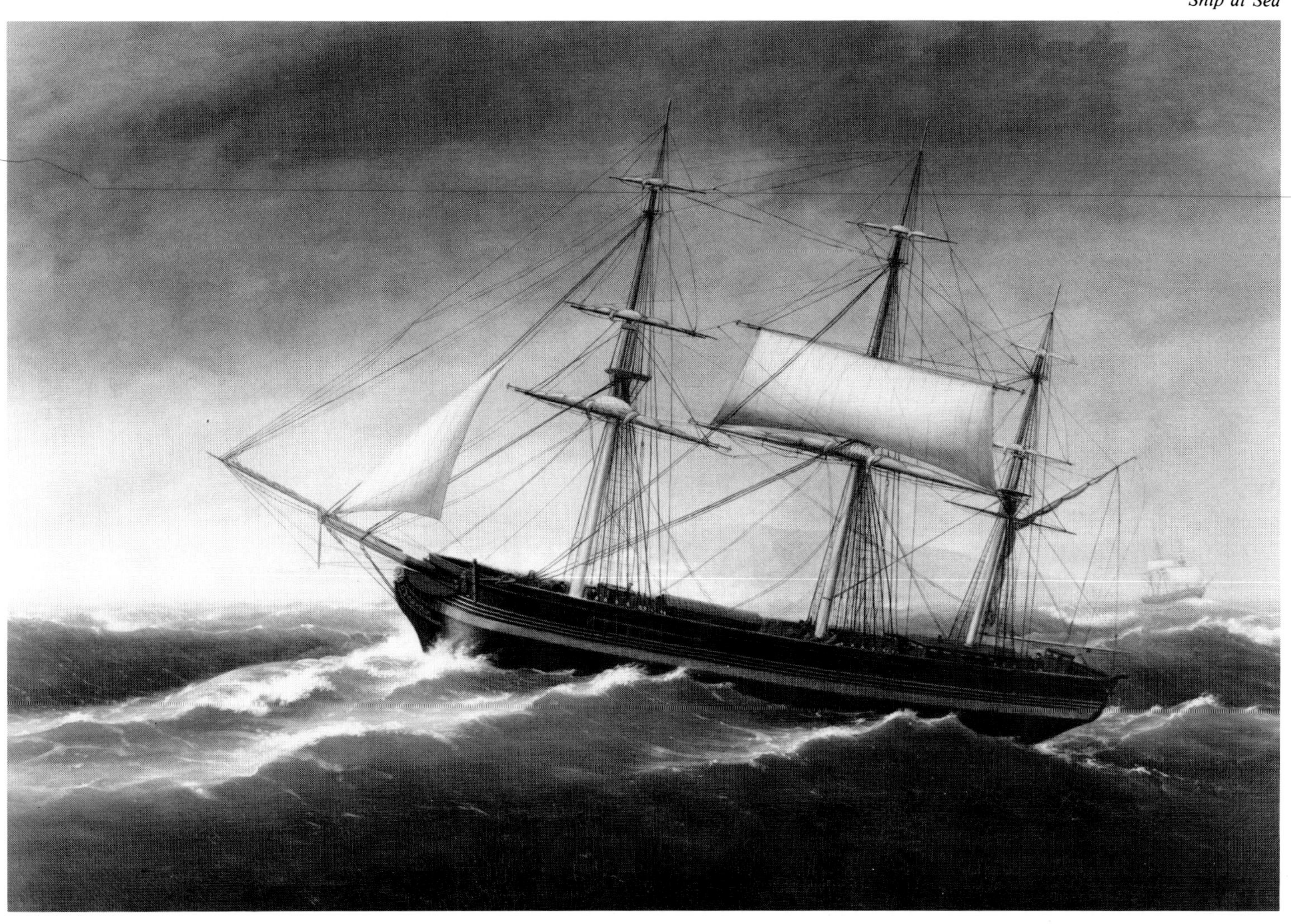

1981 Museum Purchase
(1978.101)

DAVID GILMOUR BLYTHE (1815-1865)

The Doctor's Night Caller
Oil on canvas, c.1850
25" x 30"

David Gilmour Blythe was one of America's important mid-19th century anecdotal painters. Although his personal life was filled with tragedy, his paintings were generally touched with a quality of amusing wit.

In this work titled *The Doctor's Night Caller* the moment depicted is a bleak and snowy winter night when a young and apparently excited boy has awakened a Doctor who, in robe and night cap, stands within his open door listening to the child's message. What the message is and whether the Doctor's response is one of alarm or of annoyance, we can only guess. Yet the arrangement of the two figures in the architectural setting and their expressive gestures help direct our attention on the narrative itself. Interest is further heightened by the concentration of intense light on the figures at the doorway and by the long and pointed diagonal shadows which lead the eye from the foreground to the figures themselves. And, although our attention by virtue of the strong pictorial devices used by the artist is prevented from straying from the narrative focus of the composition, the narrative itself remains as mysterious as the eerie stillness and the deep darkness which permeates the surrounding space of the composition.

Like many of America's early painters, Blythe was self-trained. He was born in 1815 near East Liverpool, Ohio and began his career as a carpenter. His own restless personality coupled with the tragedy of his wife's early death resulted in his wandering aimlessly from town to town and job to job throughout most of his adult life. Yet he was both a skillful and a prolific painter of satirical and witty anecdotal themes. The last 10 years of his life were spent primarily in Pittsburgh where, as an alcoholic and in poverty, he died in 1865 at the age of 50.

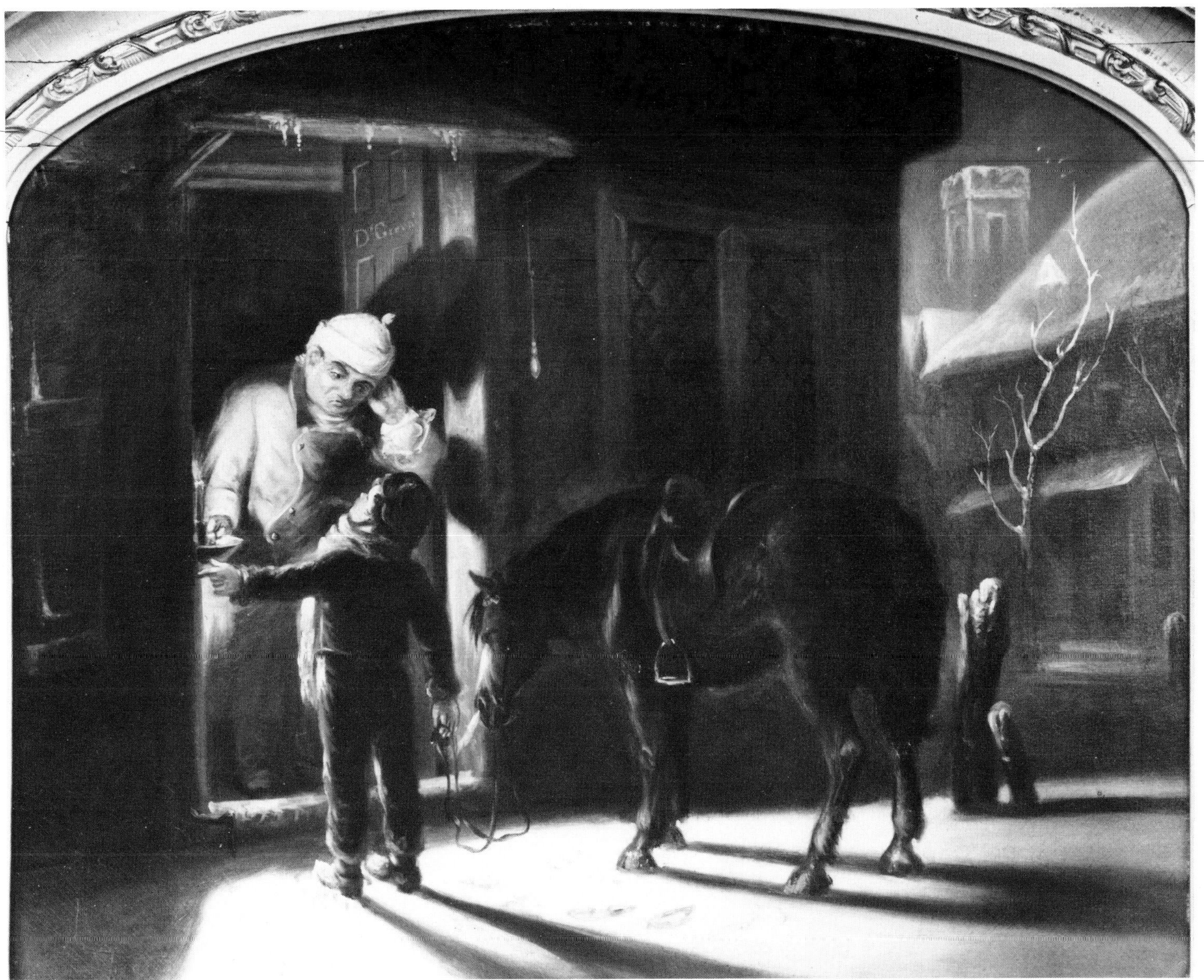

1977 Gift of Mr. Frank D. Stevens III
(1977.96)

DE WITT CLINTON BOUTELLE (1820-1884)

Beside Still Waters
Oil on canvas, 1852
33'' x 48''

The natural beauty of the American wilderness, the search for God in nature, and the fear that growing industrialization would inevitably create disharmony between man and nature were among the major concerns of a group of painters known today as the Hudson River School, active in the early and middle 19th century in America. Moved by these sentiments, many turned to the idyllic landscape, tranquil and uncorrupted, as the principal theme of their work.

One member of the school was DeWitt Clinton Boutelle, who executed this painting titled *Beside Still Waters* in 1852. Here, a winding stream, flanked by heavy clusters of luxuriant trees, carries the eye into the depths of the composition. In the far distance, a massive mountain range is almost consumed by the blue light which glows in the sky above. Near the foreground, a lone shepherd sits in quiet contemplation along the water's edge, disturbed by nothing but the sound of the stream and the slight movement of his sheep nearby. The title of the work obviously derives from the 23rd Psalm.

DeWitt Clinton Boutelle was born in Troy, New York in 1820 and as a youthful painter was much influenced by Thomas Cole and A.B. Durand, the leading exponents of the Hudson River philosophy. Although he painted in New York and in Philadelphia, Boutelle ultimately settled in Bethlehem, Pennsylvania where he established his house and studio and where he died in 1884. He was a member of the Pennsylvania Academy of Fine Arts and was elected an associate to the National Academy in 1853, the year following the completion of this work.

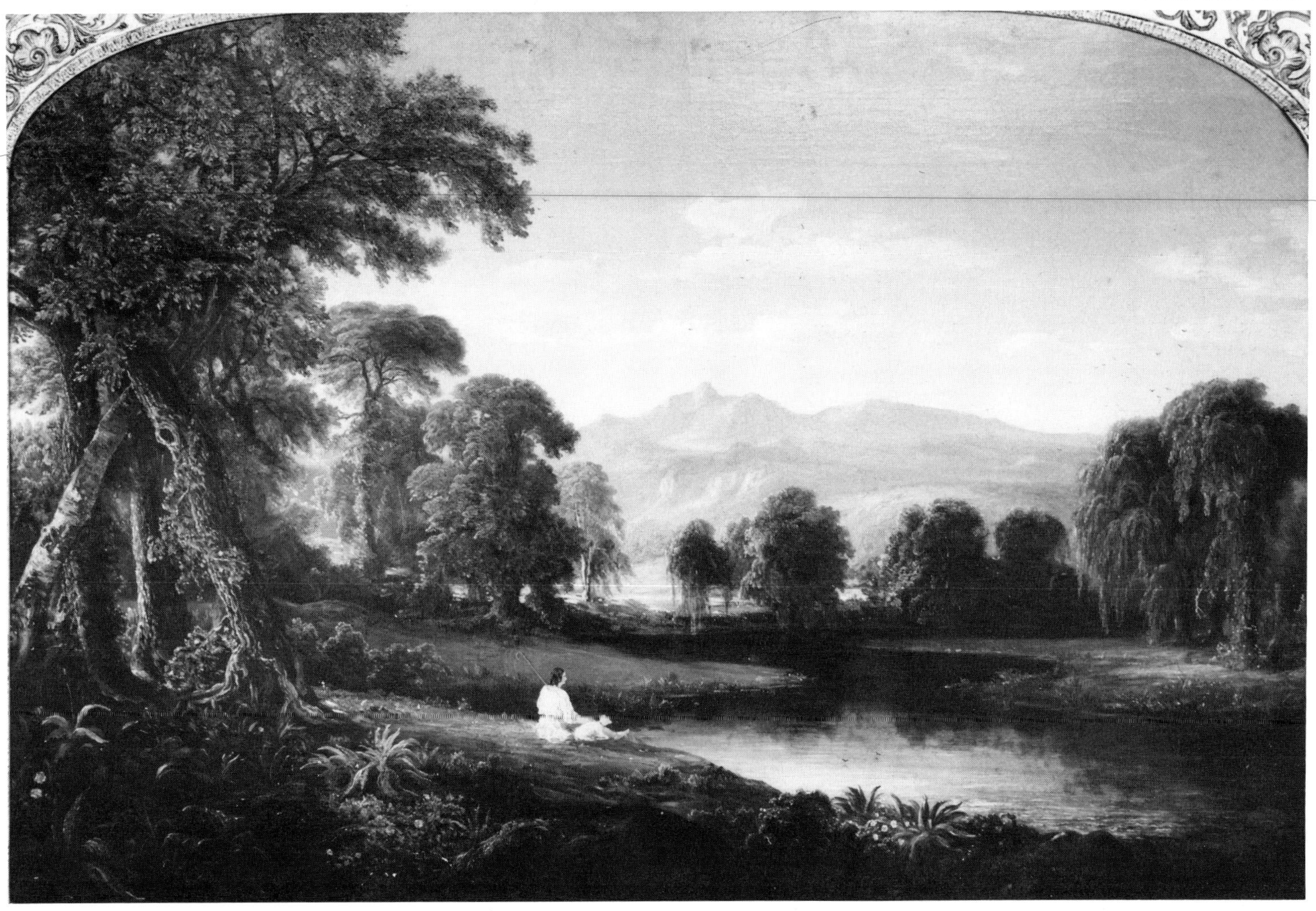

1977 Museum Purchase, Gift of Metropolitan Arts Board
(1977.98)

GEORGE LORING BROWN (1814-1889)

Near Sunset: View of Rome
Oil on canvas, 1857
32¾'' x 53⅛''

George Loring Brown was one of America's most prominent 19th century expatriate painters. Early in his career he made a brief visit to Europe where he first became acquainted with the works of the 17th century French master, Claude Lorraine, whose landscapes remained a life-long source of inspiration to Brown. In 1839, when he was only 25 years of age, he left America for Italy where he painted extensively throughout the ensuing 20 years. It was in 1857 that he executed this very handsome work titled *Near Sunset: View of Rome*. Although the painting itself depicts a European site, those features conventionally found in 19th century American landscapes are clearly in evidence, including the tall dominant tree right of center, the bushes and smaller trees scattered in and near the foreground, a tree stump in the right foreground with grazing cattle nearby and an all-encompassing atmospheric quality throughout the composition that lends pictorial reality to the romantically luminous sky overhead.

Here Brown, much in the manner of Claude Lorraine, has located all of the traditional compositional devices in such a way as to guide the eye into the distance along a zigzag path, focusing attention alternately on one side of the composition and then on the other, beginning with the dominant foreground tree at the right, then left to the tall slender tree along the edge of the dirt roadway, then to the cluster of bushes in the middle ground, then to the arched entrance of the bridge at the left, etc. Moreover, as the eye penetrates the successively receding planes of pictorial space, tonal intensity of forms correspondingly diminishes. Yet object definition is never entirely lost. Indeed, the composition presents a detailed and topographically accurate view of Rome looking south from the northern bend of the Tiber River toward Hadrian's Tomb and the dome of St. Peter's Basilica, both seen in the distant early evening mist. At the extreme left, in the foreground, is an ox cart at the base of what appears to be a terraced open-air restaurant sheltered by slender twisted vines. Slightly beyond, and spanning the Tiber, is the Milvian Bridge or Ponte Molle, which historically is of much special note as the site where, in a momentous battle in A.D. 312, Constantine the Great defeated the troops of Maxentius and thereby won the undisputed title of Emperor of Rome.

George Loring Brown was born in Boston in 1814. In his youth he worked as a woodengraver but, following the advice and encouragement of the American portraitist George P.A. Healy, he pursued a career in painting. Following his 20-year sojourn in Italy, he returned to America in 1859 and spent the remainder of his long and productive life working and exhibiting in Boston and New York. Brown died in Malden, Massachusetts in 1889 at the age of 75 years.

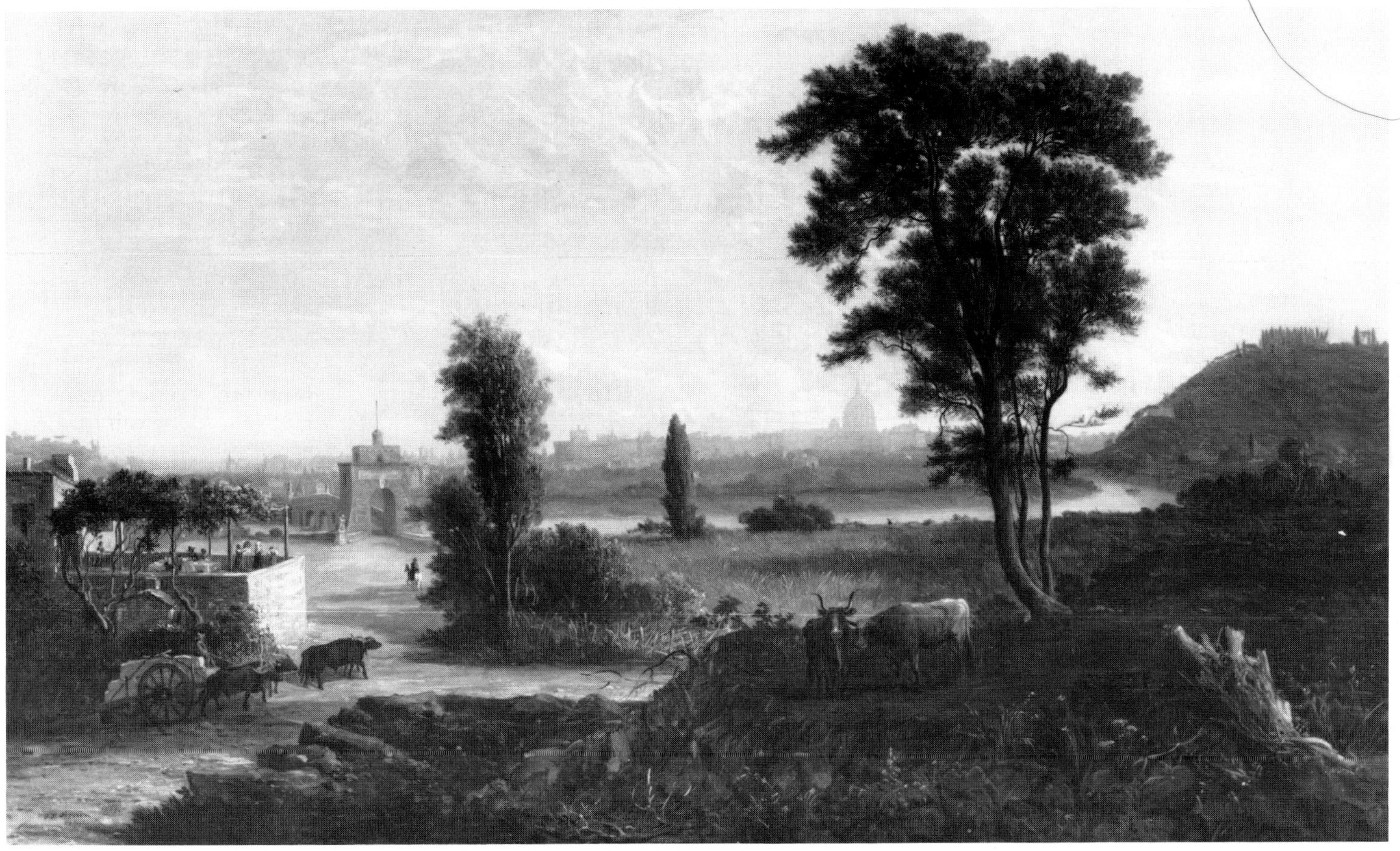

1988 Museum Purchase, Volunteer Operated Gift Shop Art Fund, Friends of the Wichita Art Museum
(1988.25)

WILLIAM SONNTAG (1822-1900)

Summer Landscape
Oil on linen, c. 1855-1860
37" x 54¼"

This summer landscape by the American artist William Sonntag was painted quite probably in upstate New York about 1855. Although the work itself is no doubt a faithful transcription of some particular site, the artist's primary objective was certainly not merely to record an exact geographic location. For, like other painters of the 19th century American landscape school, Sonntag poetically idealized the undisturbed rural setting and sought to create an image of the all-embracing beauty of the natural environment with its infinite variety of shapes, colors, textures and moods, all interwoven into an harmonious unity of life. Here the clear reflections from the still, silvery surface of the water, the cows peacefully standing along the river's edge, and the uncorrupted wilderness, mysteriously teeming with vital forces, yet strangely quiet, combine to evoke a mood of reverence and tranquil solitude.

Compositionally, spatial distance is organized in three rather sharply-defined zones, with the foreground occupied by distinct but dark forms, the middle ground by violet-toned and somewhat less distinct forms, and the background by forms that fade in the glowing light of the far distant sky. At the same time, the thick luxuriant growth of summer foliage rendered in heavy dark green masses at the right is effectively balanced at the left by the winding river which carries the eye past rocky cliffs and toward the distant and barely visible hill. Of particular interest is Sonntag's typical manner of applying tiny flicks of white and light yellow pigment along edges of the green leaves and the brown tree barks so as to create an impression of reflected speckled light.

William L. Sonntag was born near Pittsburgh, Pennsylvania, in 1822 but spent most of his youth and early adulthood in Cincinnati, Ohio, where he began his career as a painter. He was known primarily as a landscapist and, in 1862, was elected to full membership in the National Academy of Design. Rather little is known of his life except that he was married, that he visited Europe, especially Italy, in 1853 and 1855, and that he settled in New York about 1856 where he maintained a studio until his death in 1900.

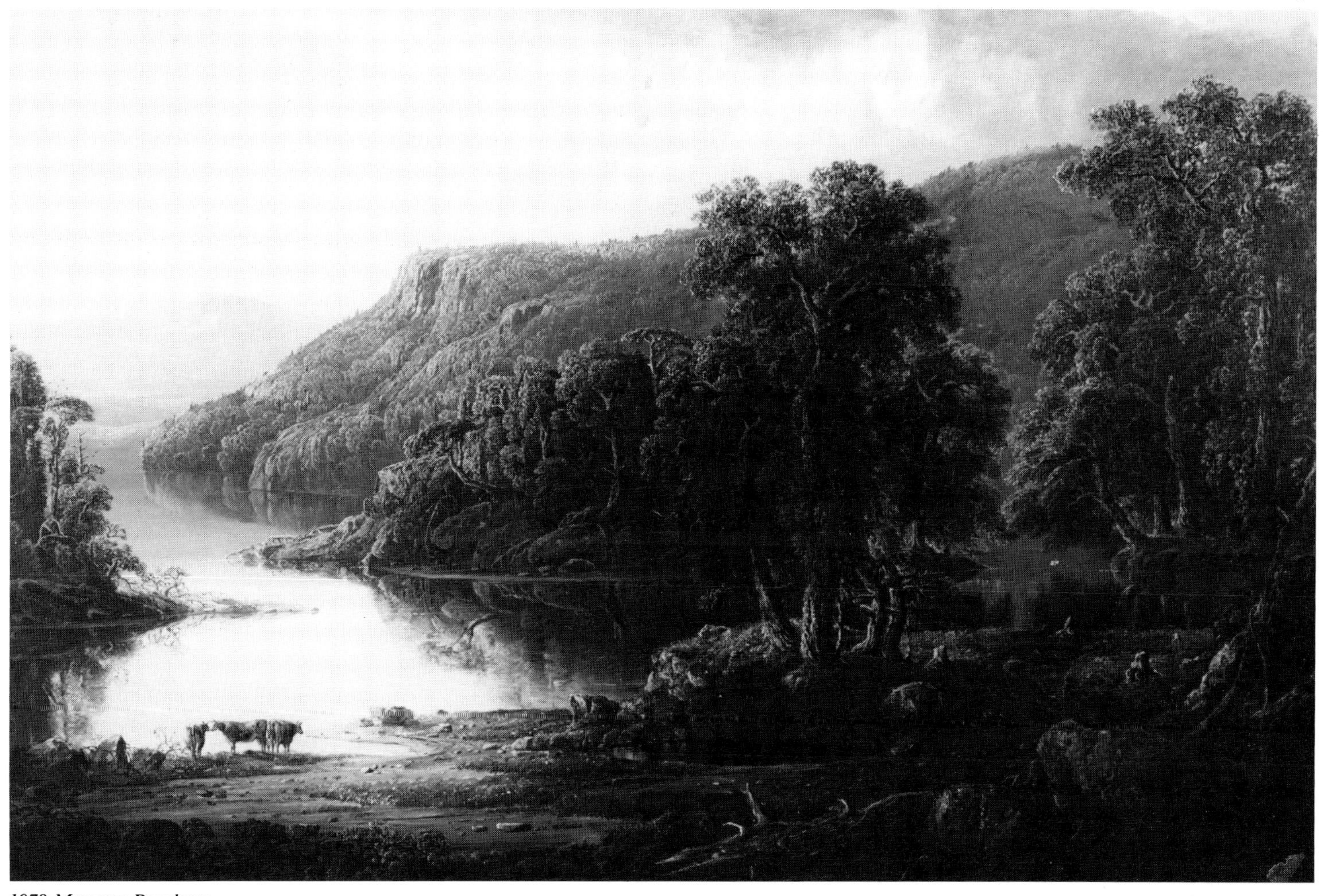

1978 Museum Purchase
(1978.90)

SEVERIN ROESEN (c.1815-1872)

Still Life with Fruits and Wine Glass
Oil on canvas, n.d.
16" x 20$^1/_8$"

One of the most prominent still life painters in America during the third quarter of the 19th century was the German born artist Severin Roesen. Little is known of Roesen's life though it appears that he was born in Germany, perhaps Cologne, quite early in the 19th century, that he was trained in Germany, that he settled in New York City most likely in 1848 when a large influx of German immigrants arrived here, and finally that he died in 1872.

Roesen gained much fame in America for his still life paintings of fruits and of flowers. In this small but elegant work simply titled *Still Life with Fruits and Wine Glass,* Roesen has painted a selection of fruits grouped together on what appears to be a slate or marble shelf. The format of the work is oval and the space of the composition appears to bulge with ripe and luscious fruits including a pear, peaches, strawberries, plums, a sliced half lemon and both purple and white grapes with sections of the grapevine branches showing leaves and tendrils. To supply a vertical accent to an otherwise essentially horizontal composition, Roesen has introduced near the edge of the shelf a tall conical wine glass containing bubbling champagne.

What is so important however is not the subject itself but rather the deceiving character of intense realism which the artist has so ably imparted to the composition by skillfully varying textures, employing multiple but harmonious colors and allowing light to play freely across all of the painted objects. The fuzz of the peach skins, the frosty sheen of the grapes, the scattered droplets of water on the surfaces of various fruits, the seeds of the berries, the crinkled leaves and the tiny bubbles of the champagne — all are handled with meticulous care and convince us that they do indeed exist as three-dimensional realities even though we know

they are merely painted forms. Moreover, the large cluster of white grapes is so painted as to appear to hang over the edge of the shallow shelf and seems to intrude into the real space which we as spectators occupy, thereby further intensifying the sense of reality of all elements of the composition.

Indeed Roesen accomplished what only a few American artists were able to achieve in their still life painting. For here we have a highly sophisticated statement of "trompe l'oeil", of tricking the eye — a technique for which Roesen was doubtlessly indebted to the 17th Century Dutch realist tradition which he very likely had come to know prior to settling in America. The final impact of the work is that we are momentarily led to believe that we can reach into the pictorial space through the open window of the picture frame and pluck one of the grapes, squeeze the lemon or even sip the champagne.

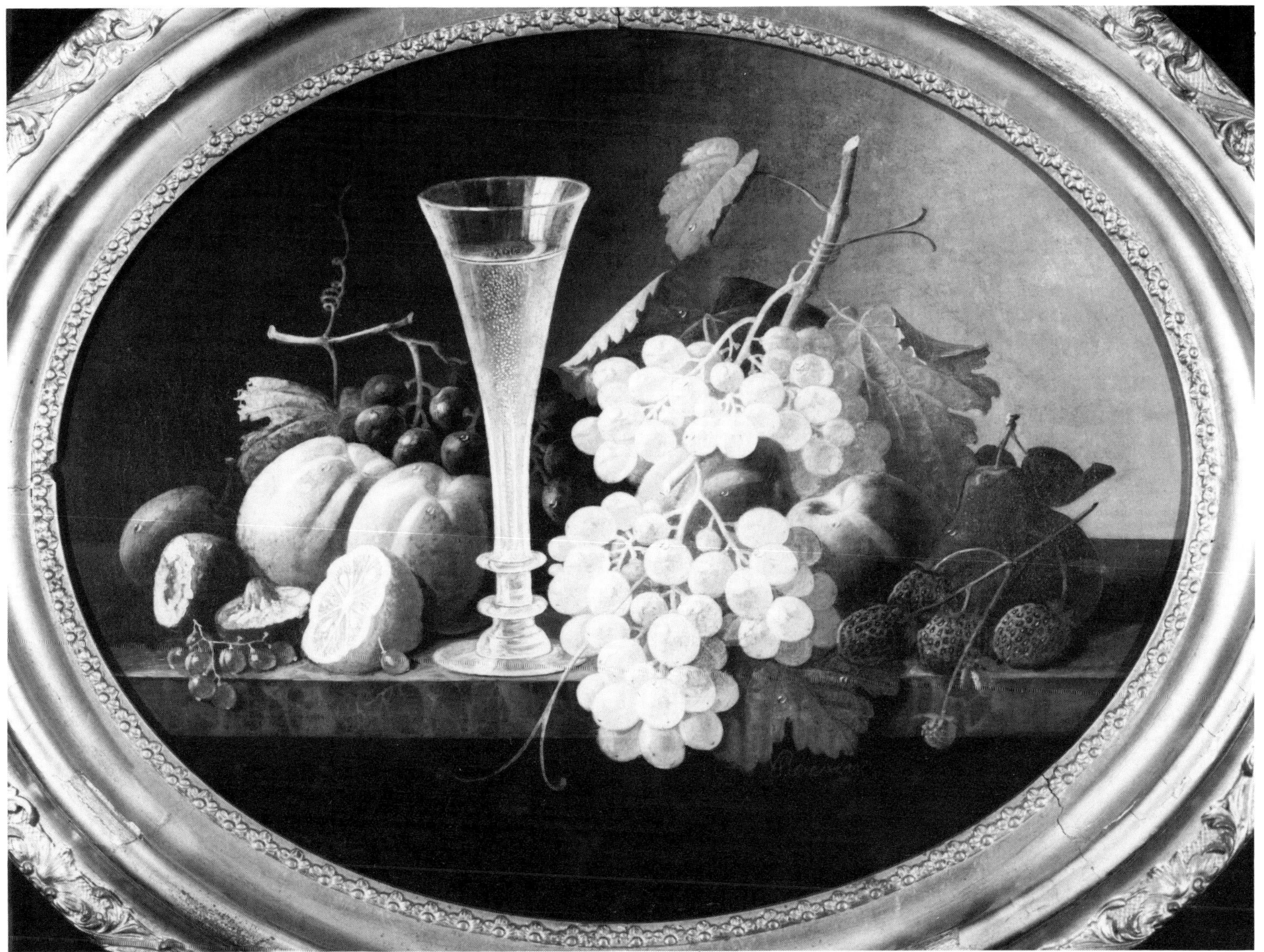

1985 Gift of Mr. George Vollmer in memory of Mrs. Lillian M. George
(1985.28)

JOHN GEORGE BROWN (1831-1913)

The Beggars
Oil on canvas, 1863
15¹/₈'' x 12¹/₈''

John George Brown was one of America's most capable and popular genre painters of the late 19th century. He was known especially for his perceptive portrayal of city street urchins — bootblacks, flower girls, newsboys and the like. In this charming little oil painting, executed in 1863 and titled *The Beggars,* the scene is a dreary street in New York. Two young and smiling street sweeps — one, a boy dressed in tattered brown trousers and jacket and the other, a girl in colorful but much over-sized hand-me-down garbs — momentarily pause from their menial chores to beg a handout from a newsboy who, reaching into his left pocket for a coin while winking at the pretty little girl at his side, gallantly obliges. His sense of self-confidence is suggested by his husky build, his sure-footed stance and the expression of authority and worldly pride on his face and in his gestures. He is obviously a man to be reckoned with: today a hard-working and prosperous newsboy, tomorrow perhaps a tycoon. The young beggars themselves servilely reach forward, but it is clear indeed which of the two he will choose to receive his philanthropy. In the background, to the left, lurks the shadowy figure of another boy beggar who, perhaps feeling unqualified to compete under the circumstances, walks off bewildered.

Although the anecdote depicted is amusing and strongly flavored with sentiment, there is much in this work that mirrors more fundamental aspects of American life during the second half of the 19th century. When this painting was executed, the Civil War was being waged, and advancing industrialization had already altered traditional values and was rapidly reshaping the lifestyle of the nation. Vast fortunes accompanied industrial growth, as inevitably did poverty, slums and child labor, especially in cities in the northeast. Such agitation as did exist against child labor was powerless in the face of the more widely accepted belief that labor builds character and that success is built on hard work. It is in these terms that Brown's paintings of street urchins were assured prolonged popularity.

Brown was of course an artist, not a social commentator. Yet by depicting the child as happy, healthy and well-adjusted to the slum conditions of 19th century industrial city life, Brown like other artists who painted similar subjects created an image through which he unwittingly contributed to the reinforcement of a myth that fostered the serious evil of child labor and child deprivation. Indeed wide acceptance of that image by Brown's many admirers effectively illustrates one way by which the age sought and found the psychological means of blinding itself to a reality in which it was deeply enmeshed.

J.G. Brown was born in England, quite probably in Durham, in 1831. He studied at the Edinburgh Academy, but as early as 1853 he had settled in New York where he continued study at the National Academy of Design. In 1863 — the same year in which he painted *The Beggars* — he was elected to full membership in the National Academy. Both the geometry and color of his compositions are carefully planned and in rendering the character, gestures and expressions of children he was excelled by perhaps no one. During his lifetime he exhibited frequently in major centers along the east coast. Brown died in New York in 1913.

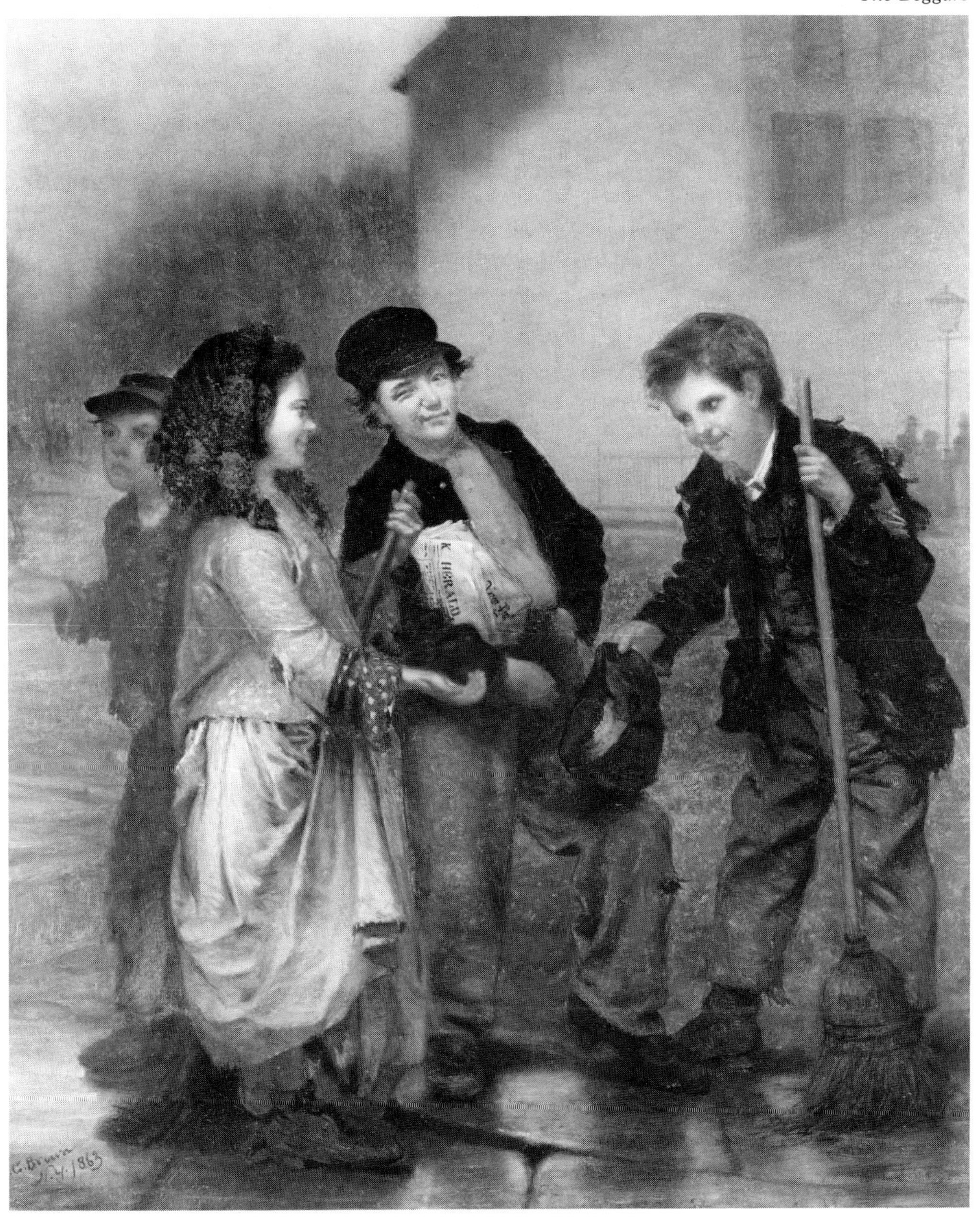

1978 Gift of Mr. & Mrs. George Ablah of Wichita
(1978.102)

R.A. BLAKELOCK (1847-1919)

Golden Autumn
Oil on canvas, c.1870
16¼'' x 24''

This mellow toned autumnal landscape appropriately titled *Golden Autumn* by Ralph A. Blakelock was executed about 1870 or shortly before and is typical of much of the finest work produced by Blakelock during the earlier years of his career. The setting might well be some location in the Adirondacks, and while the forms are fully representational, the painting itself is in no sense intended as a literal copy of any particular scene.

Here, the mood is quiet and peaceful. Figures of two fishermen are seen silhouetted against a dense forest and although small in scale are nevertheless compositionally prominent, since the artist has situated them in almost the exact geometric center of the painting. Of especial interest is the structural arrangement employed to create spatial illusion, here consisting of foreground, middle ground and background. In the foreground is a silvery gray stream with embankment and scattered rocks. In the middle ground, a stretch of trees and thick underbrush is seen, while a low and barely visible mountain range occupies the background. Yet, despite the three-part division, compositional unity is clearly achieved. For the eye quickly pierces into the depth, focusing on the two fishermen, while at the same time the waterfall in the middle ground trickles into the stream which flows gently into the foreground toward us. But of greater importance is the light which pervades the entire composition, tending to dissolve the background mountain forms and creating tiny silver toned flecks on the central mass of trees. Moreover the dashes of brightly vivid colors scattered throughout the composition effectively harmonize with the warm yellow-brown glow of light concentrated in the middle- and foreground.

It is significant that Blakelock should have selected such a relatively commonplace woodland setting, rather than a more grandiloquent scene such as characterized so many mid and late 19th century landscapes, thus setting himself apart from many of his contemporaries. Indeed, Blakelock was a self-educated artist, born in New York City in 1847. He was the son of a physician, and it was assumed that he would follow in his father's footsteps and pursue a career in the field of medicine. Instead he chose to be a painter and today is regarded as one of America's most visionary artists. Yet his life was tragic, for throughout his career he was cheated both by clients and by art dealers. And although he ultimately gained a widely respected reputation as a painter and was elected to the National Academy of Design in 1916, he spent the last twenty years of his life confined to a mental hospital and died just a few months after his release in 1919 at the age of 72 years.

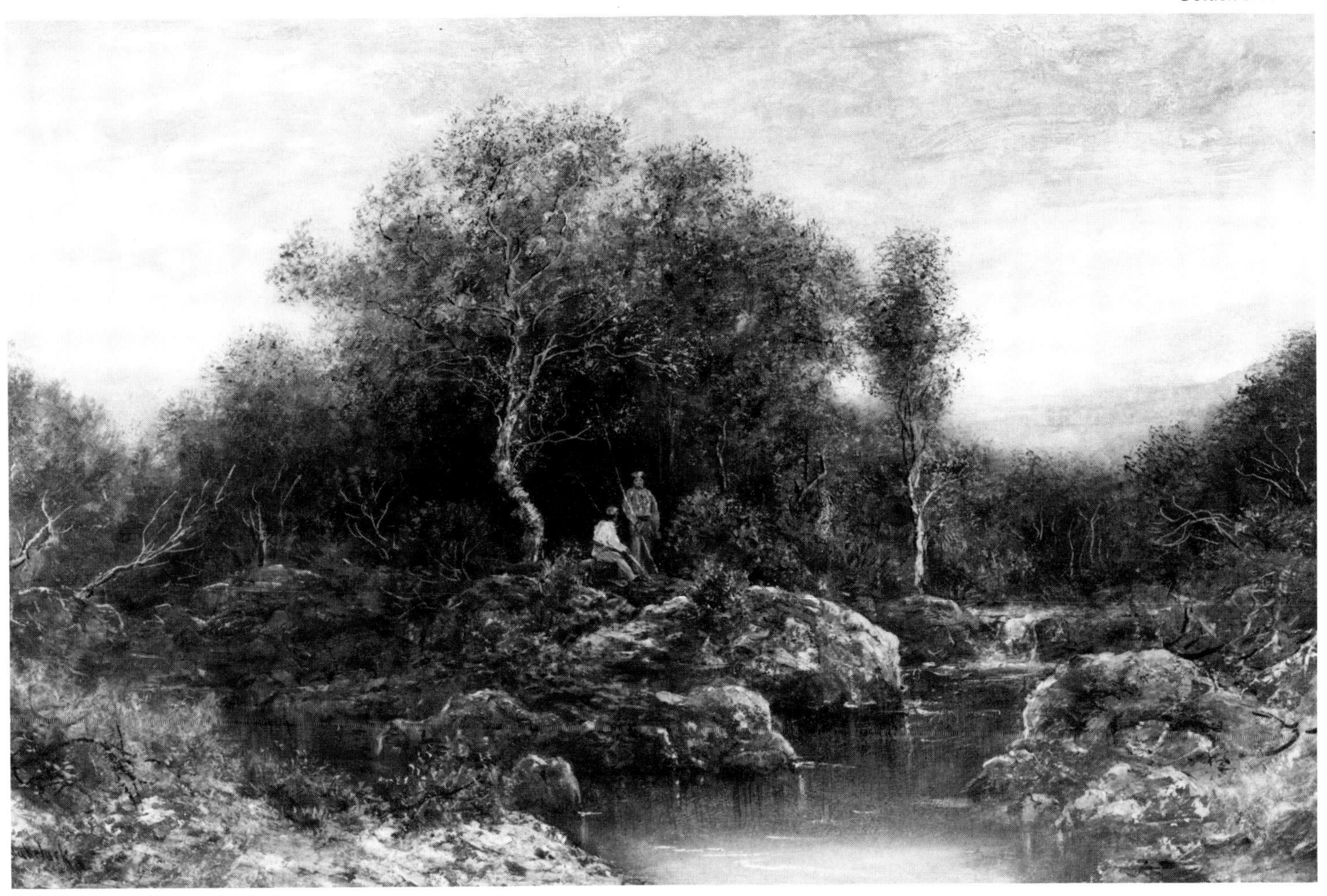

1980 Bequest of Mrs. A.L. Derby
(1980.79.1)

WILLIAM BRADFORD (1823-1892)

Midnight Sun, Labrador
Oil on canvas board, 1875
15½" x 23½"

During the 19th century, many American artists found a compelling fascination in adventurous travel to remote and sometimes largely unexplored lands where fresh experiences, exotic subject matter, strange natural forms and novel light and color effects served to excite their imaginations and ultimately to influence their art. This was certainly the case with William Bradford who throughout the 1860's made regular annual summer voyages to Newfoundland and the Arctic regions. There he found inspiration for many of his remarkable works including this superb painting titled *Midnight Sun, Labrador*. Bradford is known to have made careful firsthand drawings and completed some on-the-spot paintings during his travels. However, his paintings were generally executed in his studio where, following a rather common practice of the period, he relied heavily upon photographs taken during his numerous voyages. But Bradford did not copy directly from photographs. Instead he invented original compositions using photographs merely as sources of inspiration and of subject matter, or as he himself once stated, "...I gather my inspirations from my photographic subjects just as an author gains food from his library...."

The interest in meticulous detail and in incorporating local landmarks in *Midnight Sun, Labrador* would suggest that Bradford might have referred to photographs of the site when about 1875 he painted this handsome work. Yet the painting is more than simply a record of the physical features of Labrador for, from a compositional standpoint, just as significant is the carefully thought-out organization of harmoniously contrasting areas of light and dark. Here at the left a bold towering rock, somewhat reminiscent of the crumbling ruins of the castle fortress, is balanced by the light and comparatively open space at the right. And, from the coast in the frontal plane, the eye is carried diagonally along a narrow water inlet amidst scattered patches of dark rocks toward the luminous horizon seen in the far distance. There, attention is focused on the low sun surrounded by a hazy corona which floods the pictorial space with a strange spiritual glow, creating painterly passages of abstract color and color tones throughout the composition. Interest is heightened by the textural contrast between the rugged rocks and the frosted satin-like surface of the icy water, and by the juxtaposition of massive natural forms and the barely-visible human figures, fisherman shacks, and fishing boats. Indeed the dramatic tension established here between the eternally enduring quality of nature and the transient character of man and his physical creations — minute in scale but patiently rendered with factual precision — has strong religious overtones closely paralleling those expressed by Hudson River School painters throughout the several decades before Bradford executed this work. And this tension coupled with the eerie stillness of the scene and the pervading sense of timelessness and otherworld-ness together impart a surrealist mood to the composition which in a very real sense would seem to anticipate the works of more than one American artist of our own era.

William Bradford was born in Fairhaven, Massachusetts, in 1823. As a young man, following in the footsteps of his father, he operated a wholesale clothing business in New Bedford, Massachusetts. However, he was also a self-taught artist and, in 1857, he turned altogether from business to painting and for two years worked with the Dutch-born marine painter Albert Van Beest. In 1860 Bradford first exhibited at the National Academy and, in 1861, he took the first of his many visits to Labrador and the polar regions. In 1873 he published in England his well-known book titled *The Arctic Regions,* illustrated with original photographs taken on his numerous voyages, and was soon thereafter commissioned by Queen Victoria to execute a painting now in the Royal Collection in London. Bradford came to be the most prominent American painter of Arctic scenes but he also enjoyed a reputation as a photographer and lecturer. While on a lecture tour in New York City, he died in 1892, five days before his 69th birthday.

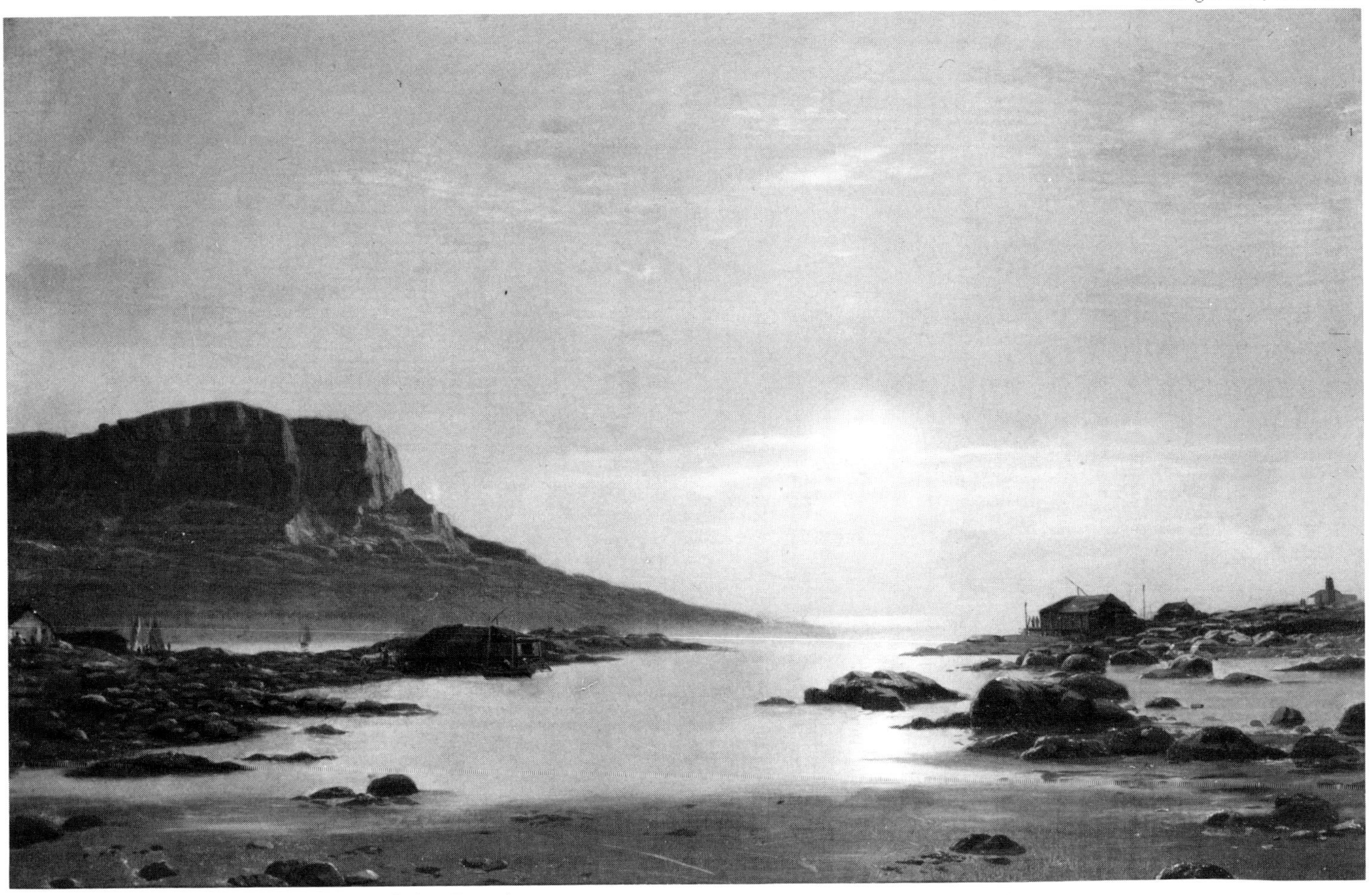

1978 Purchase, Paul Ross Charitable Foundation Donation
(1978.108)

FREDERIC REMINGTON (1861-1909)

The Bronco Buster
Cast bronze, brown patina, 1895
22¼" h., 19" w., 11¾" d.

Both in literature and in art, themes of the Wild West became increasingly popular at the close of the 19th century. By then life on the frontier was being radically transformed by the spread of industry across the continent. Fortunately many of the nation's most talented artists had traveled to the West and in time became absorbed in documenting that way of life which they recognized was rapidly fading away. Certainly one of the most competent, both as a sculptor and as a painter and draftsman, was Frederic S. Remington. *The Bronco Buster,* executed and copyrighted in 1895, was his first and indeed his most popular sculpture. Here, as in most of his works, Remington's conscious aim was to capture the authentic flavor of the Old West as he knew it.

Remington conceived this work as a 3-dimensional composition to be viewed from all directions, and his control over the material in which he worked is unquestionably one of his masterful achievements. The subject is treated in lucidly realistic terms with untiring attention given to the development of every detail, including the chaps, the stirrups, the crop, the spurs and the tooled leather saddle. But, in spite of the interest in detail, unity is not sacrificed and a quality of explosive power comes through clearly. Indeed, the exuberant forms of both the cowboy and the rearing horse are so skillfully articulated as to convey the impression of feverish energy, and the intent and earnest expression on the cowboy's face convincingly suggests unyielding determination.

Especially noteworthy is the dynamic equilibrium so dramatically achieved. For the composition is a complex system of thrusts and counterthrusts which link the forms of the cowboy and the horse and at the same time produce the net effect of precarious balance. In particular, the horse, sensitively poised on its hind legs, imparts a tenseness which reflects the precarious aspect of the action itself and calls to mind the turbulent age which is both literally and symbolically portrayed in this subject. With *Bronco Buster,* Remington invites the viewer to participate vicariously, if only momentarily, in the excitement of life in the Wild West.

Frederic Sackrider Remington was born in 1861 in Canton, New York. For a little more than a year, he attended the Yale Art School but, like C.M. Russell — that giant of the art of the Old West — he was otherwise a self-taught artist. He made his first trip to the West when he visited Montana in 1881. During the 1880's he traveled extensively throughout the West working on ranches and in mining towns where he gained first-hand knowledge of frontier life. In the course of his brief career, he received many commissions to paint and sketch western subjects which were published as illustrations in such popular magazines as *Harper's Weekly, Colliers,* and *Outing.* He exhibited frequently, won numerous awards, published many articles and several books and, in 1891, was elected an associate member of the National Academy of Design. Remington established residence in upstate New York in 1891 but, in 1909, he moved to Richfield, Connecticut, where he died six months later at the age of 48.

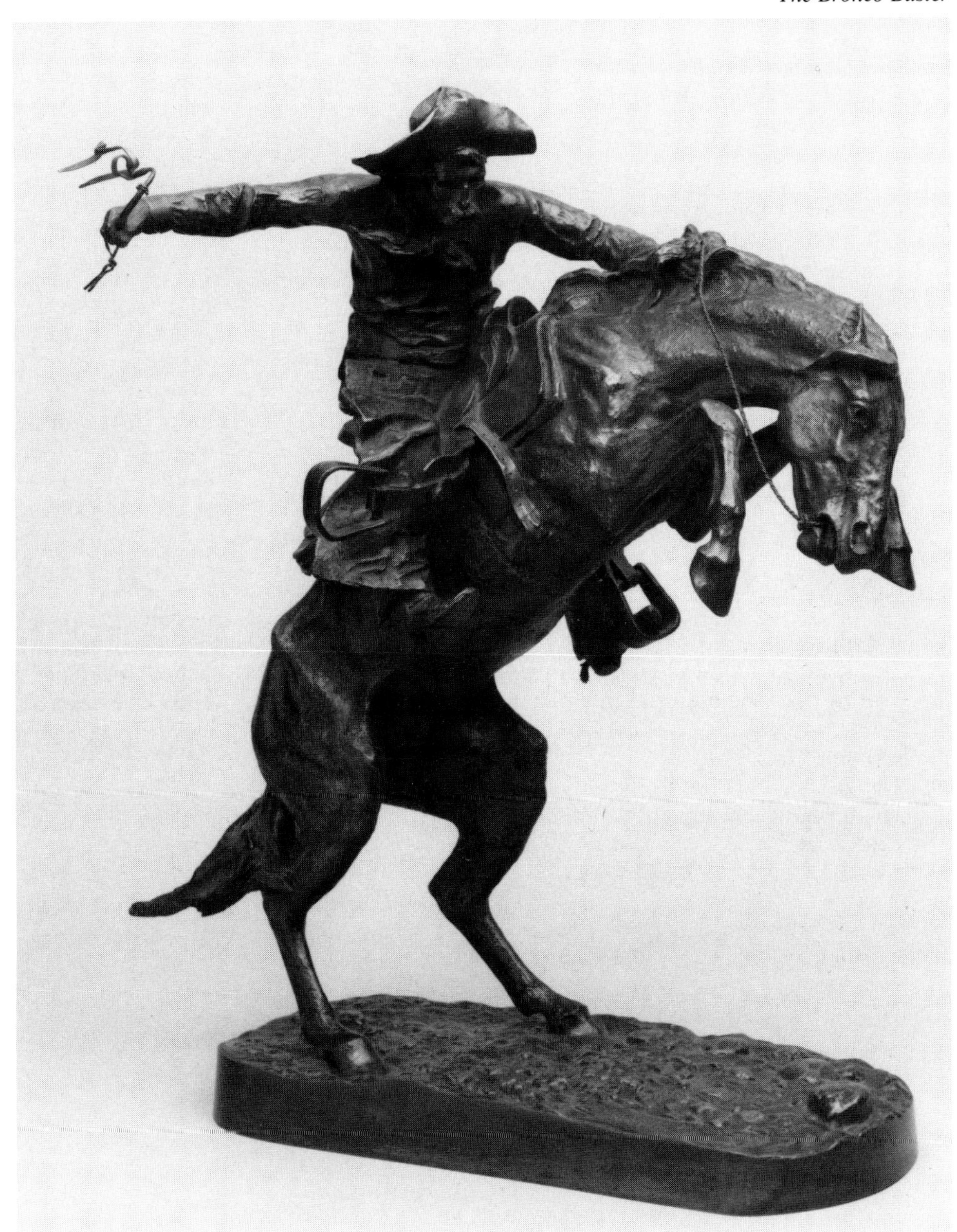

1979 Purchase, Mr. & Mrs. V. Richard Hoover of Wichita Donation
(1979.15)

WALTER LAUNT PALMER (1854-1932)

View of Venice from the Isle of St. George
Oil on canvas, 1882
36¹/₈" x 78"

For centuries, artists have been enchanted by the unique water-landscape of Venice and by the great mediaeval palaces and Renaissance churches situated along the Grand Canal. This rather monumental work, painted in 1882 by the American artist Walter Launt Palmer, is a panorama of the topography of Venice along the edge of the San Marco Canal as seen from the Isle of St. George. An all-encompassing glow unifies the open space and at the same time softens the majestic architectural forms in the distance. Yet near the left the famous domed church of Santa Maria della Salute can be distinguished, and visible at the extreme right are the Ducal Palace, St. Mark's Church and the tall campanile on St. Mark's Square.

The markedly horizontal format of the painting emphasizes the long low strip of land seen in the distance. Indeed, the composition itself is constructed essentially of two long horizontal bands: one of land and sky, the other of water. Yet this division is neutralized by a series of effective devices, as for example the subtly handled reflections of the architecture on the rippling water surface, the mirrored image of smoke rising from the barely visible tug boat at the left, and the fishing boat at the right whose bold and colorfully striped sail clearly reaches across the horizon line, visually linking the lower and upper registers.

Of special interest is the impact created by the high horizon line itself, for the continuous expanse of water between us and the horizon tends to pull us into the composition and toward the sun-drenched forms in the distance. In viewing this work, our eyes fall upon the sharply focused realism of the dark mass of heavy pilings and the rusted chain with sagging strands of wet seaweed in the immediate foreground. But our attention rests there only momentarily, for the pilings serve to introduce us to the scene and at the same time strengthen the implicit force which pulls us into the composition.

Walter Launt Palmer was born in Albany, New York, in 1854. He was the son of Erastus Dow Palmer, the noted mid-nineteenth century American sculptor. Walter Palmer studied in Paris. But far more influential on his development was the American landscapist Frederick E. Church under whom he had studied earlier for a period of approximately two years beginning in 1870. Throughout his career, Palmer was well-known for his many paintings of Venetian scenes and for his winter landscapes. He was the recipient of numerous awards both in America and in Europe. In 1877 he was elected to the National Academy of Design as an associate member and in 1897 as a full academician. Palmer died in Albany in 1932.

A point of special interest in viewing this object is the frame itself which apparently was considered an integral part of the total presentation. For in the center of the lower edge of the molding amidst the chain of hand-carved oak leaves the artist has carefully cut the word *Venezia;* and somewhat to the left is his monogram *WLP.*

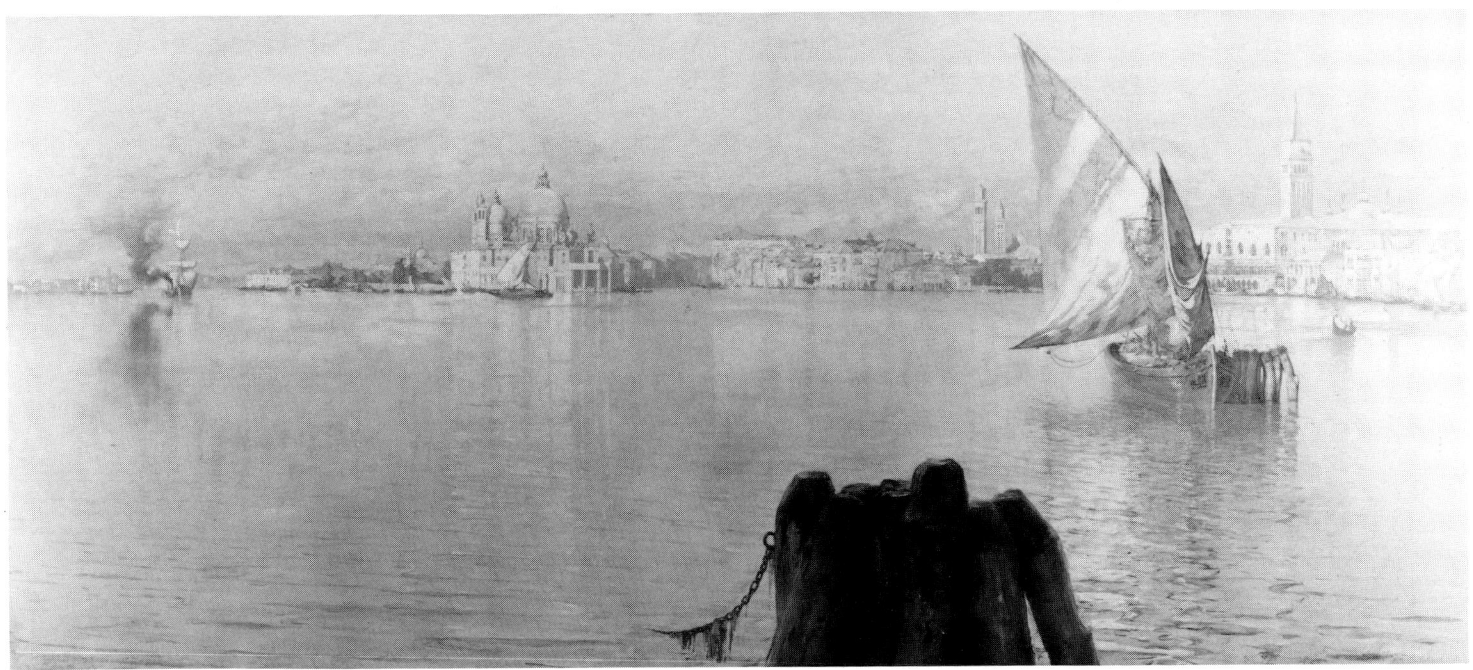

*1978 Donation by Mid Kansas Federal Savings & Loan Association in honor of Mr. & Mrs. Kenneth Brasted, Sr.
(1978.89)*

GEORGE HENRY BOUGHTON (1834-1905)

The Peacemaker
Oil on linen, 1883
27¾" x 51⁵/₈"

This painting titled *The Peacemaker* was executed by the American artist, George Henry Boughton in 1883. Boughton was primarily a landscape painter and the aesthetic interest of this piece lies largely in the refined handling of natural forms, the well organized composition and the convincing treatment of space. However, in accord with the characteristic sentiment of so many Victorian works of the period, the subject matter is concerned largely with moral teaching and in this specific instance with family unity. For here it would seem that a quarrel between the young farm wife, standing in the foreground, and her sulking husband seen at the left is being mended happily by the intervention of the country parish priest. The notion is further emphasized by what appears to be two olive branches, traditional peace symbols, which the young child in the foreground waves prominently before our eyes.

Boughton was born in 1834 in England, but at the age of three was brought to America and soon settled in Albany, New York where he studied art. At an early age, he gained wide popularity as a painter of landscapes. In 1861 when he was 27, he returned to England where he spent much of the remainder of his life. However, he was elected to the National Academy of Design in New York in 1871 and at the same time was granted membership in the Royal Academy in London. The painting for which he is best known is a work in the New York Historical Society and titled *Pilgrims Going to Church on Thanksgiving Morning* — a painting which for many years has appeared in every young school boy's and every school girl's American History book. Boughton died in London in 1905 at the age of seventy-one.

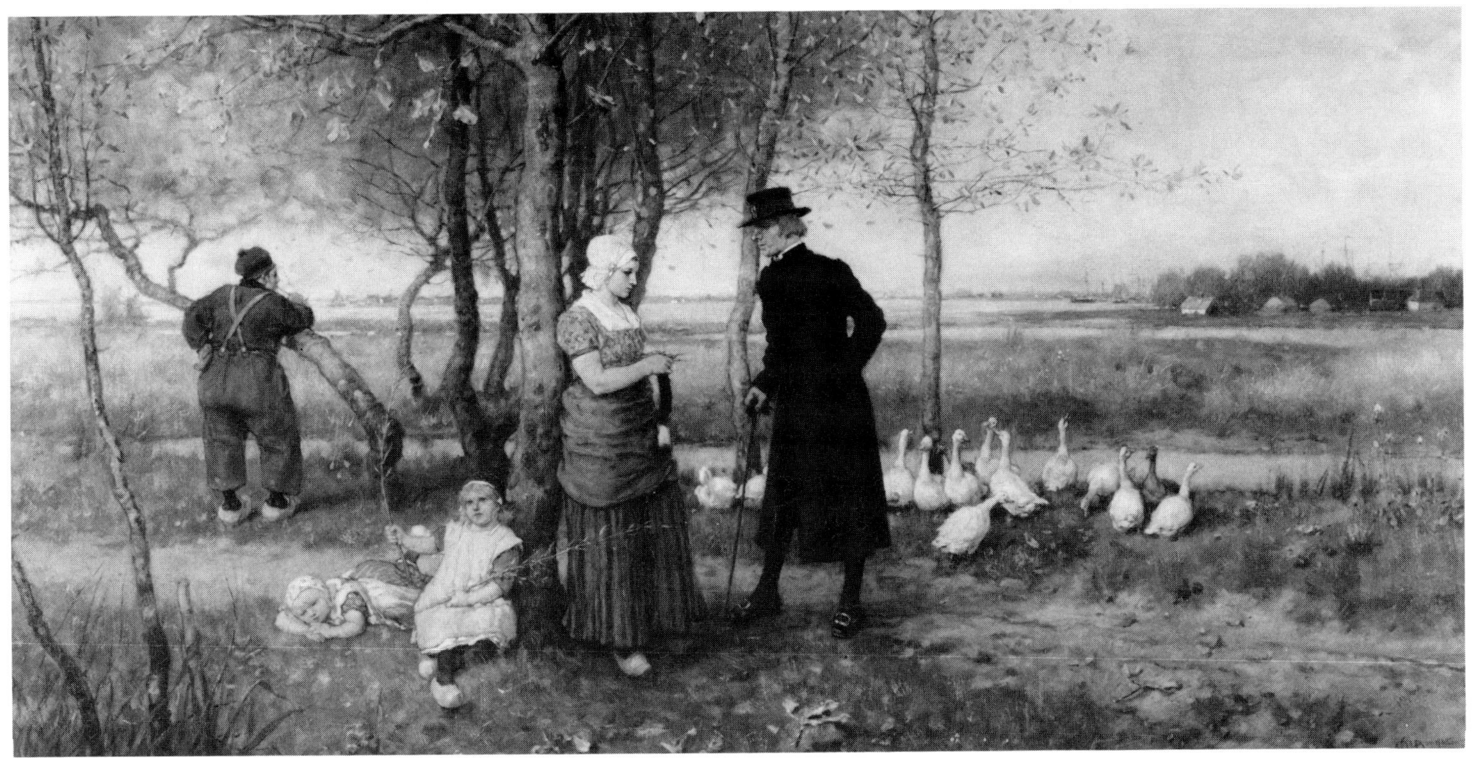

*1978 Donation by Mid Kansas Federal Savings & Loan Association in honor of Mr. & Mrs. Kenneth Brasted, Sr.
(1978.50)*

JOHN LA FARGE (1835-1910)

Autumn
Oil on canvas, 1882
55¼'' x 27¹/₈''

This large and commanding allegorical painting, titled *Autumn,* was executed by the noted 19th century American artist John LaFarge in 1882. Here, a young woman poses as she holds a large basket in which the fruits of the autumn harvest will be collected. The red-brown colors of her flowing robe which falls in deep and abundant folds coupled with the vividly rich but subtle tones in the background are appropriately employed to suggest both the mood and the color scheme of the autumn season.

Allegorical statements such as this are essentially foreign to the thought of America today. Yet a century ago when LaFarge painted this work, *Autumn,* such images were indeed popular not only as expressions of "high" culture for the homes of America's post-Civil War *nouveau riche* but also as designs for murals and large stained glass windows in churches, banks, schools, libraries and other public buildings. Like many other works of the period, *Autumn* typifies a tradition often known as the "Genteel Tradition" which found inspiration in early European sources. For not only the allegorical subject matter, but the painterly technique and the Baroque exuberance as well are quite typically European in derivation. Yet it was not the primary intent either of LaFarge or of other artists working in this manner to imitate simply for the sake of imitation but more importantly to discover, explore and transmit the heritage of the European past to American soil as a basis for elevating American taste and ultimately equipping American artists to develop a purely American style. In retrospect it becomes clear that an American art based on American imagery such as was produced by the Ash Can School at the turn of the century or the American Scene painters of the 1930s, did not emerge directly out of this Genteel Tradition but rather came about through a complete repudiation of that tradition. Nevertheless, the sophisticated approach implicit in Genteel Tradition paintings such as this work by LaFarge represents an important phase in the history of American painting and was a significant expression of one wing of American thought as the 19th century drew to a close.

John LaFarge was born in New York City of French ancestry in 1835. In 1856 he traveled to Europe. After returning to the States he studied painting under the American painter William Morris Hunt. In 1869 he was elected to the National Academy of Design and soon thereafter won much recognition as a pioneer in American mural painting and especially for works that he executed for the then recently completed Trinity Church in Boston. LaFarge also experimented in new techniques in the production of stained glass windows and executed some of the most important late 19th century murals in America including those at Bowdoin College in Brunswick, Maine; The Church of the Ascension, New York City; and the Court House in Baltimore, Maryland. It is interesting to note that LaFarge designed a massive stained glass window for the William H. Vanderbilt mansion in New York City about 1885 and used this painting as a model for one of the principal figures in that window.

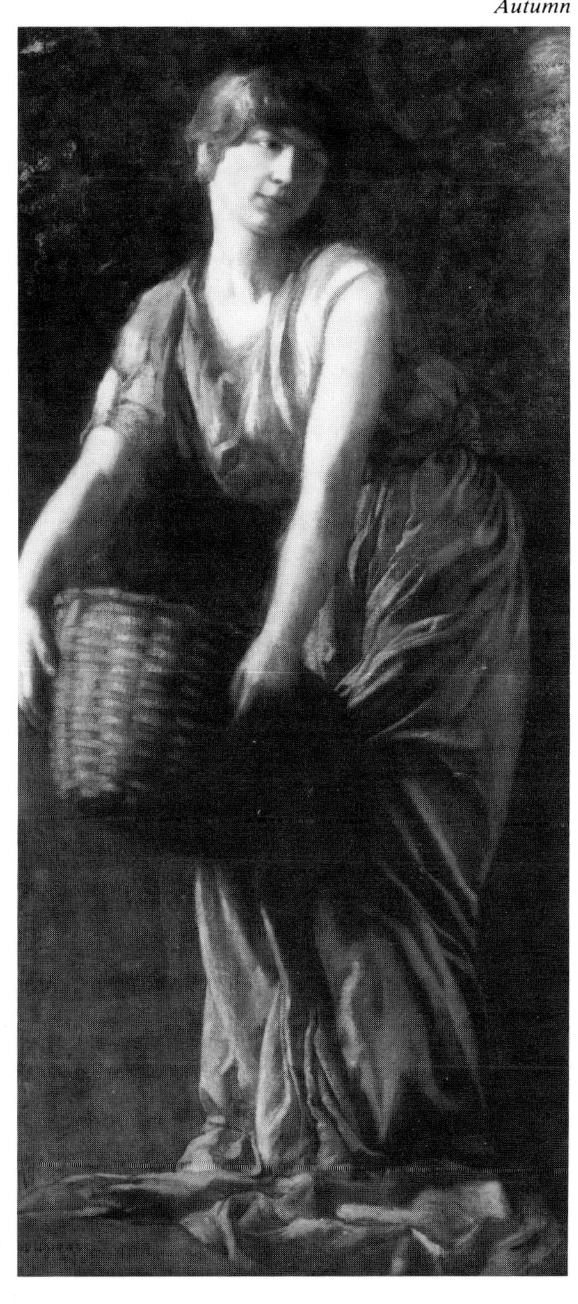

1982 Museum Purchase, Funds Donated by Vulcan Materials Company
(1982.5)

FRANCIS COATES JONES (1857-1932)

The Song
Oil on canvas, c.1905
24³/₈'' x 40³/₈''

Soon after 1900, such avant garde movements as American impressionism and ash-can realism were joining the mainstream of American painting. At the same time more conservative attitudes, rooted in the drastic social and economic changes that marked the decades following the Civil War, energetically sought to promote an image of America which could measure up to the level of refined taste typified by Old World standards. Both for subject themes and for styles, the conservative wing turned readily to ancient classical and Renaissance prototypes. With the first World War, however, that movement fell out of fashion. Only recently has it gained renewed attention by historians and critics of art who now see the period as an American Renaissance.

This handsome oil titled *The Song* executed by Francis Coates Jones no doubt soon after 1900 is a fine example of American Renaissance painting. Here, a beautiful young woman stands and holds a lyre in her left arm while singing or reciting before four young women who, seated on a marble bench, appear spellbound as they listen. All of the figures are garbed in classically inspired diaphanous chitons which fall gracefully in loose rhythmic folds. The setting is calmly serene and the scene brings to mind popular tales of Sappho, the ancient Greek poetess who is said to have devoted her life to instructing young women in poetry and music.

Technically, the work is handled with enviably meticulous refinement. Colors are vivid and throughout the composition textures are convincingly rendered, as for example the stone bench and marble tile floor, the feather fans and the quality of soft human flesh. A nearly opaque luxuriant green backdrop furnishes a flat decorative pattern against which the carefully modelled figures stand out in sharp silhouette. Yet, faint glimmers of light seep through the densely tangled green at the right, dispersing a delicate greenish tint across adjacent areas of the composition.

Of especial interest is the sense of classical design itself. For all of the figures are inscribed within a balanced triangular format with the head of the standing figure coinciding with the apex of the triangle. One side of that triangle is formed by the sloping line of the three figures on the right while the other side, extending well beyond the limits of the composition, is defined directionally by the right arm of the leaning figure at the extreme left. This geometric organization recalls the familiar arrangement of triangular pedimental sculptures found in ancient classical buildings. And indeed the three relaxed figures on the right — two leaning against each other and the third reclining — are compositionally reminiscent of a particular group of ancient marbles, the so-called ''Three Fates'' from the east pediment of the Parthenon, with which Jones was most certainly acquainted.

Francis Coates Jones was born in Baltimore, Maryland, in 1857 and was the brother of Hugh Bolton Jones, another well-known painter of the period. In 1876 he went to Paris to study at The Ecole des Beaux Arts for four years. In 1882 he settled in New York City. In 1885, Jones won the coveted Clark Medal at the National Academy of Design and became an associate of the National Academy. In 1894 he was elected full academician. Jones was the recipient of numerous art awards and served actively as a member of the Board of Directors of the American Academy at Rome and of the Metropolitan Museum of Art in New York and for more than 20 years was a trustee of the National Academy of Design, serving as Treasurer. He maintained his residence and studio in New York until his death at the age of 74 years in 1932.

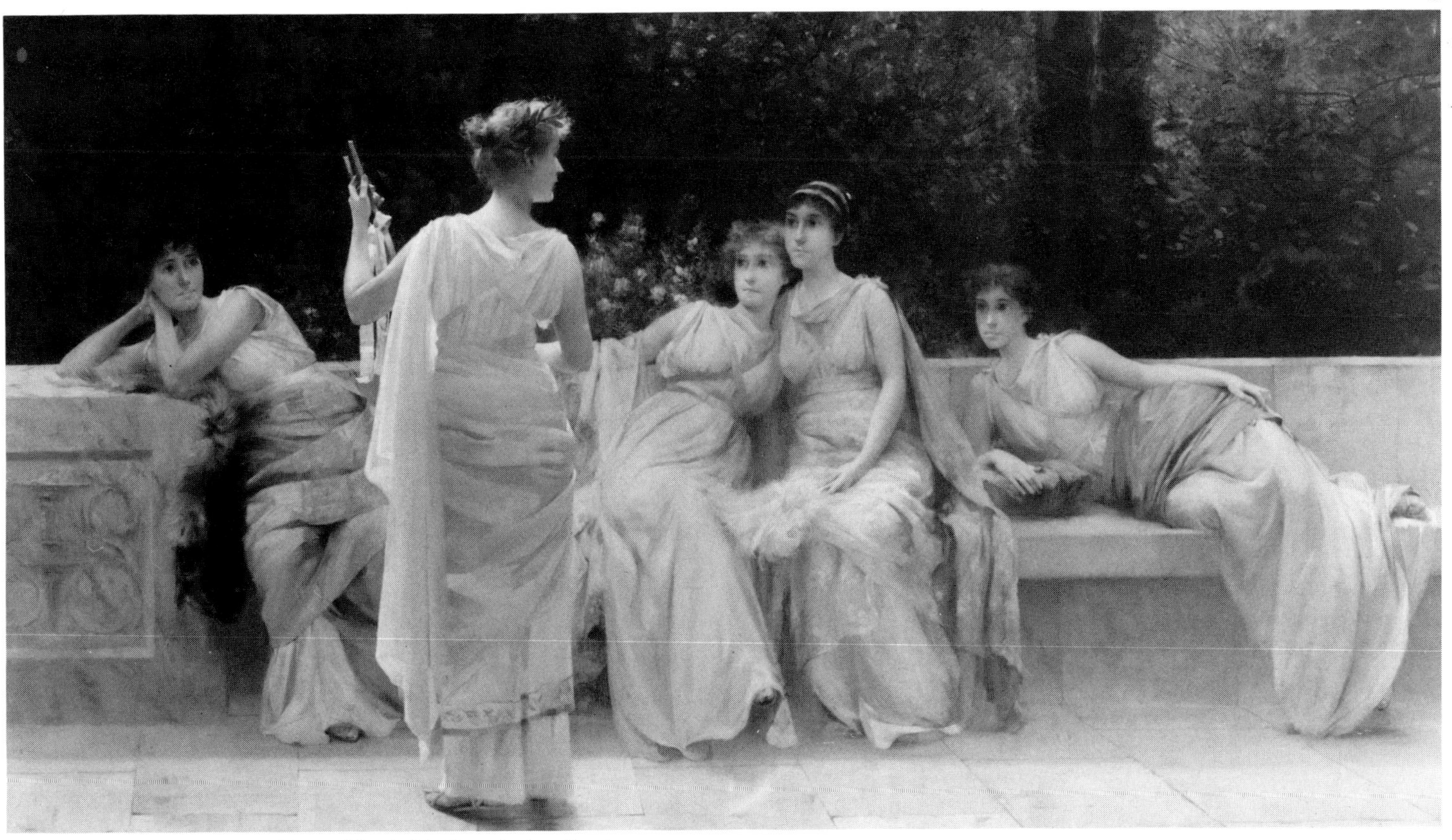

1979 Museum Purchase, Paul Ross Charitable Foundation Fund
(1979.55)

ADDISON T. MILLAR (1860-1913)

Venice from the Schiavoni Quai
Oil on canvas, c.1900
14¹/₈'' x 27⁵/₈''

Venice, the glorious city of reflections, serenades and romance, has captured the imagination of artists, both American and European, for many centuries. Indeed, few if any artists who have ever visited Venice have failed to record their personal impressions. And although all agree on its charm, no two interpret that charm in exactly the same way.

In this painting titled *Venice from the Schiavoni Quai* by the late 19th century American Addison T. Millar, the compositional structure guides the eye into pictorial depth. There we glimpse an early morning view of the mouth of the Grand Canal, bordered on the right by the stately Ducal Palace and the soaring bell tower of Saint Mark's Square, and on the left by the massive dome of Santa Maria della Salute, Venice's most famous church. Beyond are towers and the facades of typical Venetian palaces lining the canal as it winds into the distance. Of course this work is not intended to be a literal transcription of Venice's topography, for instead Millar has attempted to catch the lively mood of the city and its many varied colors and contrasts. Certainly in choosing forms and colors, he apparently was most interested in furnishing a sense of contrast between hot and cool color tones which drench the site, and between the eternal and the transient qualities which simultaneously are ever present. For here the monuments of the past are bathed in bright light and stand boldly silhouetted against a changing luminous violet sky, while colorful sailboats and gondolas — some with and some without canopies — glide gracefully along the rippling blue-green waters. Streaks of white clouds swirl around the still visible moon, echoing the varied architectural outline that stretches across the horizon. In essence, this painting is simply Millar's impression of the beautifully satisfying harmony experienced in the multiple contrasts that typify the unique character of Venice.

Addison T. Millar was born in Warren, Ohio in 1860. For a while, he was a pupil of William Merritt Chase in New York and subsequently he studied in Paris. Throughout his career he was best known for his etchings and aquatints, representative examples of which are found in the collections of the New York Public Library and the Library of Congress in Washington, D.C. However, he also produced a large body of paintings and was represented in many turn of the century private collections and in such public collections as the Detroit Museum of Art and the Rhode Island School of Design. Millar is one of the many artists who flourished in the late 19th and early 20th centuries but who today have been almost entirely forgotten. Little is known of the late period of his life except that he was killed in an automobile accident in 1913 in South Norwalk, Connecticut.

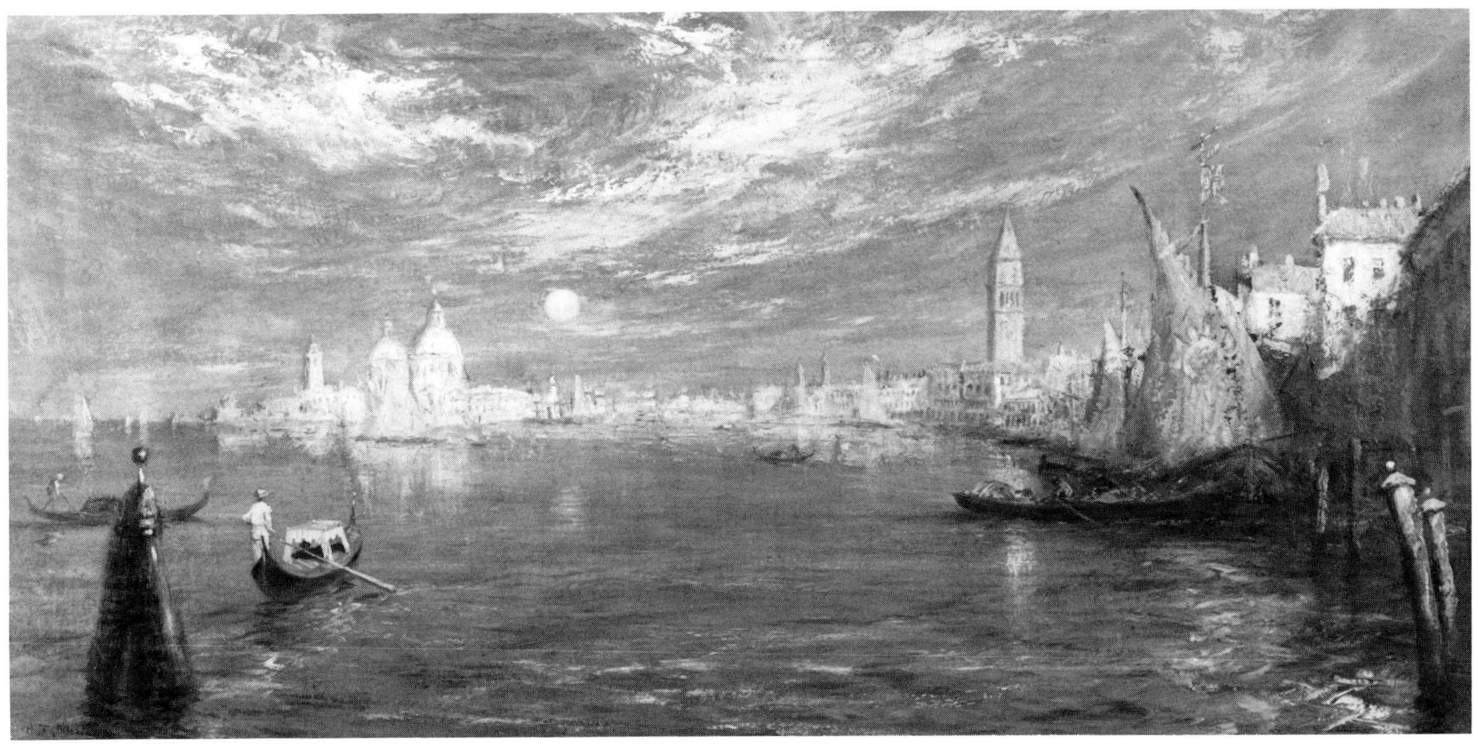

1980 Bequest of Mrs. A.L. Derby
(1980.79.4)

ALFRED H. MAURER (1868-1932)

Still Life with Flowers
Oil on card, c.1912
$21^5/_8$" x $18^1/_8$"

Alfred H. Maurer was indeed a true pioneer of contemporary American painting. He was born in New York City in 1868, attended the National Academy of Design and worked briefly as a lithographer. In 1897 he went to Paris where he studied painting at the Academie Julian. Soon, however, he revolted against the conservative academic training and by 1905 he fell under the spell of the French avant garde painters, and most especially Matisse and Cezanne. Maurer lived in France until 1914 when, because of the War, he returned to New York and resided in his parents' home for the remainder of his life. However, during his extended stay of 17 years in Paris his works had been included in exhibitions in France as well as in America, and in both 1909 and 1910 he showed prominently in Gallery "291", the noted Photo-Secession Gallery headed by Alfred Stieglitz in New York.

In this striking painting titled *Still Life with Flowers,* Maurer produced a work which clearly reflects the influence both of Cezanne and, even more, of Matisse. Here, the subject matter consists of a vase of brightly colored flowers placed in the center of the composition. Yet in no sense is this merely a traditional floral painting. For although Maurer has not abandoned recognizable form, his intent here was certainly to create a statement of color harmony and to furnish a sensation of vitality through the expressive use of a wide range of richly contrasting colors. Moreover, his sweeping brushstrokes charge the composition with a flamboyant quality, intensifying the liveliness of color choices. In addition, the flattened space which he uses here takes on the character of material reality by virtue of the light pastel colored patches applied throughout the surrounding areas. Thus his space as well as the forms contained in the space are in a very real sense constructed essential-

ly of pure color. By the same token, the colorful shadows both in the lower right and along the left edge function clearly as independent compositional motifs and as a result would seem to have a material reality of their own.

All of these features are quite characteristic of the many major changes that had begun to appear soon after the turn of the century in French painting and which were particularly evident in the works of the group derisively known as the *Fauves,* or "wild beasts". It was through his contacts with these painters during his early years in Paris that Maurer came to absorb the conceptual tenets of the modern movement which he helped transmit to America. But although he exhibited frequently in America during his career, the public and the art critics remained hostile to his works. In addition, his aged father, Louis Maurer the noted painter and lithographer for Currier and Ives, became increasingly unsympathetic to Alfred Maurer's work. In 1932, his father died at the age of 100 years, Three weeks later Alfred Maurer, apparently in ill health and in a deep depression, hanged himself in New York. Today he is recognized as perhaps the first American modernist and one of America's greatest 20th century painters.

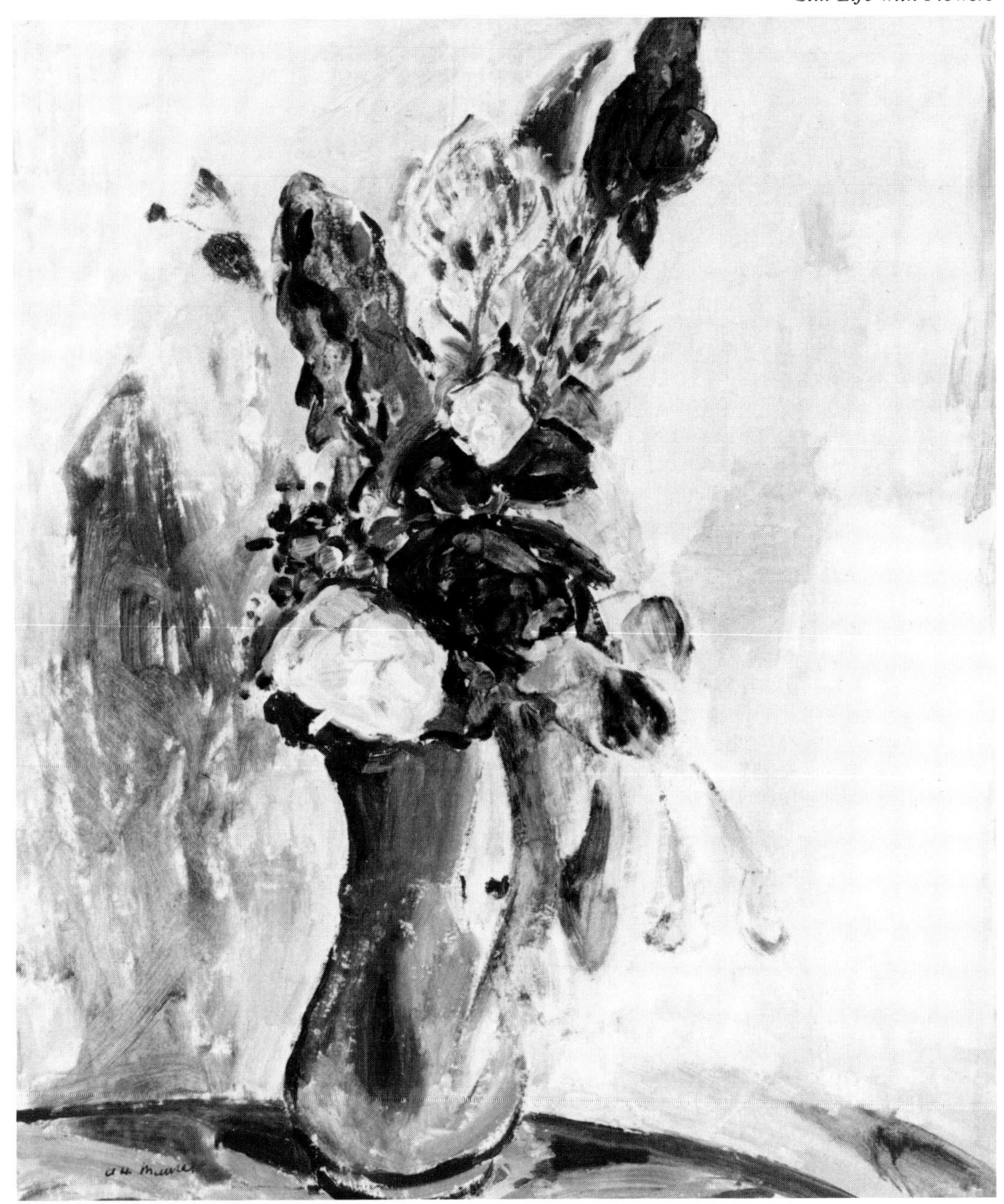

1983 Museum Purchase, Friends of the Wichita Art Museum Art Fund
(1983.15)

STUART DAVIS (1894-1964)

Storm over Pawtucket
Oil on canvas, 1912
30⅛" x 38¼"

The well-known American painter, Stuart Davis, is sometimes looked upon as the father of Pop Art. And understandably so, since so many of his paintings of the 1920s include such word images as *JAZZ* as well as various depictions of product advertising objects such as labels or cigarette packets, together organized in purely abstract designs. But Davis began his career by painting scenes of everyday life, and in 1913 when he was only 19 years of age he was represented in the well-known Armory Show with five paintings. At that time his work showed strong evidence of the influence of Robert Henri under whom he had studied, and his technique reflected not only Henri's influence but also his own special enthusiasm for such modern European masters as Van Gogh and Gauguin.

This work, titled *Storm over Pawtucket,* is one of Davis' very early paintings, executed in 1912. Here the high horizon and sweeping diagonals impart a dynamic compositional quality which in turn is intensified by the restless movement of blown leaves and bent trees and bushes that suggests the high winds of a brewing storm. In the lower right hand corner a small child wearing a red jacket clutches her mother, while in the upper left a man hastens to take shelter from the storm. But the theme alone would be less effective in communicating this mood were it not for the lively bravura in the handling of the brushstrokes. Even more significant, however, is the manner in which Davis relies upon the counterplay of colors, especially throughout the right side of the composition where, for example, the child's red jacket plays sharply against the luscious dark green trees above and at the same time dramatically contrasts with the fluttering white dress worn by the protective mother. This energetic color sense is in turn harmoniously keyed to the rather animated organization of the forms themselves. And in a very real sense these are the formal ingredients that Davis came to use later on in his more mature abstract compositions.

Stuart Davis was born in Philadelphia in 1894. His mother was a sculptress and his father was the Art Director of the Philadelphia Press where Davis had the unique opportunity to meet many of the young illustrators on the news staff who later became famous as the Ash Can painters, including Sloan, Luks, Shinn and Glackens. At the age of 15 Davis settled in New York City and studied with Robert Henri. In 1913 he was represented at the Armory Show. By 1920 his style had shifted into a strong abstract manner which characterized his works throughout the remainder of his career. During the 1930s Depression under the Federal Arts Project of the Works Progress Administration, he executed a number of important abstract murals in such sites as Radio City Music Hall and the World's Fair of 1939. His works are found in major collections throughout the world. At the age of 69 Davis died in New York City in 1964.

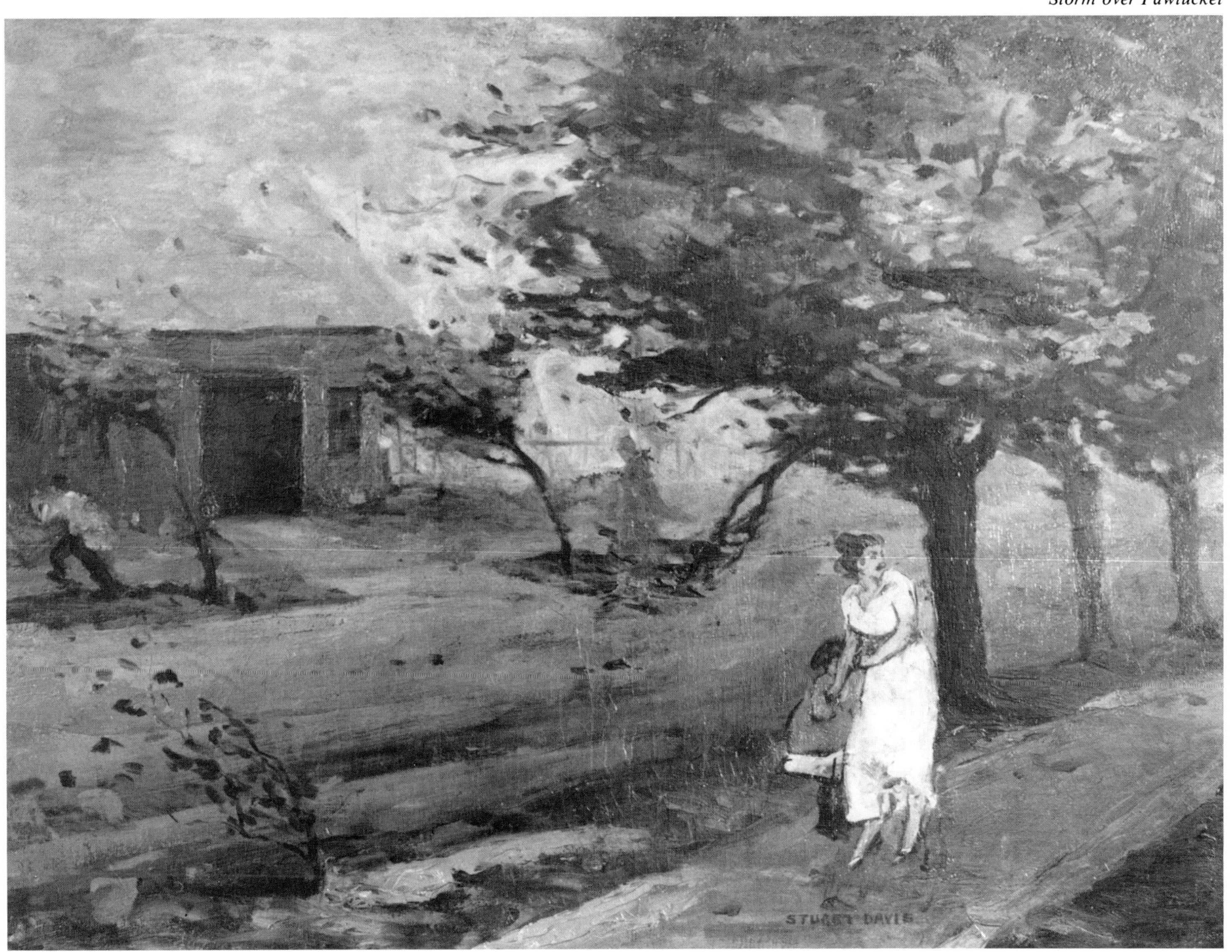

*1980 Gift of Mr. & Mrs. Kurt Olden, New York City
(1980.93)*

HUGO ROBUS (1885-1964)

Man & Horses
Oil on canvas, 1916
28" x 34¹/₈"

This stunning painting was executed in 1916 by the American artist Hugo Robus. It was, of course, as a sculptor that Robus earned the distinction for which he is so widely remembered today. Yet, during the early years of his career, he devoted his attention exclusively to painting, and his importance lies in the fact that he was among the early and more innovative American experimenters in abstraction who worked under the influence of French cubist doctrine coupled with German expressionist teaching.

One of the few paintings that Robus both signed and dated is this work titled *Man and Horses*. Here the viewer at first struggles to identify within the composition those forms that resemble a man and horses. Only on close searching do shapes emerge that are convincingly discernible. In no sense, however, is this painting intended to be imitatively representational for, instead, it is largely a record of the artist's sensitive response to some situation which he had experienced and which stimulated the production of forms — the shapes, colors, directions and relationships — that we see on the canvas.

What are especially interesting are the fluid sculpturesque masses, the overlapping folds, the interplay of angles and curves and the exquisite colors and color tones that maintain their respective independence yet at the same time so closely interrelate, creating a kind of spectrum-like unity. Indeed, both the forms and the strong color patterns are clearly reminiscent of some of the early 20th century expressionist works that Robus had obviously come to know during an extended European sojourn just before World War I. At the same time, the merging of masses and the seeming fusion and interpenetration of figural masses with surrounding spaces together bring to mind the so-called "passage" device employed by the early French cubists, thus quite conclusively demonstrating that the extremely contemporary aesthetic tendencies that Robus had absorbed before his conversion to sculpture.

Hugo Robus was born in Cleveland, Ohio, in 1885. He attended the Cleveland School of Art and, in 1908, moved to New York City, where he studied at the National Academy of Design. Between 1912 and 1914, he studied in Paris. It was in 1920 that he shifted his efforts from painting to sculpture which almost exclusively commanded his attention for the remainder of his life. However, it was not until the early 1950s that he won the professional recognition which his skill and creative accomplishments deserved. Robus taught at Columbia University, The Brooklyn School of Art and at Hunter College. He died in New York City in 1964.

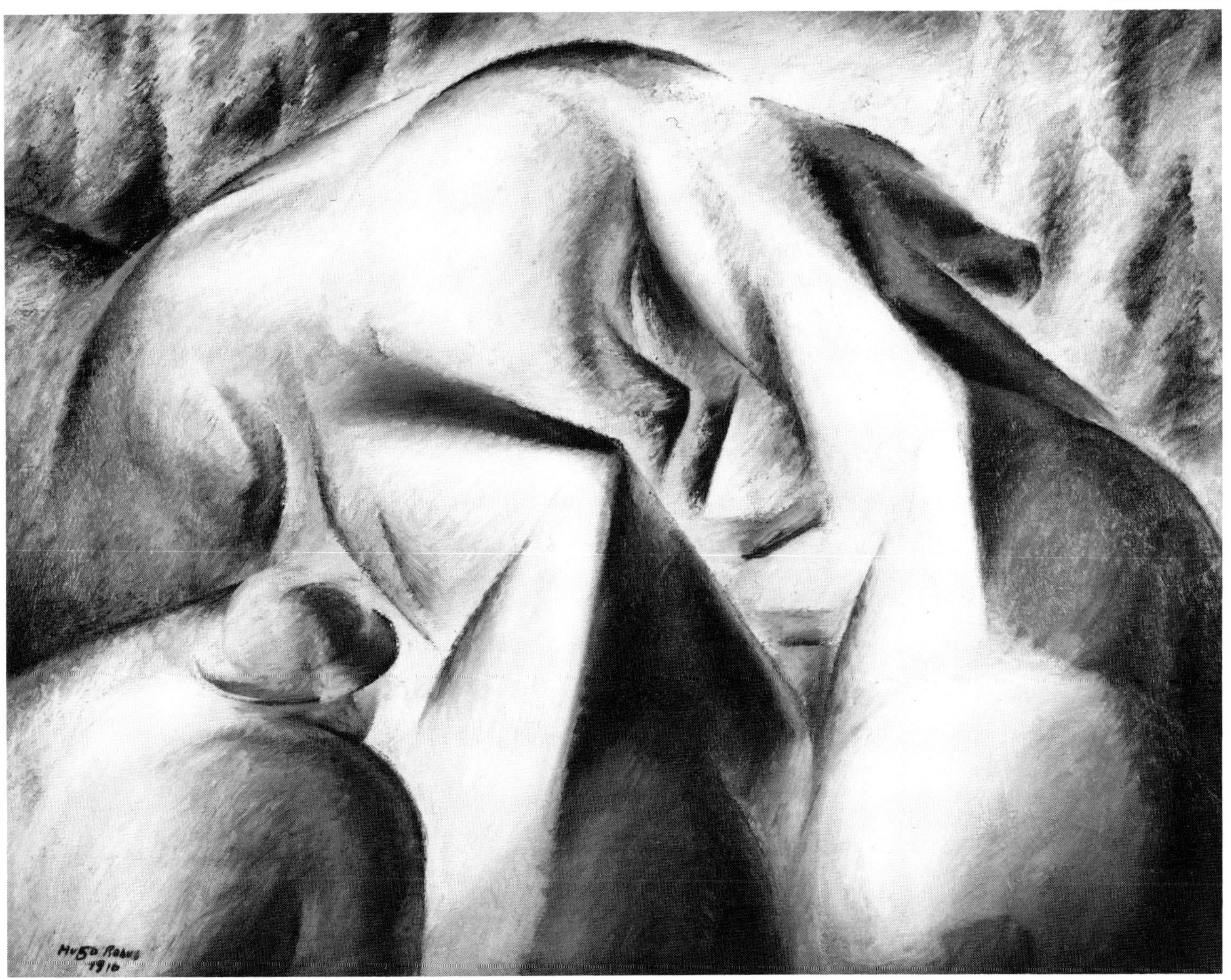

1984 Museum Purchase, Friends of the Wichita Art Museum Art Fund
(1984.30)

J. ALDEN WEIR (1852-1919)

The Connoisseur
Oil on linen, 1889
42¼" x 30³/₈"

In this refined oil on linen titled *The Connoisseur* and executed in 1889 by the American artist J. Alden Weir, the figure of a contemplative young woman wearing a pale blue-green gown of sheer fabric with loosely hanging kimono-like sleeves is seen leisurely gazing at a large scroll drawing which she holds before her. Her soft reflective facial expression, the sensitive handling of her features, the subdued tonal harmonies and the subtle treatment of forms throughout are together the vehicles through which a mood of tranquility and quiet solitude is effectively evoked. The result is an image of idealized womanhood and self-containment so popular in late 19th century American painting.

Of especial interest is the formal organization, for the vertical lines of the gracefully poised figure and the horizontal position of her right arm are complemented by the sweeping curve which proceeds from her neck and left shoulder through her left arm and hand and carries uninterruptedly across the arched line of the outstretched paper that she holds. Indeed it is through this compositional device that the drawing which she so admires becomes essentially an extension of the young woman herself, thus suggesting the appropriateness of the title *The Connoisseur*.

Julian Alden Weir was born in 1852 at West Point, New York, where his artist-father, Robert W. Weir, was professor of drawing at the United States Military Academy. Alden Weir studied first under his father and later in Paris at the Beaux-Arts Academy. During numerous early European study trips, he was much influenced by Manet in France and Whistler in England. He was a member and President of the National Academy of Design and a founding member of the Society of American Artists. At about the time that he executed *The Connoisseur* in 1889, his works were becoming less academic as his interests turned more toward the impressionist manner. Thereafter his palette became brighter and the surfaces of his canvases more tactile. He was one of the original members of the American Impressionist Painters who first exhibited together in 1898 under the label of *The Ten*. Weir died in 1919 at the age of 67. His paintings and etchings are included in most major museum collections throughout the nation.

The Connoisseur by J. Alden Weir was purchased in 1978 and was dedicated to Elizabeth S. Navas whose enviably sensitive and inquiring connoisseurship built the distinguished Murdock Collection held by the Wichita Art Museum.

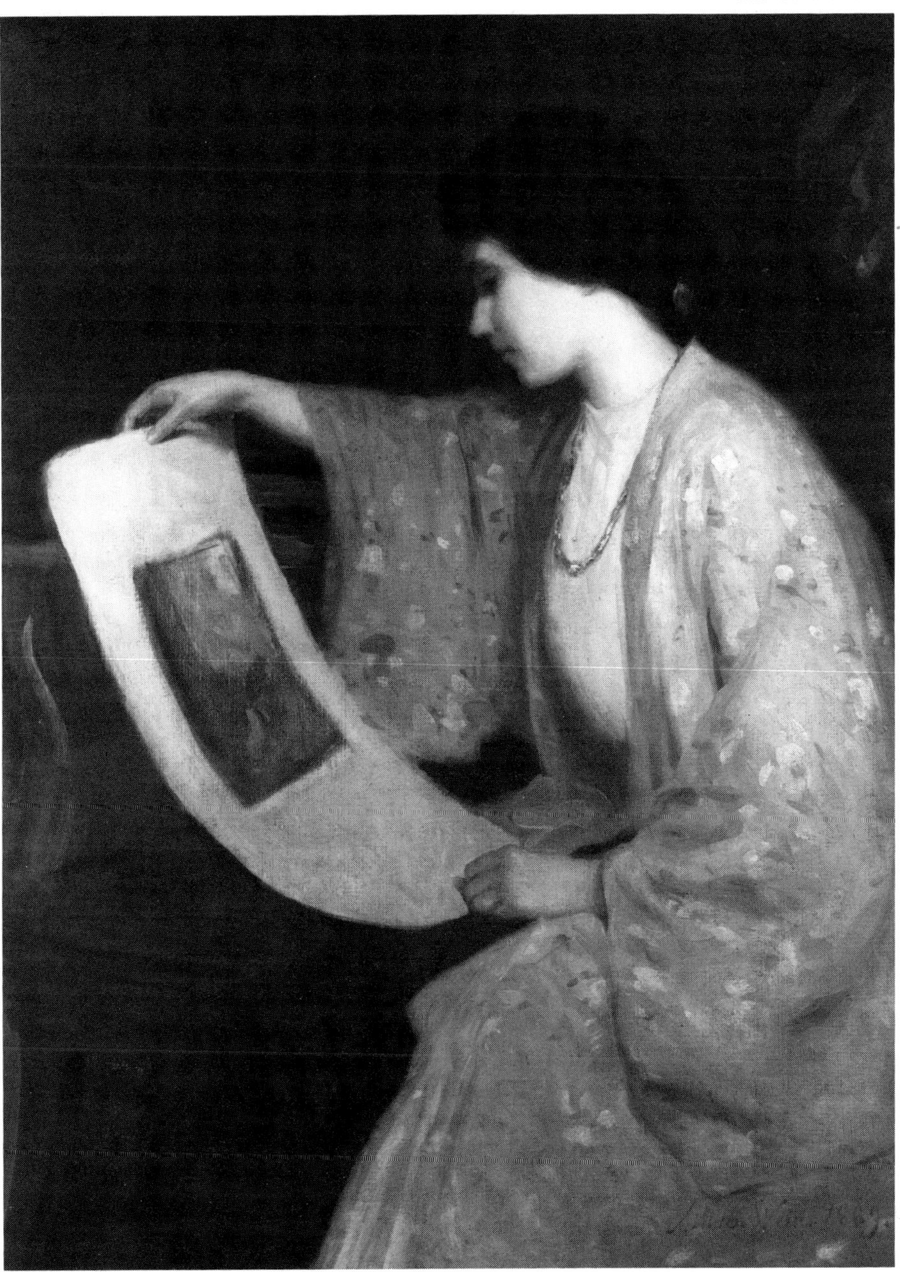

1978 Museum Purchase, Director's Discretionary Fund, Friends of the Wichita Art Museum (1978.91)

WILLIAM MERRITT CHASE (1849-1916)

Portrait of Alice
Oil on canvas, c.1890
22" x 18"

The noted American painter William Merritt Chase executed this handsome oil on canvas in approximately 1890. The work is titled *Portrait of Alice* and the subject is the artist's wife.

Especially interesting is the lively painterly quality consisting of broad sweeping brushstrokes which so effectively impart a feeling of spontaneity and moving vitality throughout the entire composition. The subject's face is enframed by her black hair and the black chiffon-like dress which she wears, and at the same time her beautiful features are accented by the red rose worn in her hair and the warm radiance which glows from the lovely features of her face.

Chase was born in Nineveh, Indiana, in 1849. His initial training came from local and regional artists. However, in 1869 he went to New York and studied at The National Academy School and in 1872 he enrolled in The Royal Academy of Munich where he studied under the renowned artist Karl von Piloty. During his stay in Munich, he travelled to major art centers in Europe and in 1878 returned to New York and accepted a teaching position at the Art Students League. His first one-man show was held in 1886 at the Boston Art Club and in 1890 he was elected to the National Academy of Design. Throughout his career, Chase strongly supported American art at a time when European styles were much in vogue. He was a prolific painter and one of the most actively influential art instructors in the history of American art. For more than 35 years he taught at major art schools including The Art Students League, The Pennsylvania Academy of Fine Arts, and The Brooklyn Art Association. He also founded the Shinnecock School in Southhampton, Long Island, and The Chase School of Art in New York City. In addition, for many years Chase conducted summer classes in European centers until shortly before his death in New York City in 1916.

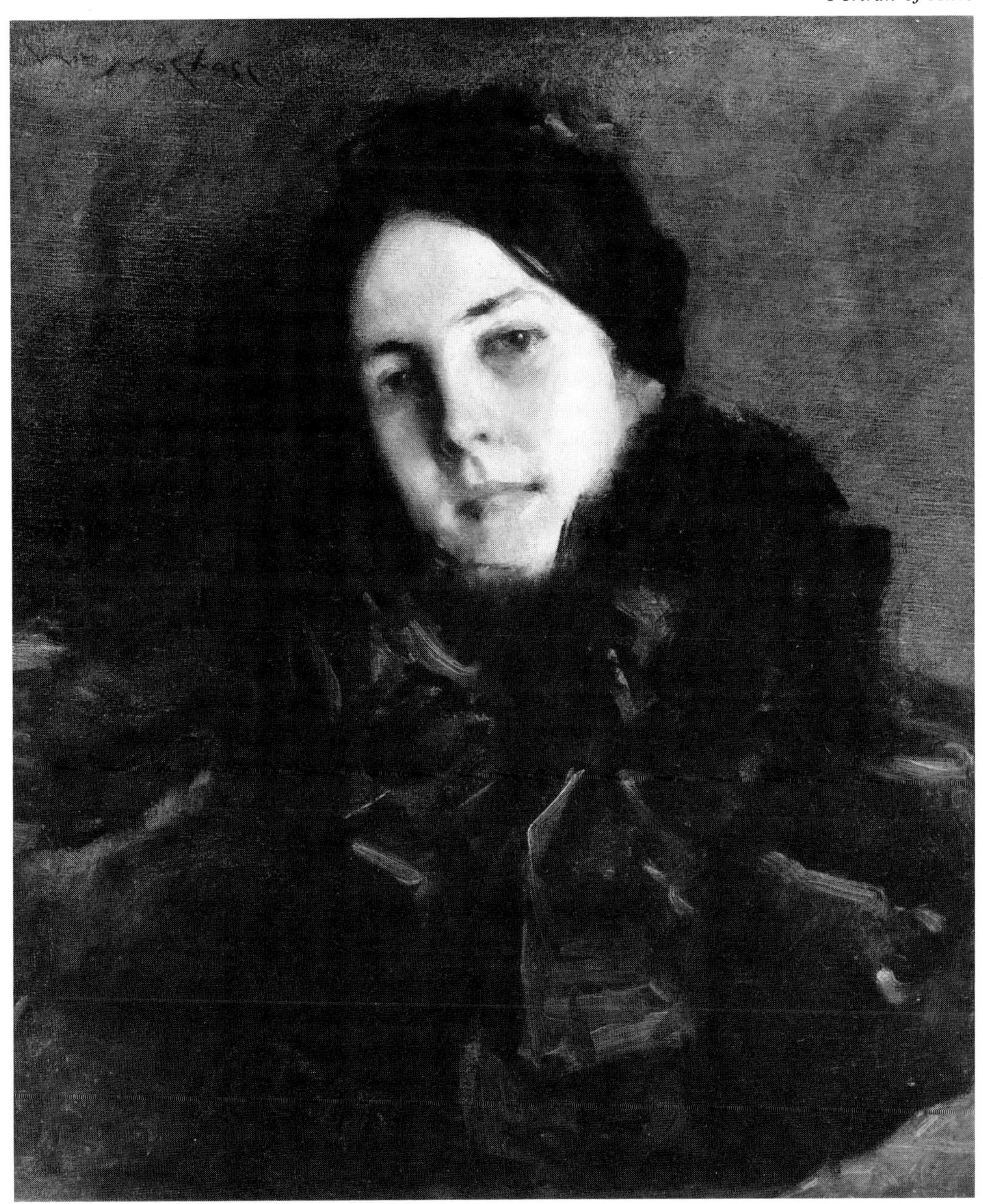

1977 Gift of Sam P. Wallingford Foundation, Wichita, Kansas
(1977.67)

WILLIAM MERRITT CHASE (1849-1916)

On the Sound
Oil on canvas, c.1890
17^1/$_8$'' x 28^5/$_8$''

William Merritt Chase was one of the most noted painters in America during the late 19th and early 20th centuries, and certainly an artist who through his teaching exerted tremendous influence on a vast generation of younger artists who followed in his footsteps. Even though he openly acknowledged the influence of many early masters, his own compositions were invariably executed in an entirely new and original manner.

This work titled *On the Sound* was painted by Chase about 1890. Here a wide expanse of water is broken by a line of low and barely visible hills at the distant horizon and by the sharp diagonal of the pier seen at the right and by a single wooden stake in the left foreground. Near the end of the pier a figure appears to be standing and at the far end a cluster of moored row boats is suggested. What is especially interesting and significant is the strong but highly simplified geometry of the composition. For here the horizon is extremely high and the pier, cropped-off at the lower right hand edge, sharply pierces the open space pulling the viewer into the composition. Such compositional dynamics clearly testify to the impact which Japanese woodblocks had on the aesthetics of both European and American painting at this time.

In defining three-dimensional forms as well as the quivering reflections along the water surface, Chase has employed loose and lively brushwork. Even more significant, his masterful skill in adjusting close color values enabled him to achieve exquisitely subtle tonal harmony and the impression of an all-embracing misty atmosphere. In turn, a quiet and tranquil mood is caught and at the same time the character of a fleeting moment in nature is effectively captured. These features are indeed quite reminiscent of the work of J.A.M. Whistler whose paintings Chase much admired.

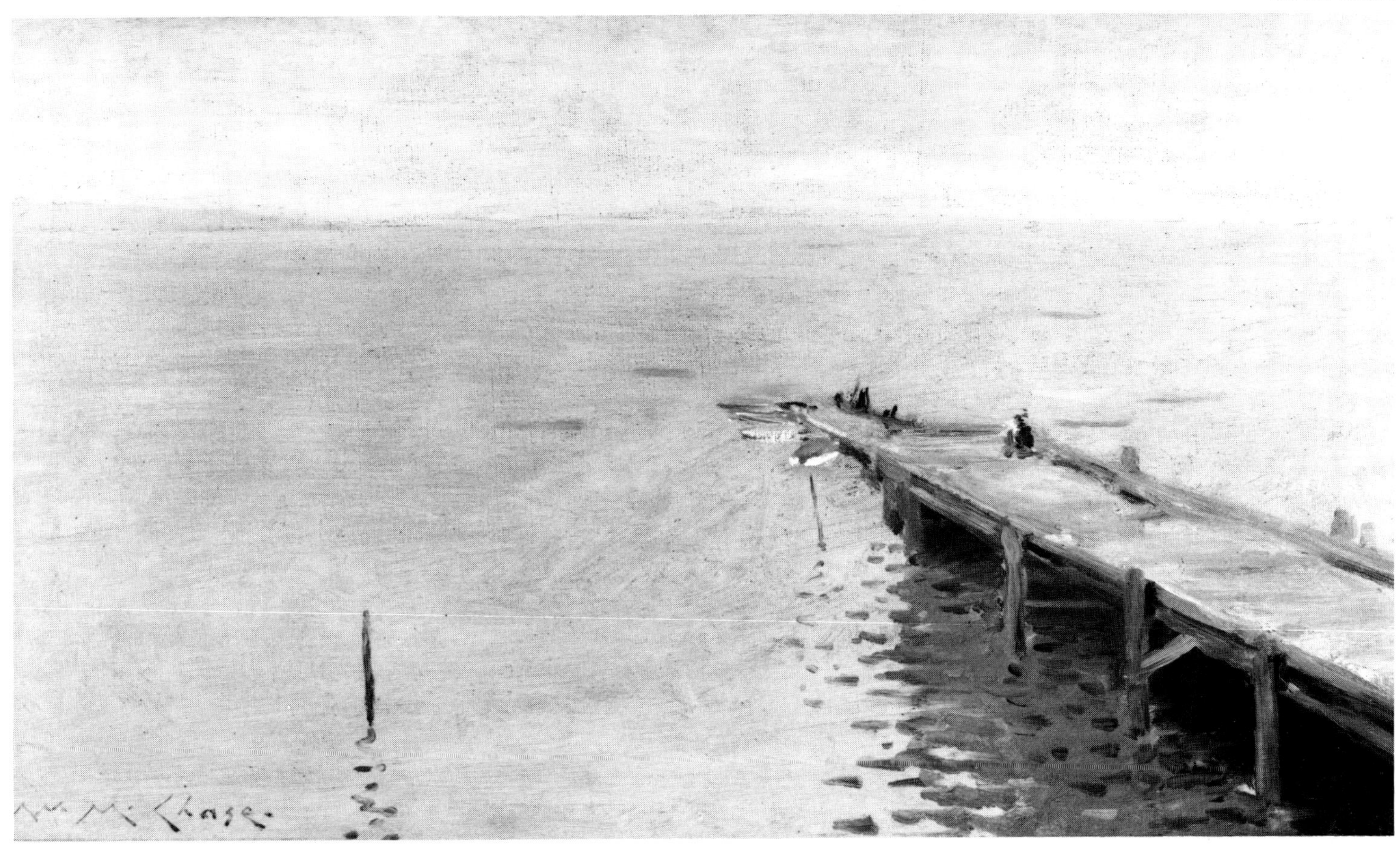

1983 Museum Purchase, Paul Ross Charitable Foundation Fund
(1983.66)

WILLIAM MERRITT CHASE (1849-1916)

Reflections
Oil on canvas, n.d.
24¹/₈'' x 18¹/₈''

Silence, tranquility, and a sense of mystery pervade this very simple still life composition titled *Reflections* by the American artist, William Merritt Chase. But what is especially significant here is the strong geometry of the composition consisting solely of four basic geometric forms, *viz.* a cylinder, a circle, a rectangle and a sphere, so organized as to create a right triangle that cuts into the pictorial space at a slight diagonal and imparts a quality of mathematical purity and structural stability to the work.

Like many American artists during the closing decades of the 19th century, Chase found inspiration in the aesthetics of Japanese art forms including prints, wall hangings, pottery, fans, and the color patterns of Japanese batiks. That interest is clearly echoed here in the particular props selected as well as in the general decorative treatment of shapes and textures. Moreover, in this instance as in many of Chase's compositions, the strong influence of Whistler, with whom he had become closely acquainted on a visit to London in 1885, can quite readily be seen in the mottled, seemingly shimmering space that encompasses the still life arrangement and in the subtle color harmony and the narrow range of delicate tones used throughout the composition.

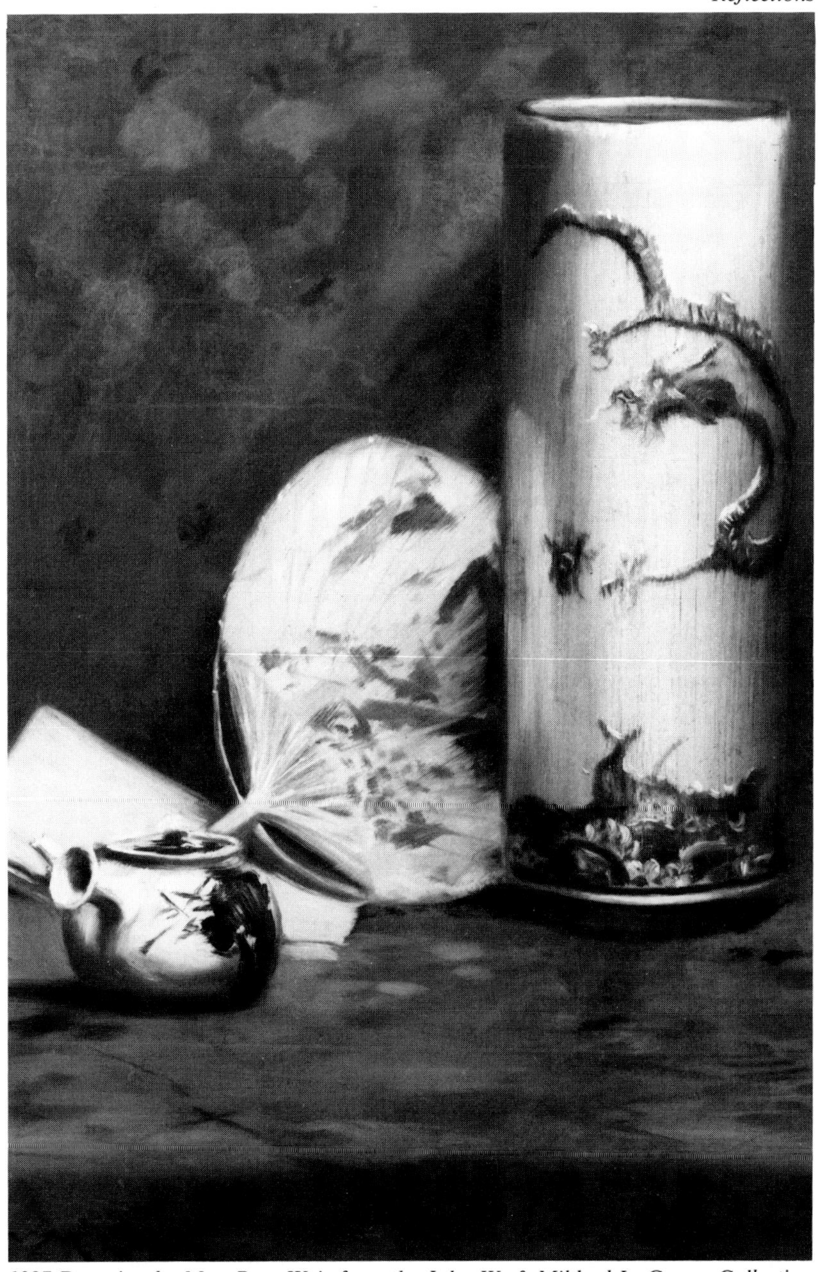

1987 Donation by Mrs. Ross Weir from the John W. & Mildred L. Graves Collection (1987.8)

BIRGE HARRISON (1854-1929)

Old Sawmill
Oil on canvas, c.1910
30¼" x 40"

Since the beginning of the 19th century the natural landscape tradition has been a dominant force in the development of American painting. But while artists of the early and mid-19th century treated the landscape with much attention to precise detail, most turn of the century landscapists focused on mood rather than fact, on suggestion rather than on descriptive detail thereby more intimately relating to the subtle effects of nature while employing the natural scene as a point of departure for conveying both impression and sentiment.

One of the most sophisticated groups of landscapists working at the end of the 19th century represented a movement that flourished between 1880 and about 1915 which today is known as Tonalism. Birge Harrison was certainly one of the leading spokesmen of this movement and this work painted by Harrison about 1910 and titled *Old Sawmill* rather clearly epitomizes tonalist aesthetic theory. Here an old sawmill stands in an open expanse of snow-covered ground near the foot of a hill. Wheel tracks in the snow, as seen at the lower left, carry the eye to the middle distance. But actually the subject of this work is not so much the sawmill as it is the experience of the quiet setting itself on a cold and gloomy winter day at dusk when the misty atmosphere suppresses all detail and like a diaphanous veil faintly blurs the bushes and trees and the outline of the distant hill. Human figures are altogether absent from the composition, and it is the magic of the broad view into open natural space which evokes a mood of complete quiet, tranquility and solitude, a mood much intensified by the dominant subdued gray and blue-gray color tones, extremely close in value much as in a black and white photograph. What is especially interesting is that the same tonal proximity that contributes to the mood of this painting also occurs in nature at early dawn, at dusk and at moonlight and during the late fall and winter seasons, a fact which explains the time-setting most often chosen by the tonalists. Indeed, all of the characteristics of this painting typify the aesthetic doctrine to which the tonalist group rather uniformly adhered.

Although the Tonalist movement itself was clearly related to the parallel development of American Impressionism at this time, the two were certainly not identical, for tonalism was more directly inspired by the work of the French Barbizon painters and by the avant garde paintings of the American expatriate James A.M. Whistler. Perhaps the most significant aspect of tonalist painting was its obvious reaction against the literal transcription of nature and its interest instead in simplified form, thus in one sense heralding the abstract formalism which came early in the 20th century.

Birge Harrison was born in Philadelphia in 1854. He attended the Pennsylvania Academy of Fine Arts and subsequently studied in Paris with the noted painter and teacher Carolus-Duran. In the course of extensive world-wide travels he spent considerable time in England where he became much inspired by the light and spaciousness expressed in works by John Constable and by the muted color tones used by the Norwich school painters, especially John Crome. On his return to the U.S. in 1897, Harrison settled in Woodstock, New York where he offered classes under the auspices of the Art Students League. Harrison was a prolific painter and as a teacher and writer exercised much influence on other artists. He wrote extensively for such periodicals as the *North American Review, Craftsman, Century Magazine, International Studio* and others, and in 1909 published a book titled *Landscape Painting*. In 1910 he was elected to full membership in the National Academy of Design. Harrison's works are represented in major museum collections throughout the U.S. He died in Woodstock in 1929.

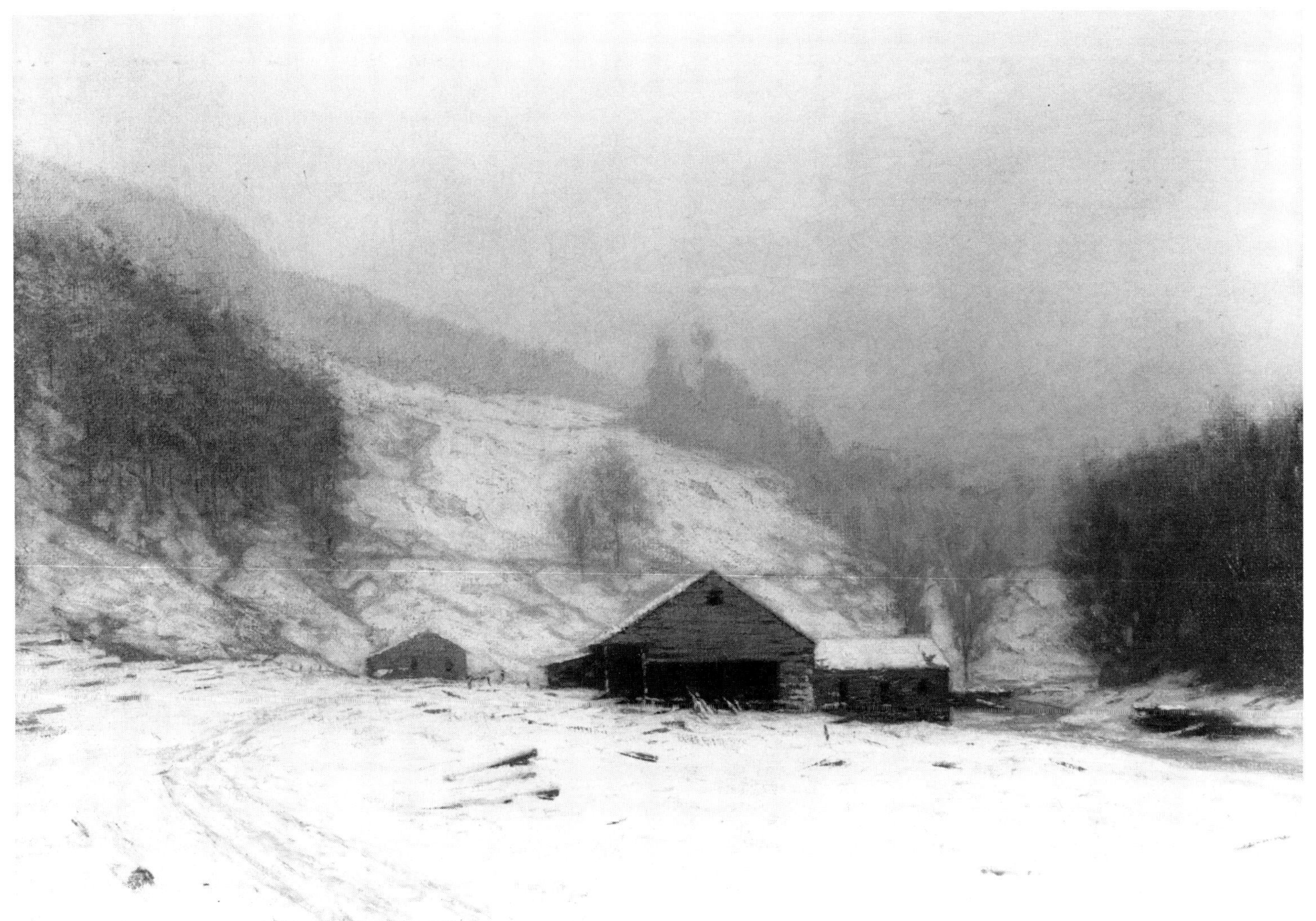

1982 Museum Purchase, Roland P. Murdock Collection Addition, Elizabeth Innes Galland Bequest (M169.82)

ERNEST LAWSON (1873-1939)

Saint John the Divine, New York City, in Winter
Oil on canvas, c.1907
16$^1/_8$" x 23"

Throughout his career, the noted 20th century American impressionist Ernest Lawson was deeply absorbed in the beauty of the American landscape and in capturing momentary impressions of the changing seasons and the changing times of day. Lawson painted in many regions of the United States, Canada and Europe but his favorite site was the area around New York City.

This oil on canvas titled *Saint John the Divine, New York City, in Winter* is a highly accomplished work and one of Lawson's finest early compositions. Based on the artist's stylistic development and the constructural stage of the cathedral as shown here, the date of execution would quite probably be 1907.

The specific subject matter depicted is the Cathedral of Saint John situated on a snowcovered hill with a dense thicket of bare winter trees at the left and a small footbridge near the base of the hill. One of the delights here is the sense of winter chill which the artist has so skillfully caught. Even more significant, however, are the gentle calm of the luminous atmosphere and the haunting tonal nuances of the glowing winter sky at twilight which effectively harmonize with the blue-gray shadows cast across the snow-covered foreground and the erect but wispy trees. Added interest is achieved in the contrast between the stately architecture and the soft shimmering quality of the setting. Yet the two seem clearly to belong together: one symbolizing stability and permanence, the other expressing the reality of fleeting change.

Lawson was a gentle and contemplative individual and a profoundly dedicated painter whose prolific accomplishments won him eminence within his profession and full membership in the National Academy of Design. But at the same time his life was surrounded by tragic sadness. He was born in Halifax, Nova Scotia in 1873 and at 15 years of age in 1888 settled briefly in Kansas City, Missouri. As a young artist, he studied with John Twachtman and J. Alden Weir and made several trips to Paris where in 1893 he met Somerset Maugham and some years later was fictionalized as the painter "Frederic Lawson" in Maugham's novel *Of Human Bondage.* Lawson exhibited with The Eight in 1908 and again in the Armory Show in 1913.

In 1916 with his wife and daughter he visited Spain where he executed a number of paintings. Although his early career had brought him fame and on some occasions considerable fortune, changing tastes and times following World War I and during the Great Depression of the 1930s led to extreme financial hardships, discouragement and ill health. In the final decade of his life he spent much of his time as a guest of close personal friends in Florida and in 1939 he died destitute in Miami.

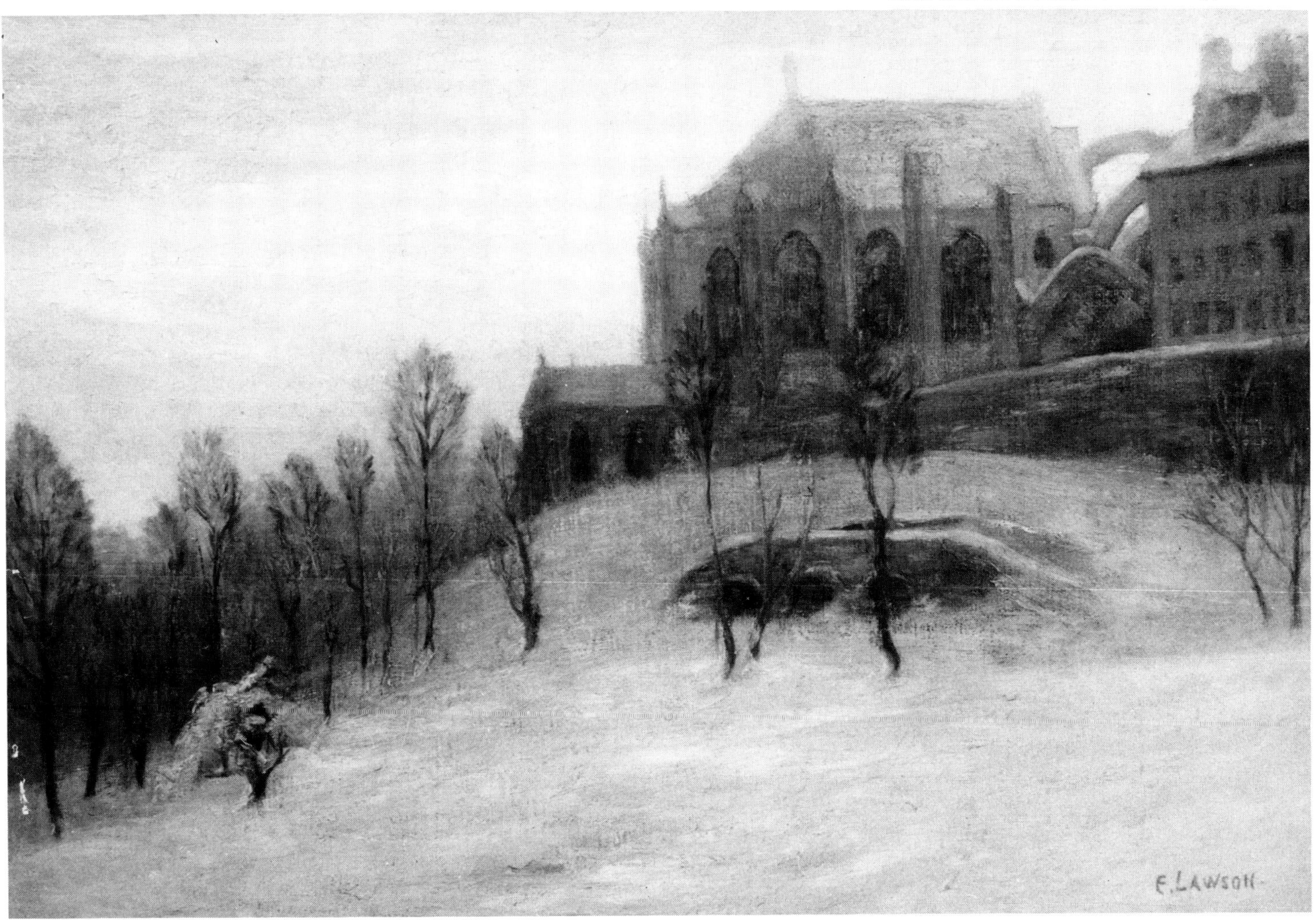

Saint John the Divine, New York City, in Winter

1981 Gift of Mr. & Mrs. Duane Buckley in memory of Floyd T. Amsden
(1981.31)

JOHN NOBLE (1874-1934)

Harbor by Moonlight
Oil on canvas, c.1915
33³/₈" x 33³/₈"

This tranquil scene titled *Harbor by Moonlight* by the Wichita-born artist John Noble was painted quite probably in Etaples, France shortly before the opening of World War I. The subject matter is fully announced in its title. But what is more important than the subject matter itself, is Noble's creative rendering of that subject: the bravura brushwork, the sensitive orchestration of colors and color forms, the lyricism imparted to a commonplace setting and the uplifting visual experience afforded by the exaggerated point of view when looking down from above.

Especially noteworthy is the narrow arched upper register of the work consisting of a network of color patches which the eye magically transforms into a fishing village with clustered red-roofed houses stretching along the water's edge. In like manner, the composition contains summarily treated yet readily identifiable forms, as for example the fishermen's boats painted with loosely applied strokes of black-gray and dark brown pigment and thus appearing to be in deep shadow. And silhouetted against the dark blue sea these forms stand out in bold contrast with the delicate tones of the background town itself.

But perhaps the focal point of the composition is the bright splash of cold yellow moonlight glowing from the quiet surface of the water. Yet no element here is in any sense a copy of any specific object. Instead the entire work is a freely created interpretation of an experience which the artist knew and understood and which in this rather impressionistic manner he communicated more effectively than he could possibly have done had he produced a detailed photographic likeness. Of course, it was this capability which was the genius of John Noble and which so fully expressed his own creed that art should be creative rather than imitative.

John Noble was born in Wichita on March 15, 1874. As a boy he had no formal schooling and instead worked with his father driving cattle over the Chisholm Trail. Eventually, however, he went to Cincinnati where he studied for a short time at the Cincinnati Academy of Fine Arts. In his early career he worked as a newspaper cartoonist and painted portraits of nudes for public bars. One of these paintings was the celebrated *Cleopatra at the Bath* which hung behind the bar of the Carey Hotel in Wichita and it was that painting which won notoriety when it was gashed by the zealous social reformer, Carrie Nation in 1901.

While still a young man, Noble went to Paris and studied at the Julian Academy as well as at the Ecole des Beaux Arts in Brussels. In 1906 he married a French girl and settled in Brittany where he worked as a fisherman with a sardine fleet. It was during this period and in the succeeding years spent in Etaples and in London that he gained fame as a painter of the sea. In 1920 he returned to the United States where he spent the remainder of his life. Noble was active both in New York and in the well known Provincetown art colony and actually founded the Provincetown Art Association, serving as its first president. He was a true individualist and a true romantic, but his life was a turbulent one. He suffered from chronic alcoholism and in 1934 died in Bellevue Hospital, New York City, from paraldehyde poisoning.

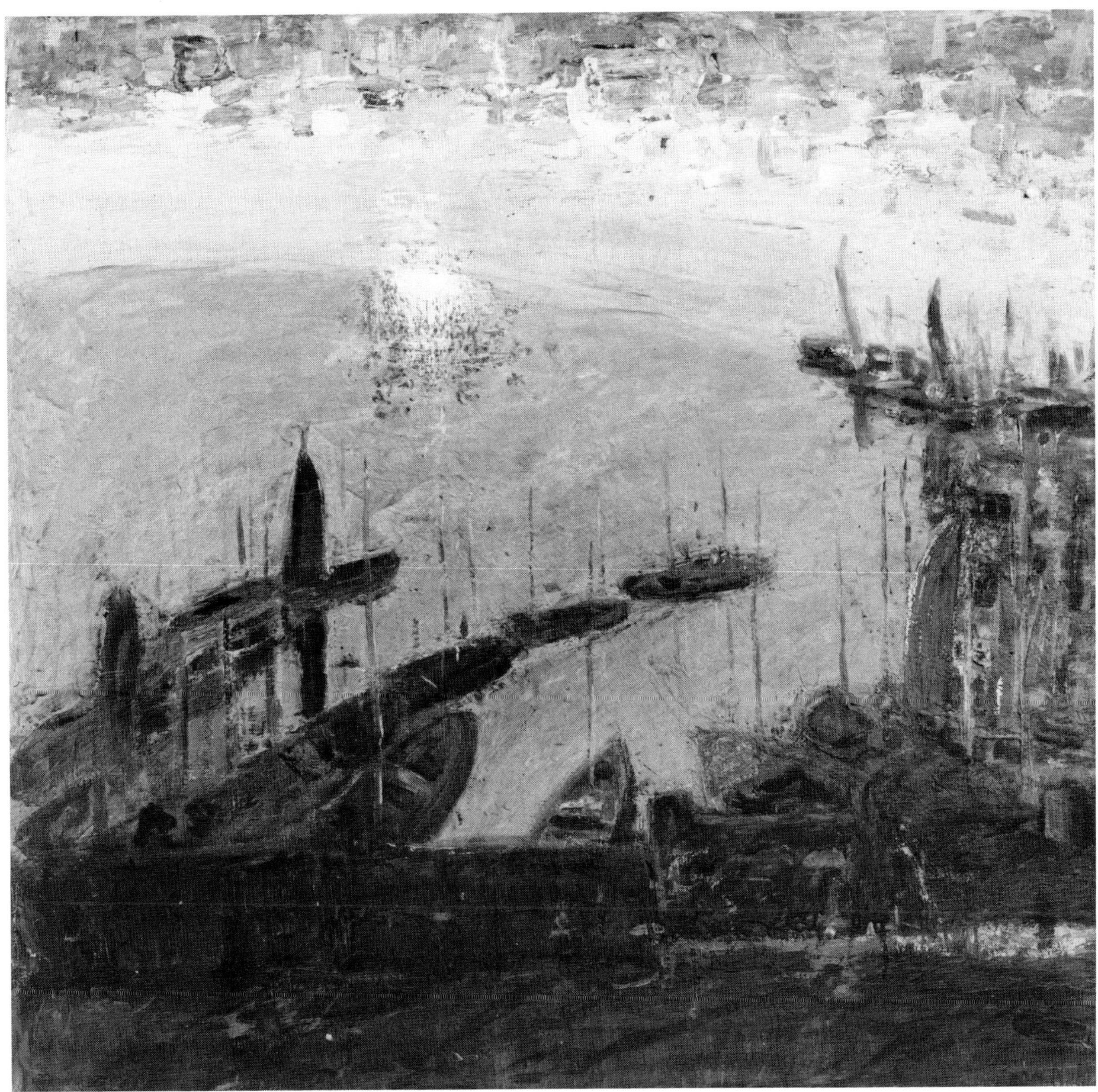

1980 Museum Purchase, Paul Ross Charitable Foundation Fund
(1980.92)

WILLARD LEROY METCALF (1858-1925)

Old Willows in Spring
Oil on canvas, 1923
26" x 29"

In his day, Willard Metcalf was regarded as the truly American Impressionist. And he was especially known as a painter of seasonal landscapes for in his works he so ably caught both the visual character and the changing mood of each passing season.

In this painting, executed in 1923 and titled *Old Willows in Spring,* Metcalf has effectively captured the essential spirit of spring as a glorious triumph over the winter which it inevitably displaces. Here the setting is early spring with its clean fresh colors, its clear and cool atmosphere and its sense of delicate yet lively vigor. Of course green is the dominant color, loosely applied in soft edge patches and in a wide spectrum of closely related but not identical tones, with the most vivid appearing in the immediate foreground, the less vivid in the middle ground, and the least vivid in the distance where dark purple tones also are introduced to describe the distant hills. This recession of color intensity produces an impression of spatial depth which in turn is further emphasized by the narrow winding stream that carries the eye into the pictorial distance. But the crystal-like clarity and the surface stillness of the stream intensify an overall mood of tranquility and expand our awareness of space by sharply reflecting nearby forms.

What is so interesting here is the element of spatial ambiguity introduced by virtue of the distortion of scale, especially evident when we compare the size of the grazing cattle on the hills in the far distance with that of the little fisher-boy seated by the stream near the foreground. While the two are a vast distance from one another, the more distant cattle do not appear smaller than the nearby fisher-boy in the foreground. Still another element of ambiguity arises from the strong sense of solidity and permanence introduced in many of the physical details while contrarily a transitory mood implicit in the seasonal cycle is otherwise clearly evoked. Such ambiguity arouses viewer attention and thus heightens aesthetic interest and discovery.

In French impressionist painting, a sense of flux is generally evident but is far less common in American works, a fact which would suggest that the American mind more readily accommodates change that occurs within a system of permanent stability. Indeed what Metcalf has achieved so enviably well here is the depiction of the sense of place typical of American painting. And in so doing he has made a visual statement that defines the stability of existence as a harmonious and continuing relationship between mankind and the natural environment to which all humanity is inseparably linked, both biologically and historically.

Willard Metcalf was born in Lowell, Massachusetts, in 1858. He studied in Boston and at the Academie Julian in Paris and was a founding member in 1898 of the American Impressionist group known as the "Ten". Metcalf painted throughout New England and most particularly in Connecticut until his death in 1925 in New York City.

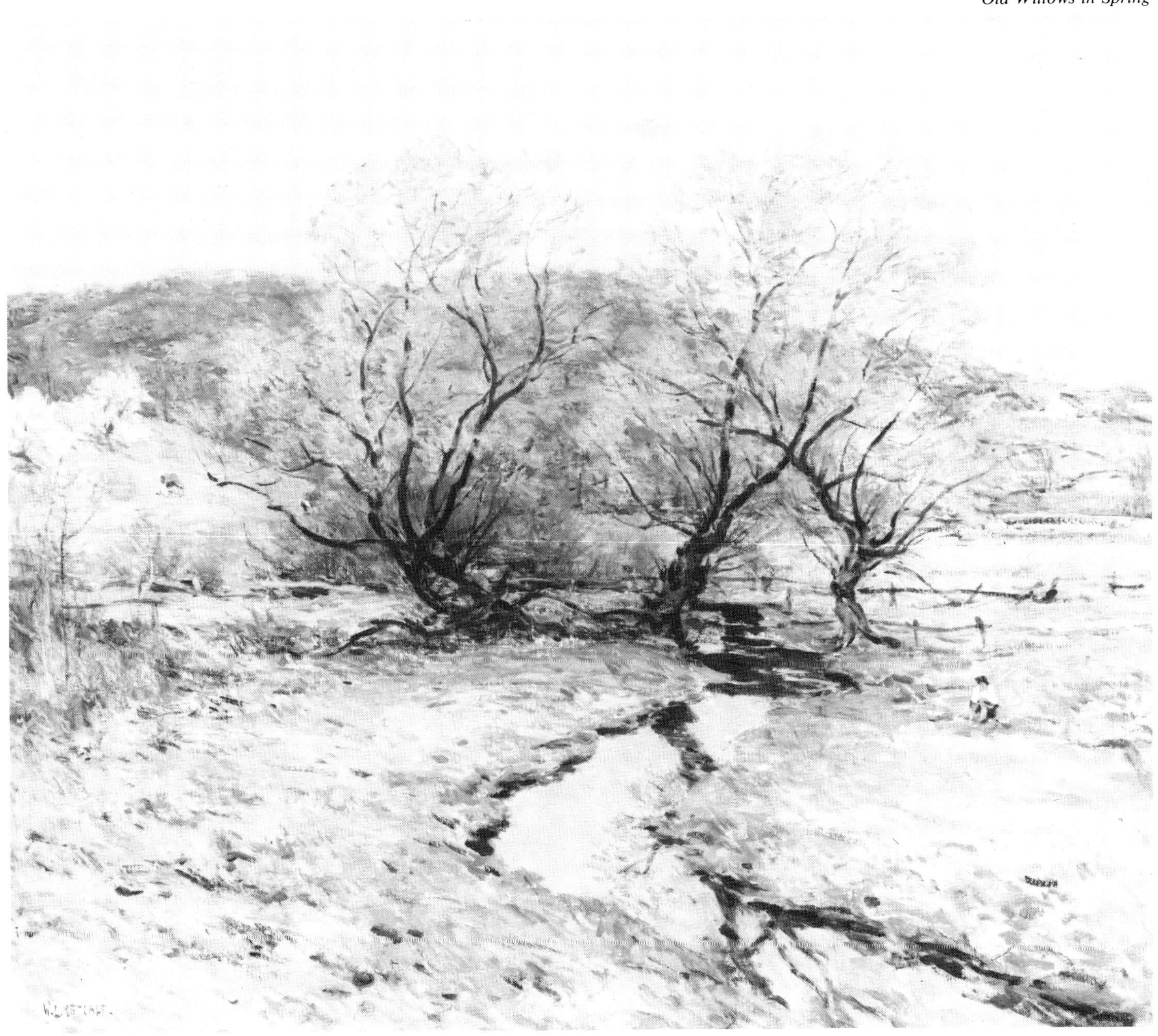

*1988 Donation by Mrs. Ross Weir from the John W. & Mildred L. Graves Collection
(1988.17)*

FREDERICK CARL FRIESEKE (1874-1939)

The Black Shawl
Oil on canvas, c.1910
32" x 23¾"

The Black Shawl is a striking example of the finest work painted by the American impressionist Frederick C. Frieseke (1874-1939). Frieseke was born in Owosso, Michigan and studied briefly at the Art Institute of Chicago and at the Art Students League in New York City. In 1898 he sailed to France and enrolled in the Academie Julien in Paris. Except for a few brief trips to the States, he retained permanent residence in France for the remainder of his life. Soon after settling in France, Frieseke adopted the impressionist manner. He became closely acquainted with Monet and other French Impressionists and purchased the house in Giverny that was originally occupied by Theodore Robinson.

Almost without exception, the subject of Frieseke's paintings was the female figure. In this particular work the setting is an interior view portraying a young woman dominantly placed in the center of the compositional format. She is seen in a three quarter rear view and wears a black fringed shawl over her shoulders and a long flowing satin gown with deep irregularly shaped folds that flare widely at the base. Background space is flat and consists of striped wall paper and, at the far right, a two-dimensional oriental folding screen decorated with a surface pattern of dappled colors. Moreover the amorphous quality of color masses that loosely flow across the surface of the fabric covering what seems to be a small sofa at the left confirms the decorative flatness of the composition. Here Frieseke has presented his statement more in post-impressionist terms than as purely traditional impressionism. What is so interesting of course is that the figure of the young woman, though handsomely modeled and appearing to be standing in a three-dimensional space as she views herself in the little hand mirror that she holds, is at the same time tightly linked with the flat space of the background. For the folds of her gown tend to repeat the patterns of the sofa cover, and the dappled coloration pattern of her black shawl echoes that of the screen at the right. As a result, the compositional dynamic is one of spatial ambiguity and emphasizes the theoretical dictate of the late 19th and 20th centuries that the foremost reality of a painting is the flatness of the picture plane.

Frieseke was actually a second generation American Impressionist and it is understandable that much of his work discloses an interest in strong design and flattened composition that were typical of the post-impressionist movements of the early 20th century. Indeed in every sense he was considered one of the most talented and highly respected American artists living abroad during the period. Frieseke died in Normandy in 1939 at the age of 65 years.

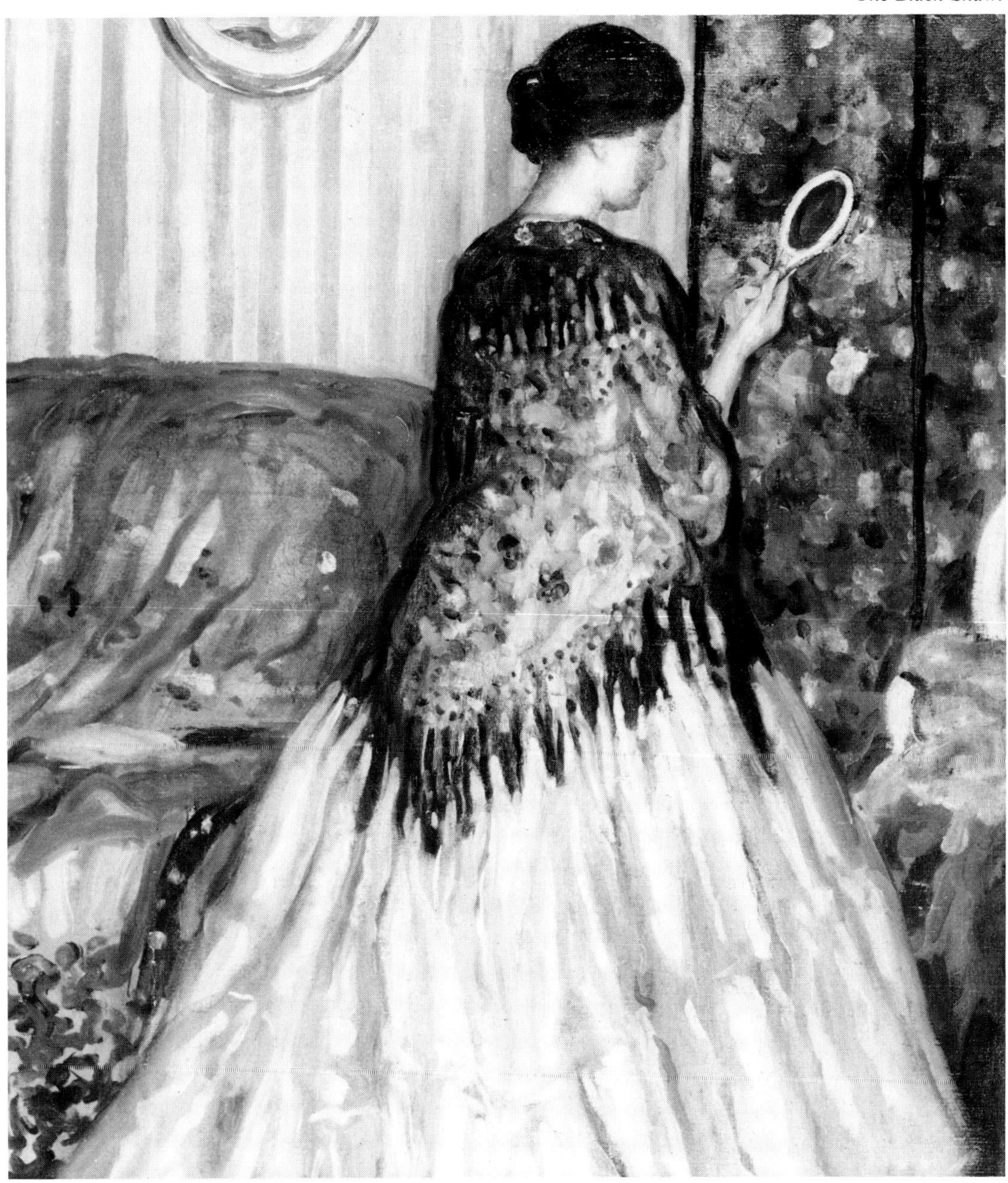

1986 Museum Purchase, Paul R. Ross Charitable Foundation Fund
1986.19

THOMAS W. DEWING (1851-1938)

Conversation
Oil on canvas, c.1925
16$^{1}/_{8}$'' x 25$^{1}/_{8}$''

A mood of poetic calm and quiet enigma pervades the atmosphere of this refined oil on canvas titled *Conversation* by the American impressionist, Thomas W. Dewing. The work was painted quite probably soon after the turn of the century and in every sense is clearly a masterpiece of understatement.

The setting is the interior of a spacious but sparsely furnished room. A flat multipanelled wall serves as a backdrop extending across the full width of the composition and is interrupted only by a centrally-located fireplace and mantle over which hangs a large mirror. Two young women dominate the space of the room, one standing at the left and the other seated at a circular table to the right of center. The only other objects in view are a small winged head on the mantle and two small windsor chairs, one near each end of the composition. Space is otherwise completely open and empty but alive, readily recalling the abstract spatial treatment so often found in 18th and 19th century Japanese prints.

Compositionally this work is of much unusual interest for it is clearly a combination of symmetrical and asymmetrical concepts, the backdrop wall being essentially a symmetrically balanced design while the seemingly vast space of the room is entirely asymmetrically organized. Three carefully plotted spatial coordinate points — the standing woman at the left, the seated woman at the table near the center and the small chair at the far right — define a straight line which pierces the room diagonally and imparts an energetic charge to the space. Indeed, both the visual appeal and the emotive impact derive from the powerful relationship of the two opposing points of view, so effectively integrated here through the use of geometry as the instrument of disciplined control.

The subject of this work is only superficially identified by the title *Conversation,* for the true thematic content itself remains ambiguous. However, it is quite likely that the artist is alluding here to woman's view of the meaning of existence in terms of the cult of virtuous womanhood that typified the thinking of one segment of the cultural climate that lingered on well beyond the turn of the century. For a dreamlike quality of remoteness and isolation, a cool detachment, is suggested. And that quality is of course heightened by the interest in the classically inspired gowns in which the slim figures are clad as well as by the use of pale tonalities and soft, blurred forms throughout the composition.

With slight variations, Dewing repeated this general composition many times during his career, using exterior as well as interior settings. And over and over again he used the same models, often dressed in the same gowns. Yet each of his works seems fresh and alive and each has the same evocative quality and the same compelling poetic refinement that we see here in *Conversation.*

Thomas Wilmer Dewing was born in Boston in 1851. From 1876 to 1879 he studied in Paris but thereafter settled in New York City. In 1887 he became an associate of the National Academy and in 1888 was elected a full Academician. Dewing was a member of a group of noted impressionist artists known as *The Ten American Painters* who exhibited together in New York in 1895. During his lifetime, he failed to receive the popular acclaim enjoyed by many of his contemporaries, though numerous major collectors and quite a few museums, both here and abroad, were perceptive enough to acquire his works. He died in New York in 1938 and today is recognized as one of the most original American masters of his period.

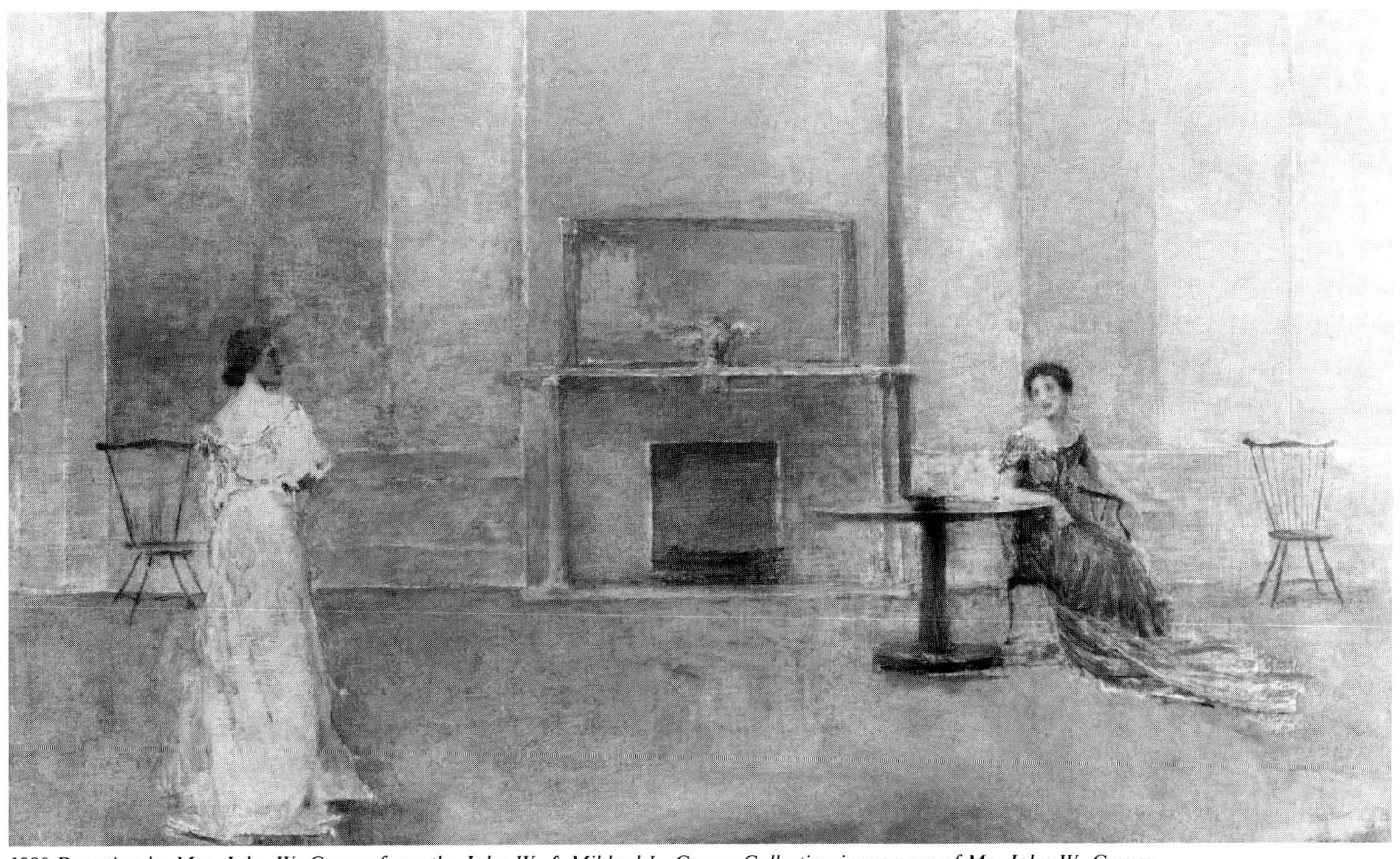

1980 Donation by Mrs. John W. Graves from the John W. & Mildred L. Graves Collection in memory of Mr. John W. Graves (1980.31)

GUY WIGGINS (1883-1962)

New England Christmas
Oil on canvas mounted on masonite, 1920
32" x 32"

A joyous Christmas mood reverberates through the clear night atmosphere of a small New England town in this 1920 oil painting by the American Impressionist Guy Carleton Wiggins and fittingly titled *New England Christmas.* In the background, the tall slender steeple of a typical Federal style church reaches upward beyond the top edge of the canvas. And immediately before the church stands a brightly lighted Christmas tree, capped with the traditional star of Bethlehem. In the foreground, amidst the cluster of leafless bushes and trees, a small crowd has congregated, perhaps preparing to return home following a midnight service on Christmas Eve. House lights dot the snow-blanketed hills of the village seen in the sloping distance to the left.

A feature of special interest is the symbolic parallel established between the tree and the church. Together they constitute the axis around which the entire composition is built, for both carry the eye upward toward the sky and both stand out brightly against the dark winter night, suggesting immortal life and the eternal victory of light over darkness. Moreover, the dignified proportions and delicately adapted classical forms of the church architecture are together echoed in the stability and stately balance of the tree and its refined strands of sparkling ornament. Indeed, by virtue of the close physical proximity of the tree to the church, we are suddenly made aware that the church building is essentially a geometric abstraction of the form of the tree itself. But, as is so typical of impressionist painting, the composition here is completely informal. And while each figure is readily discernible, detail is intentionally de-emphasized, for more important to the impressionist artist is his interest in surface tactility and his use of color and the creation of atmospheric effect.

Guy Carleton Wiggins was born in Brooklyn, New York, in 1883. He studied at the National Academy of Design and also with Robert Henri, and made several visits to Europe, especially to France. However, the influence of the impressionist manner on his work came primarily from other American painters, particularly Childe Hassam, and the themes which most appealed to him were winter landscapes of New England and snow-covered street scenes in New York City. Wiggins spent much of his mature life in Old Lyme, Connecticut, located on the Connecticut River in a region which, because of the many American impressionists working there, is sometimes referred to as the Giverny of America. Indeed, the church depicted here is the Old Lyme Congregational Church built a century before this painting was executed. Wiggins was a member of the National Academy, the Salgamundi Club, the Lotus Club and other art organizations, and today his works are included in major museum collections throughout the country. He died in Old Lyme in 1962.

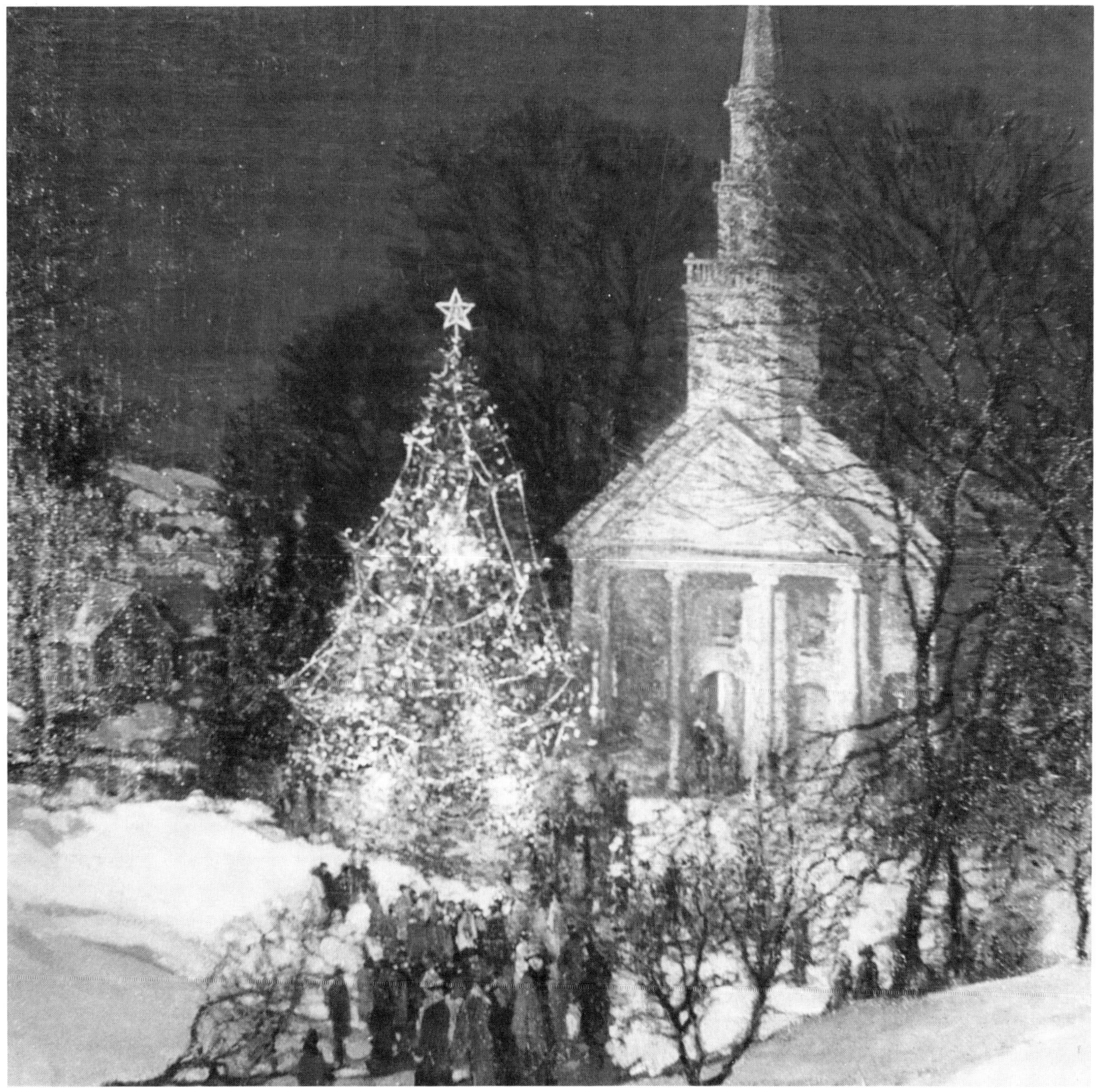

1977 Donation by the late Mr. & Mrs. Robert Carroll in memory of Mrs. Benjamin Robert Carroll (1977.55)

CHILDE HASSAM (1859-1935)

Jelly Fish
Oil on canvas, 1912
20$^1/_8$'' x 24$^1/_8$''

Throughout his long and highly prolific career, Childe Hassam was one of the dominant figures of the impressionist movement in American painting. Moreover the stylistic and technical diversities of Hassam's accomplishments over the years quite clearly testify to an active experimental interest that no doubt accounts for many of the advancements made by him in the cause of Modernism.

In this work titled *Jelly Fish* and painted in 1912, the setting is quite likely the Isles of Shoals off the New Hampshire coast where Hassam found inspiration for many thematically related paintings of the period. Here the solid forms of a jagged rocky mass reach out into a surrounding sea. And within the inlet between the arms of that rocky mass, jelly fish speckle the dark mossy water but except for supplying a touch of variety, offer nothing of significance to the composition.

In defining form, Hassam has employed thick and vigorous brushstrokes much in the pure impressionist manner, applying horizontal strokes to suggest quivering movement along the surface of the sea, and vertical and diagonal strokes along the solid rocks to suggest contours, textures and steep and irregular forms. What is so especially interesting is that the forms in this composition do not dissolve beneath the intensity of direct sunlight or behind a misty veil of color and atmosphere such as might be found in many earlier impressionist works but instead remain permanent and sharply focused. And it would seem likely that at this particular moment of Hassam's career he was interested in exploring the more enduring rather than the ephemeral qualities of nature. In that sense he was adopting a post-impressionist point of view as opposed to the pure impressionism of his earlier painting.

Certainly of equal interest is the fact that Hassam has furnished us with a bird's-eye view of the scene depicted. No horizon line is seen and traditional spatial concepts are absent. Instead what we see from above approximates a flattened surface view which imparts a powerfully abstract quality to the total composition, again suggesting a post-impressionist reaction to a traditional impressionist treatment. Indeed it is flattened space, bold and simplified design, the near purity of color and the unity of contrasts which together characterize this particular work making it one of Hassam's most successful and forward looking compositions of the period.

Frederick Childe Hassam was born in Dorchester, Massachusetts in 1859. He studied at the Boston Art Club and at the Lowell Institute. As a young artist he worked as a book illustrator and wood engraver and drew plates for such magazines as *Scribner's* and *Harper's Weekly*. That early background undoubtedly contributed to his remarkable accomplishments in etching and lithography after the turn of the century. Hassam is best known, however, for his painting of urban scenes — of Boston and more often of New York City.

In 1886 he sailed to France to study at the Academie Julien and while in France became acquainted with leading American impressionists including Metcalf, Twachtman and Robinson. On his return to America in 1889 he taught at the Art Students League and in 1898 became a founder member of the *Ten American Painters*. Hassam painted in New York City and quite frequently at various sites off the New England coasts. He died at East Hampton in 1935.

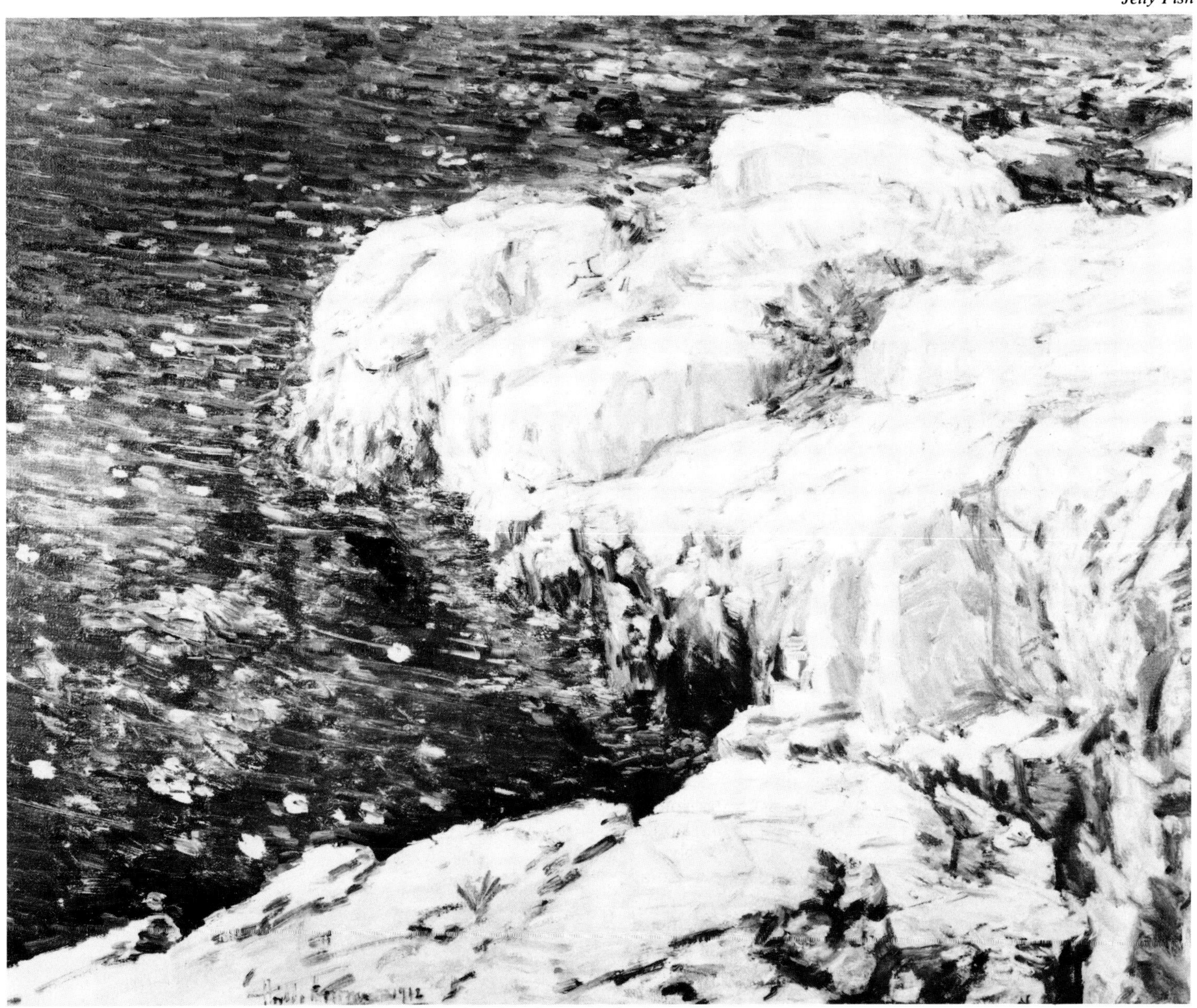

1986 Donation by Mrs. Ross Weir from the John W. & Mildred L. Graves Collection
(1986.50)

CHILDE HASSAM (1859-1935)

Childe Hassam was one of the most prominent painters among America's impressionists. He spent three years from 1886 to 1889 in Paris where he gained both knowledge and inspiration from the French Impressionist painters, although the style which he developed bears only superficial resemblance to theirs. In 1898 he joined with other American painters including J. Alden Weir and John Twachtman to form the well known impressionist group known as "The Ten".

Hassam painted actively throughout a long career. One of his comparatively late works, executed in 1921, is titled *The Spirit of the Harvest*. Here long strokes of cool colors, primarily blue, green, light yellow and white, appear to be scambled rapidly and spontaneously across the surface of the canvas. Yet actually these strokes are so organized as to create space, form and atmosphere in terms of color rather than of linear definition and conventional modeling. The result creates the impression of a dazzling sunlit field ripe for harvest. Slightly to the left of center stands a nude nymph-like figure holding up a bundle of freshly threshed grain. But while space consists only of a pattern of pure colors, the nymph figure is defined by sharply drawn contour lines and is modeled in soft pink body tones applied in short dashes of color. Indeed, the nymph actually seems to emerge out of the surrounding space and maintains its own distinctness and individuality by virtue of its outline and modeling, in contrast with the more vibrant surrounding space and background.

It is interesting that Hassam would have introduced a nymph in this composition. He employed such motifs in many of his works during the late teens and throughout the 1920s and was sometimes criticized for so doing. Yet the significance of such mythologically derived imagery is perhaps too often ignored. For here the nymph, distinct from and at the same time an inseparable part of the natural surround, would seem to clearly represent the secret soul of the harvest, the generative force of nature given visible form as the victory of continuous rebirth and renewal in the life cycle. Symbolically, the suggestion is one deeply rooted in human thought and, moreover, is certainly one that has found expression in much American painting throughout the 19th and 20th centuries, a fact which places Hassam squarely within the American tradition, even though his formal technique generally reflected the continuing influence of French impressionism.

Beginning in 1919, Hassam spent summers in East Hampton, Long Island, where this work no doubt was painted. In 1935 he died in East Hampton.

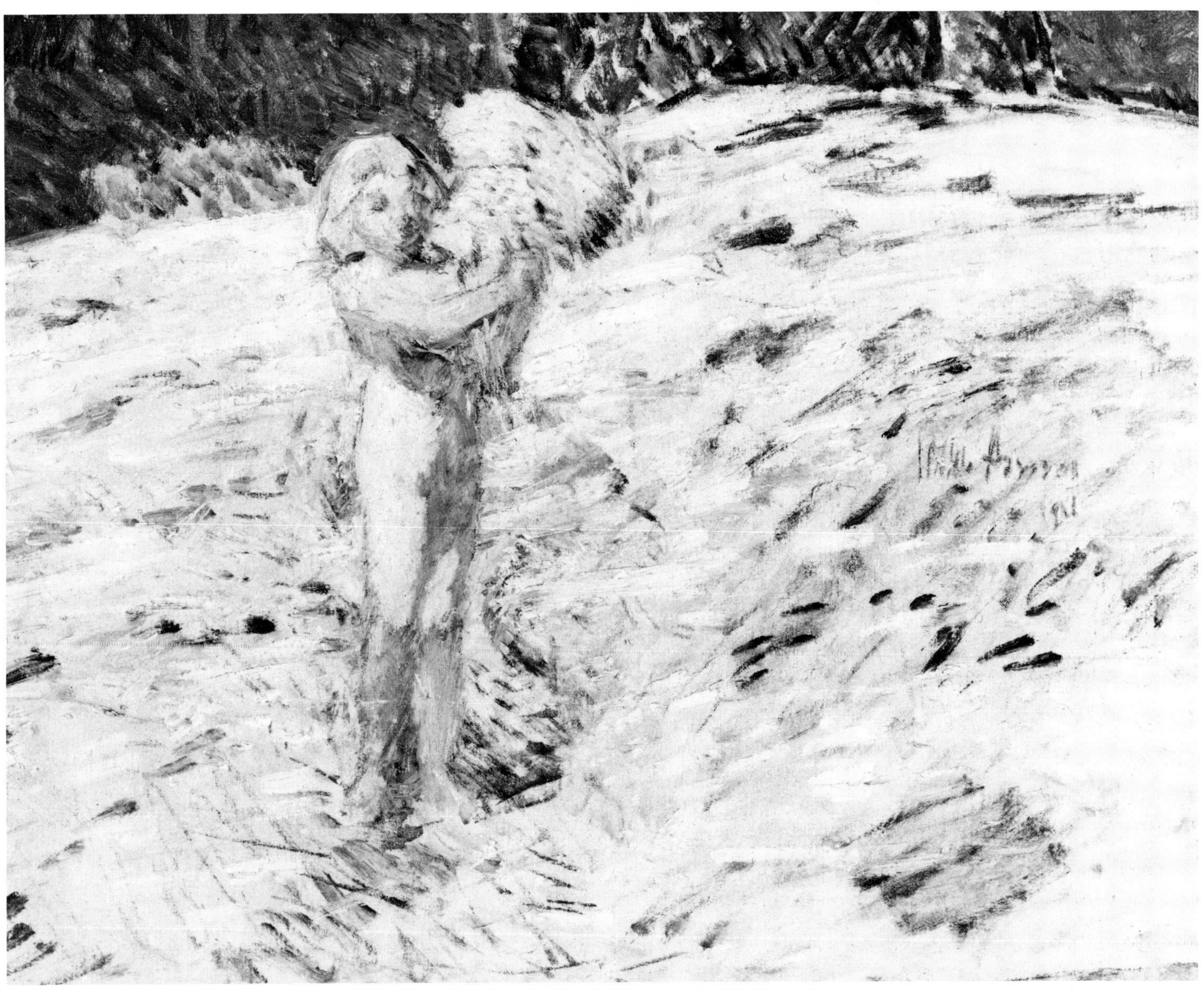

1983 Museum Purchase, Volunteer Operated Sales/Rental Gallery Art Fund, Friends of the Wichita Art Museum (1983.14)

EDWARD POTTHAST (1857-1927)

The Bathers
Oil on canvas, c.1915
30¹/₈'' x 24¹/₈''

For centuries, many artists, both in America and abroad, have been denied adequate and well deserved public recognition during their lifetimes and for many years following their deaths. Such was certainly the case with Edward Potthast whose paintings were to no small degree largely ignored from the time of his death in 1927 until just a decade or so ago.

Like many of his American contemporaries of the early 20th century, Potthast was interested in composing scenes that consisted of people engaged in rather commonplace amusement. A subject which he most favored and in which he brilliantly excelled was one of people vacationing at the beach. Certainly among his finest paintings in that genre is this lively work simply titled *The Bathers* which he executed about 1915. Here groups of bathers are shown standing in the rather shallow waters near the edge of the beach. In the distance is seen a rough surf with lashing waves that crash into white foamy masses. The bathers are arranged in two groups, one of five figures standing in a wide broken circle, and the other of three figures grouped in a triadic relationship at the far left. In addition, two figures — one in the distance at the far right and the other in the center foreground — are apparently swimming, for their bodies are completely immersed and only their heads are visible above the water surface.

Potthast's palette consists of greens, blues and various shades of mauve with scattered dabs of bright reds and yellows. What is especially interesting is the manner in which he relates those vivid colors to one another, modelling the forms and at the same time creating variety and vigorous movement across the surface of the composition. Throughout, features are generalized and are painted in a thick impasto with clearly visible brushstrokes. Vitality and a spirited sense of gaiety are further imparted by the bright sunlight which pervades the composition and by the strongly accented contrasts between shadows and adjacent dashes of colored highlights.

Potthast was born in 1857 in Cincinnati, Ohio where as a youth he worked as a lithographer. However, from 1882 to 1885 and again from 1887 to 1889, he studied painting in Munich and in other major European cities. By 1896 he settled permanently in New York City where he worked with other noted impressionists. Most of his paintings were executed out of doors rather than in the studio. Although he received considerable recognition as an artist and developed an extensive buying public, he was apparently an unusually modest man who regarded most of his works as simple sketches. His consistent refusal to participate in major painting competitions no doubt accounts in part for the neglect which his paintings experienced until quite recently. Potthast died a bachelor in New York in 1927.

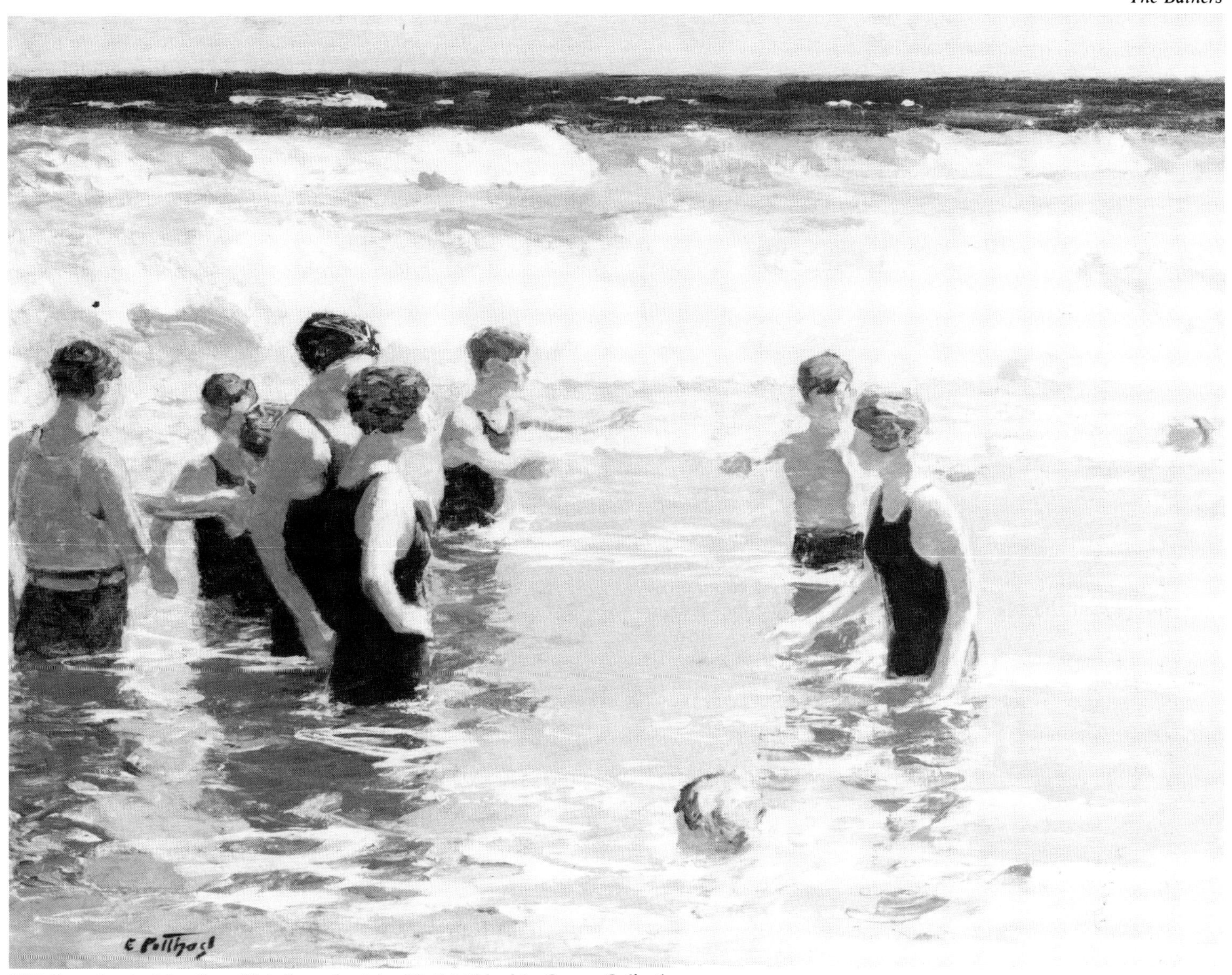

*1985 Donation by Mrs. Ross Weir from the John W. & Mildred L. Graves Collection
(1985.1)*

JEROME MYERS (1867-1940)

The Playground
Oil on canvas, 1925
18" x 22"

Jerome Myers was one of the most active artists in America during the early 20th century. Stylistically, the serenity and poetic sensitivity of his paintings echoed his own gentle personality, and certainly these qualities are fully realized in this delightful work titled *The Playground* which Myers executed in 1925. As the title indicates, the setting here is a spacious playground enclosed within a heavy wooden fence and crowded with gaily dressed young children. Perhaps what most delights the viewer are the candid poses and dainty gestures, the happy expressions and the harmonious interaction of the children at play, some quietly seated on benches or wooden crates, some frolicking about, others absorbed in conversation. Moreover, the forms of the many children scattered across the surface of the canvas produce a spirited effect much heightened by the loose and vigorous brushwork within clearly delineated contours, a quality that so typically characterized the artist's style.

One of the most striking features of this work is the effective use of a rather somber tonal background as a foil, enabling the many daubs of soft colors to scintillate, and thereby enlivening the composition and imparting an overall accented surface pattern reminiscent of that of an embroidered Gothic tapestry. But above all else the most compelling aspect of this work is Myers' ability to communicate so vividly his own tender affection for the gentle simplicity and joyous innocence of children.

Both in theme and in style, Jerome Myers worked much in the manner of the ash can painters who were his contemporaries and his friends. Yet he obviously was influenced also by the American Impressionist movement of the late 19th and 20th centuries. At the same time the dark tones commonly found in his works clearly reflect the 19th century Munich school technique which was popular in America at the turn of the century.

Myers was born in Petersburg, Virginia in 1867. As a young boy he moved first to Baltimore and then to New York City where he studied at the Cooper Union and the Art Students League. Myers traveled widely in Europe but throughout his career insisted that he could find the most meaningful and most satisfying subject matter among the immigrant people — and especially the children — of New York's lower East Side. He was an associate member of the National Academy and participated in the well-known Armory Show in 1913, and throughout much of his career was closely associated with Robert Henri. Shortly before his death in 1940, he completed his highly informative autobiography titled *Artist in Manhattan.*

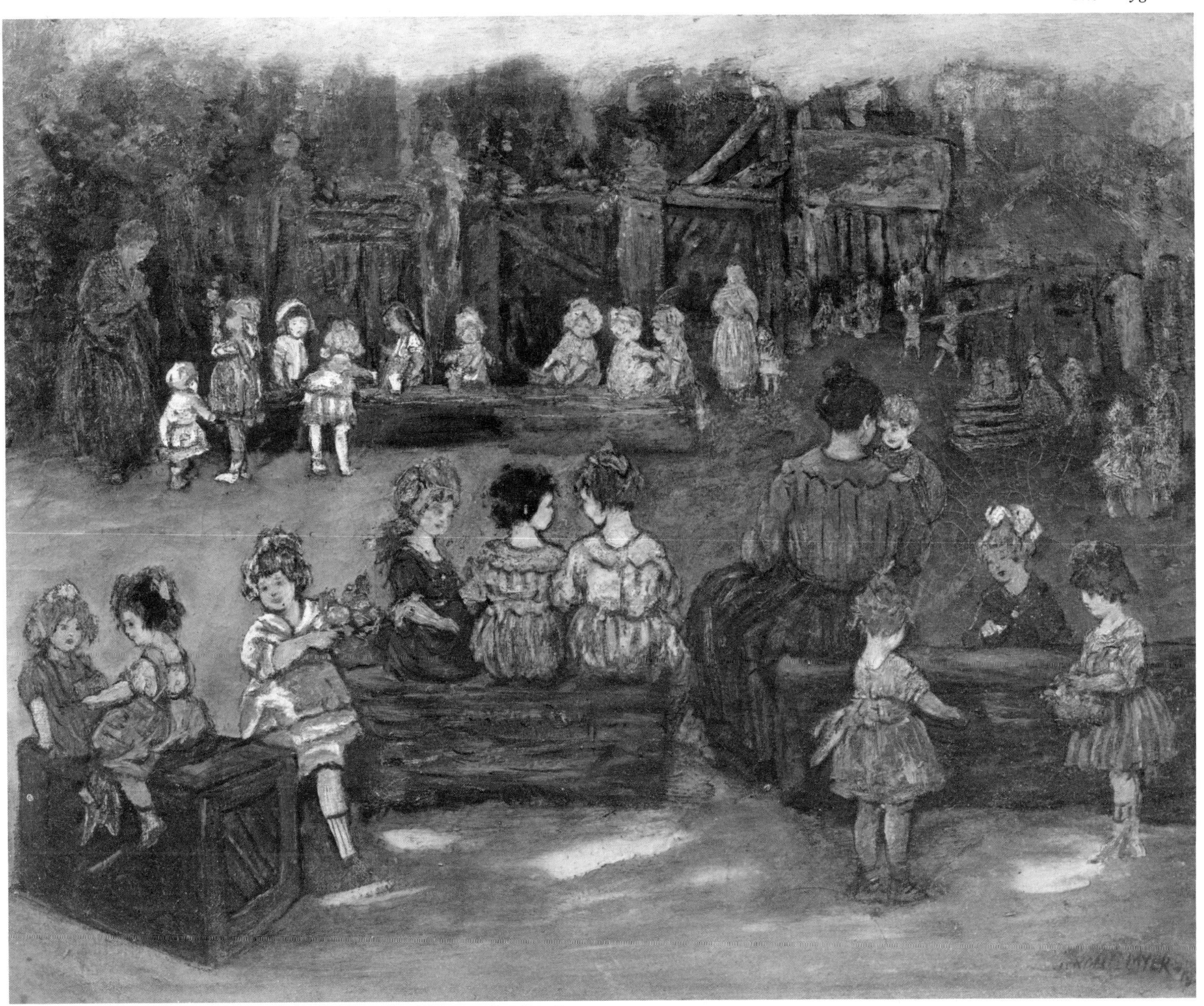

1984 Museum Purchase, Friends of the Wichita Art Museum Art Fund
(1984.40)

ELLIOTT DAINGERFIELD (1859-1932)

Glowing Sunset
Oil on canvas, c.1920
14" x 20"

One of America's most popular painters during the late 19th and early 20th centuries was Elliott Daingerfield. In his long and prolific career, he produced works in a wide variety of types and styles. Yet his best known paintings were romantic landscapes that often evoke a melancholy mood and that are stylistically reminiscent of the painterly qualities characteristic of the French Barbizon artists of the period.

In this work titled *Glowing Sunset* executed by Daingerfield about 1920, a shepherdess and two sheep are seen in a rustic setting with a hazy sun sinking in the distance at the close of an early autumn day. Rich colors are employed throughout the composition and a lively surface is achieved by the employment of thick and sometimes swirling brushstrokes. A distinguishing feature is Daingerfield's interest in developing misty, softened forms and in placing closely related color tones adjacent to one another throughout much of the composition. And while all forms maintain their identity, they tend at the same time to merge within the encompassing space. The overall impression becomes one of a fuzzy veil stretched across the surface of the canvas blurring the forms which thus appear as though seen in a dream passing fleetingly in a brief instant of time. Indeed it is this poetic, dream-like effect rather than the theme of a shepherdess which is actually the dominant subject of this painting.

Elliott Daingerfield was born in Harper's Ferry, West Virginia in 1859. His youth was spent in Fayetteville, North Carolina where he studied with a porcelain painter and subsequently served as a photographer's apprentice. In 1880, at the age of 21, he settled in New York City and studied at the Art Students League. Within a few years, he became closely associated with George Inness whose influence is strikingly evident in many of his landscapes including *Glowing Sunset*. Daingerfield was a noted author and critic as well as an artist, and published the biography of George Inness and wrote critical accounts of other artists of the period, including Ralph Blakelock. His works are included in major museums and private collections throughout the nation. He was 73 years of age when he died in his studio in New York City in 1932.

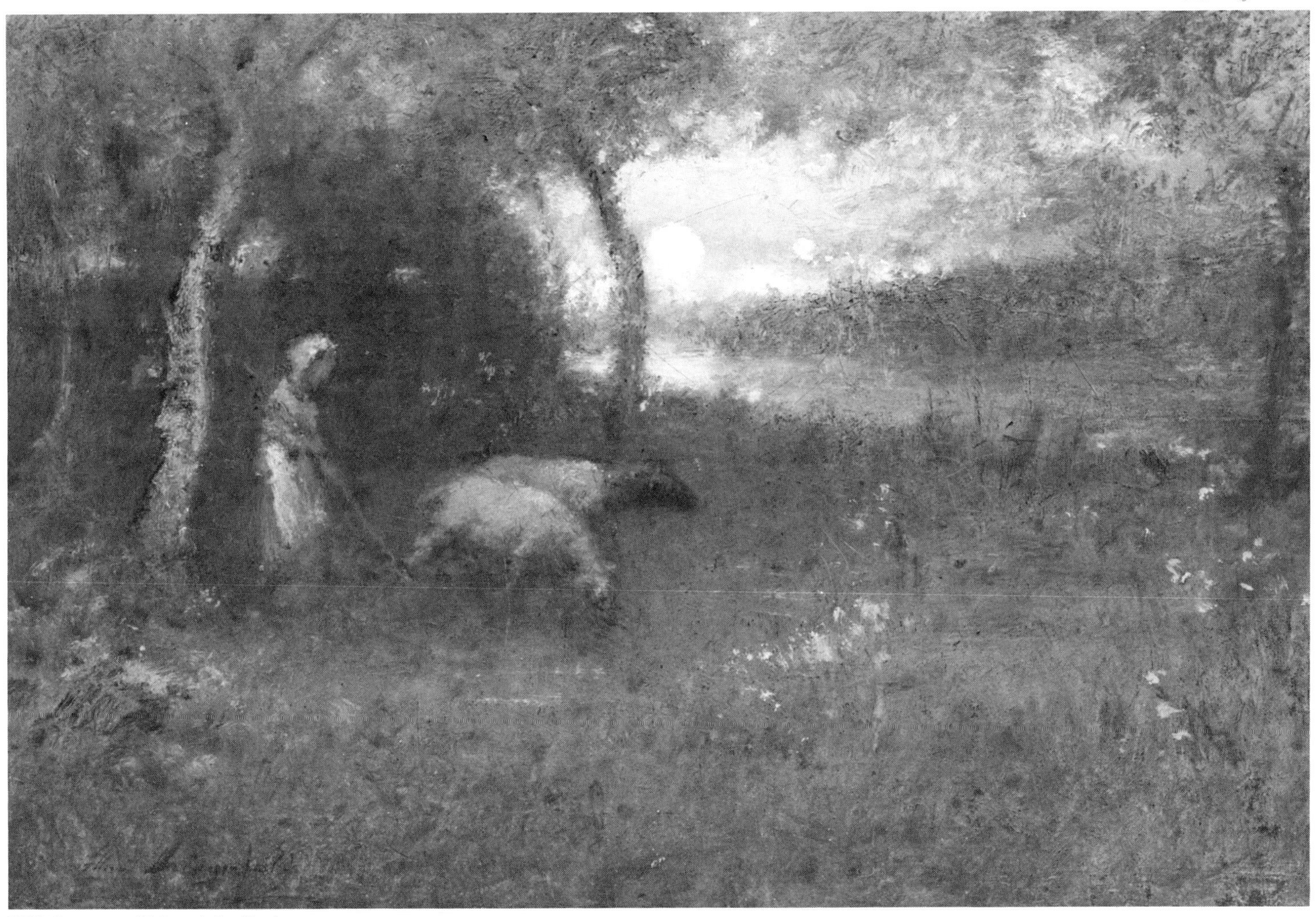

1980 Bequest of Mrs. A.L. Derby
(1980.79.2)

EUGENE HIGGINS (1874-1958)

A Mountain Home
Oil on canvas, c.1925
18¹/₈" x 24¼"

Eugene Higgins was born in Kansas City, Missouri in 1874 and died in New York City in 1958. Throughout his long and productive career as painter and etcher, a profoundly sentimental compassion for the downtrodden and the oppressed dominated the theme of almost every work he produced. For Higgins was a member of the democratic realist school and worked within the early 20th century Ash Can tradition of painting, attempting to record life as it was rather than as it should or might be. He was never a pessimist, but neither was he oblivious of tragedy in the lives of society's casualties, of the poor and homeless or simply of the weary and toil laden.

In 1925, Higgins visited Ireland, the source of inspiration for this painting titled *A Mountain Home : Achille Island, Ireland.* Here a sturdy old peasant woman, slightly bent over and carrying a basket on her arm, trudges towards her home situated on a hill at the end of a mountain road. Her bulky form echoes the crudely built stone house with its thatched roof and animal shed at the left, and the rugged rocky terrain of the desolate setting as a whole. Deep shadows, dark and somber tones and a fading afterglow in the distance together evoke a mood of melancholy. Yet Higgins saw honor and self-respect in toil and here in the figure of the Irish peasant woman he imparts a sense of dignity, substance and sureness of purpose. At the same time he introduces a sense of hope and individual achievement by the billow of smoke which rises from the chimney and suggests the warmth and security of home.

As a young man, Higgins studied at the Ecole des Beaux-Arts in Paris. Yet his works reflect no strong academic interest but instead are highly generalized symbolic statements with little or no emphasis on particularities. Moreoever, his repeated use of somber tones and the application of broad masses of thick opaque pigment recall the technique of the American romantic visionary, Albert Pinkham Ryder. At the same time his treatment of the human figure bears obvious resemblance, both in sentiment and in style, to works by the noted 19th century French painter Millet and, to a lesser degree, Daumier.

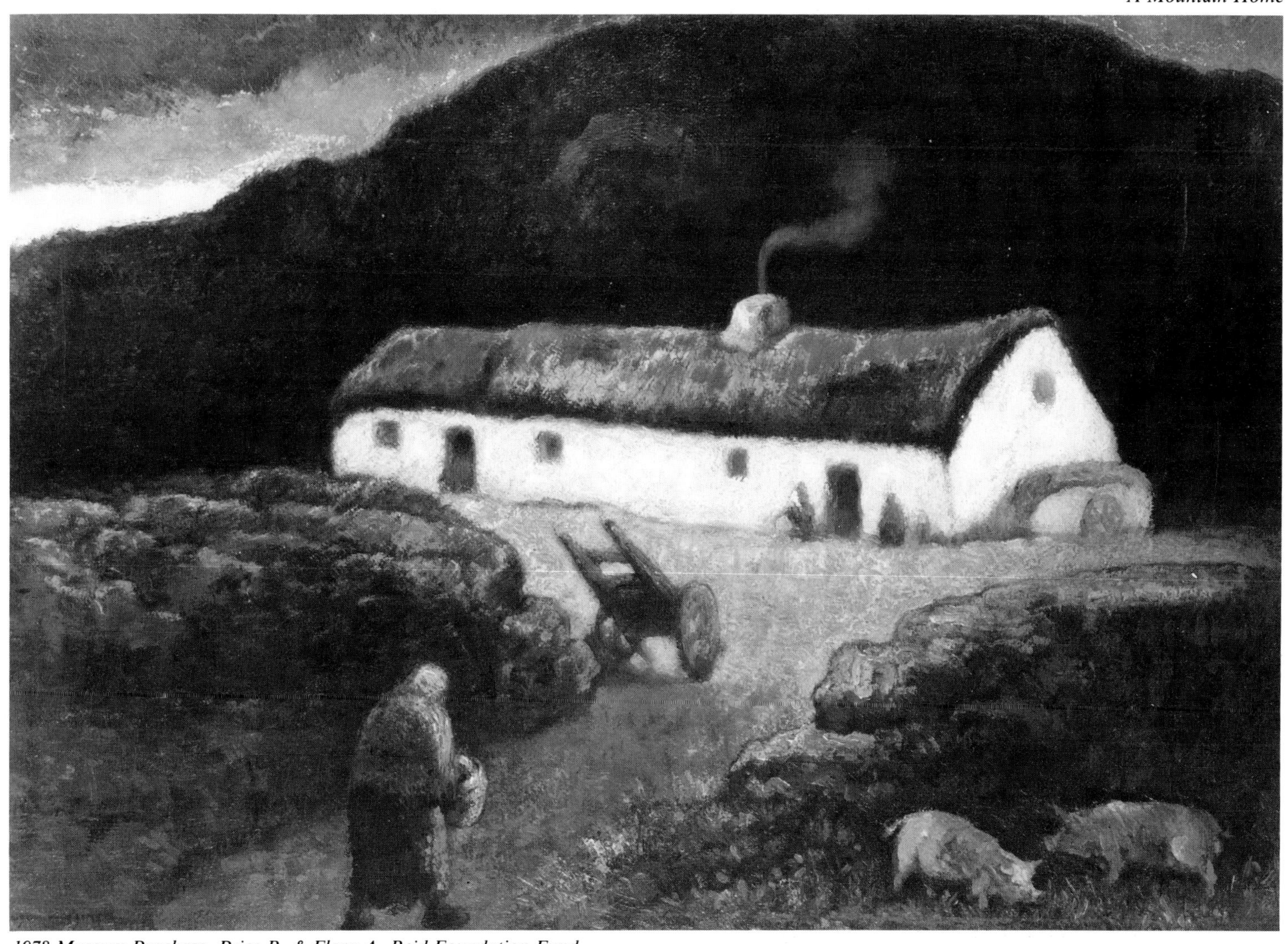

1978 Museum Purchase, Price R. & Flora A. Reid Foundation Fund
(1978.104)

ISABEL BISHOP (1902-1988)

Self Portrait
Oil on canvas, 1927
14¹/₈" x 13"

Isabel Bishop was one of America's most admired contemporary artists. She was born in Cincinnati in 1902, spent her early years in Detroit, and while still a rather young girl in 1918, settled in New York City. There she studied at the Art Students League during the 1920s with the noted painter and teacher, Kenneth Hayes Miller, and worked closely with such artists as Reginald Marsh, Edward Laning, Guy Pene du Bois and many others whose studios were then concentrated in New York's Union Square section. In 1933 she held her first solo exhibition at the prestigious Midtown Gallery which continued to represent her until her death in February, 1988.

From the beginning of her career Isabel Bishop proved herself to be a masterful draftsman and a keen observer of human life and of the manner in which human beings relate to one another in the everyday world of urban living. That keen power of observation is the force that has enabled her to penetrate so deeply into personality and discover and express qualities of universal humanness. What is so fascinating is that she could apply that rare capability to herself as well as to others, as is so evident in this engaging self-portrait executed more than 60 years ago in 1927 when she was only 25 years old and living in a loft on West 14th Street in lower Manhattan.

In this work, the subtle modeling and the delicate handling of flesh tones has enabled the artist to render her own distinctive physical features with care and exactness. But the success of the portrait as a work of art depends upon numerous factors other than physical likeness alone. Of particular interest is the fact that the soft focus realism which was to become so characteristic of Bishop's work is already in evidence here, as for example in the treatment of the fur shoulder wrap which merges with the warm tones of the nondescript background, allowing the face alone to stand out prominently in high relief. Moreover, the head tilted slightly and gently turned to our left, partly faces forward so that our attention is grasped by the radiantly penetrating eyes. But perhaps the most compelling feature of this work is the thoughtful facial expression itself, emphasized by the expressive left hand drawn to her face with the little finger delicately touching her lips. This is indeed the image of a young and vitally creative person who with but the slightest glimmer of a smile on her face is in contemplative thought as she looks outward observing us and the world about her. And it is the clarity of vision, so convincingly suggested here in this very early work, that came to be the determinant of both the style and the content of Bishop's paintings throughout her long and enormously successful career.

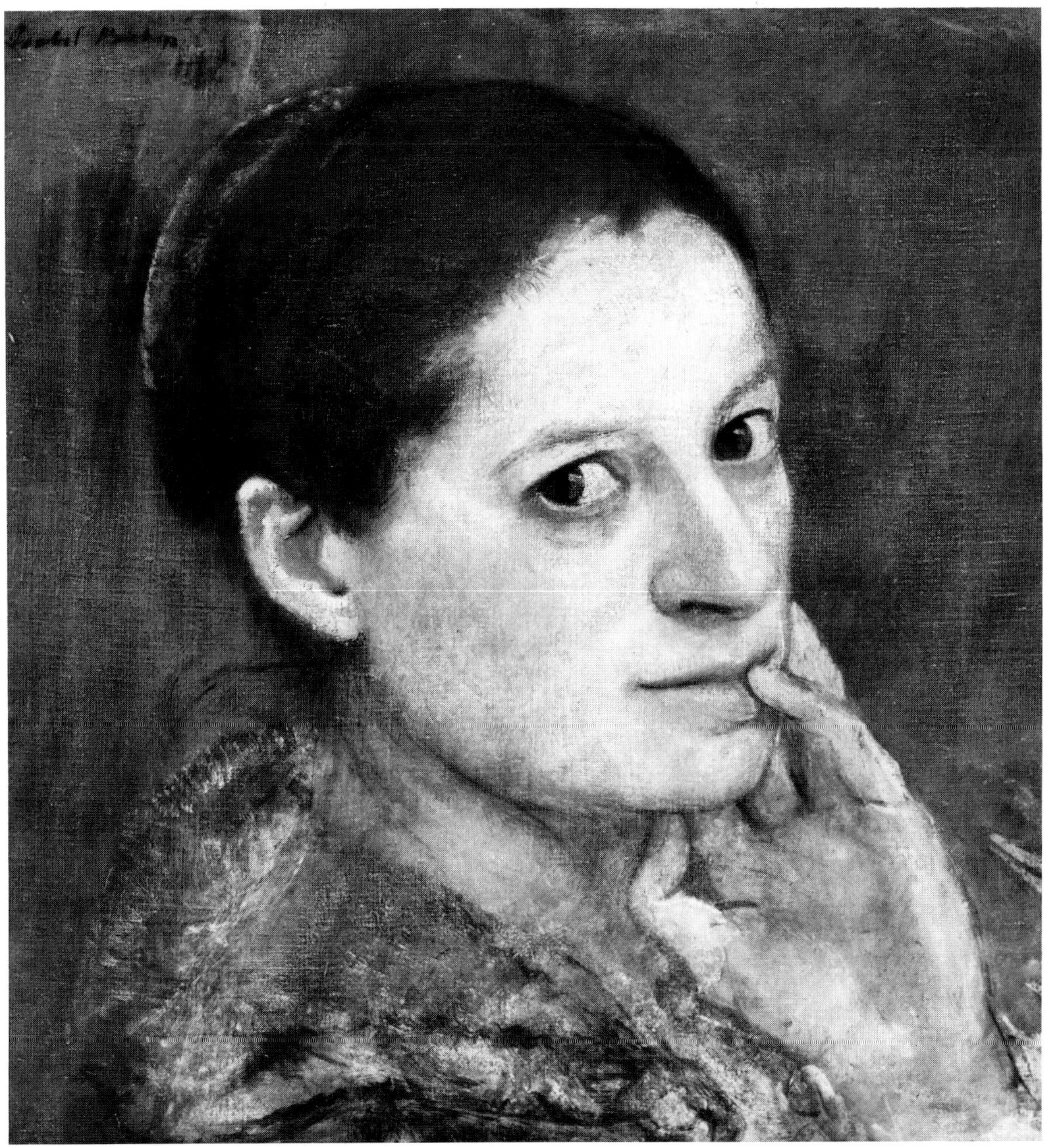

1981 Museum Purchase, Friends of the Wichita Art Museum Art Fund
(1981.34)

GEORGIA O'KEEFFE (1887-1986)

East River No. 1
Oil on linen, 1926
12$^1/_8$" x 32$^1/_8$"

It was in 1926, while living in New York City, that Georgia O'Keeffe painted this romantic view of the East River as seen from the window of her 30th story apartment in the Shelton Hotel in Manhattan. The work, titled *East River No. 1,* is one of the earliest and possibly even the first in a series of similar New York views executed by O'Keeffe between 1926 and 1928.

Most of O'Keeffe's earlier works had been abstractions, some pure geometric abstractions in color and some derived from close-up observations of flowers. However, by the early 1920s she began to move stylistically toward semi-abstract and more realist works. In this particular painting, the composition is, of course, representational and the scene is a familiar view which, at first glance, suggests a black and white photograph. Indeed, the use of only black and white pigments momentarily recalls photography more than painting, and a point of much interest here is the possible influence of the well-known photographs of Alfred Stieglitz, whom O'Keeffe had married just two years earlier. But, unlike a photograph, this painting contains only the essential forms and relationships necessary to communicate general impressions and evoke mood. All excessive detail that might obscure the truth of vision or feeling is discarded. That keen ability to reduce to absolute essentials while at the same time retaining clear recognition of figurative reality has been one of O'Keeffe's distinguishing accomplishments throughout her career.

While *East River No. 1* may be said to be what we call a *realist* painting, it is also very much an abstraction, in this instance a pleasing arrangement primarily of lines and rectilinear shapes and one sensitively rendered in the most subtly contrasting tonal variations ranging across the entire black-white value scale. Furthermore, when we closely investigate the compositional structure of this work, we find that it consists basically of three horizontal registers: the foreground buildings which hug the near edge of the river, the ice-covered river itself, and finally the smog-engulfed factories on the far side of the river. Although these three horizontal divisions stretch across the entire length of the painting, they are nevertheless harmoniously united both by a carefully orchestrated tonal scheme which pervades the entire composition and by virtue of the strong perpendicular emphasis imparted by the vertical thrust of some of the buildings. This is especially evident in the case of the center smoke-stack which rises in the frontal plane and moves upward across the icy river, penetrating into the top register and binding the three registers together. Then, too, this smoke-stack in effect bilaterally cuts the composition in half, thus tending to neutralize the otherwise dominant horizontality.

Georgia O'Keeffe's life was as interesting and exciting as were her paintings. She was born in 1887 in Wisconsin and, at the age of 10, decided to become an artist. It was in 1915 that her works first came to the attention of the eminent artist-photographer, Alfred Stieglitz, who operated the avant garde Gallery 291 in New York. From 1918 to 1949, she lived primarily in New York City and married Stieglitz in 1924. Throughout that period, she held frequent exhibitions at Stieglitz's several galleries, and it was at his Intimate Gallery that *East River No. 1* was first shown. In 1949, O'Keeffe took residence in Abiquiu where she remained until shortly before her death in 1986.

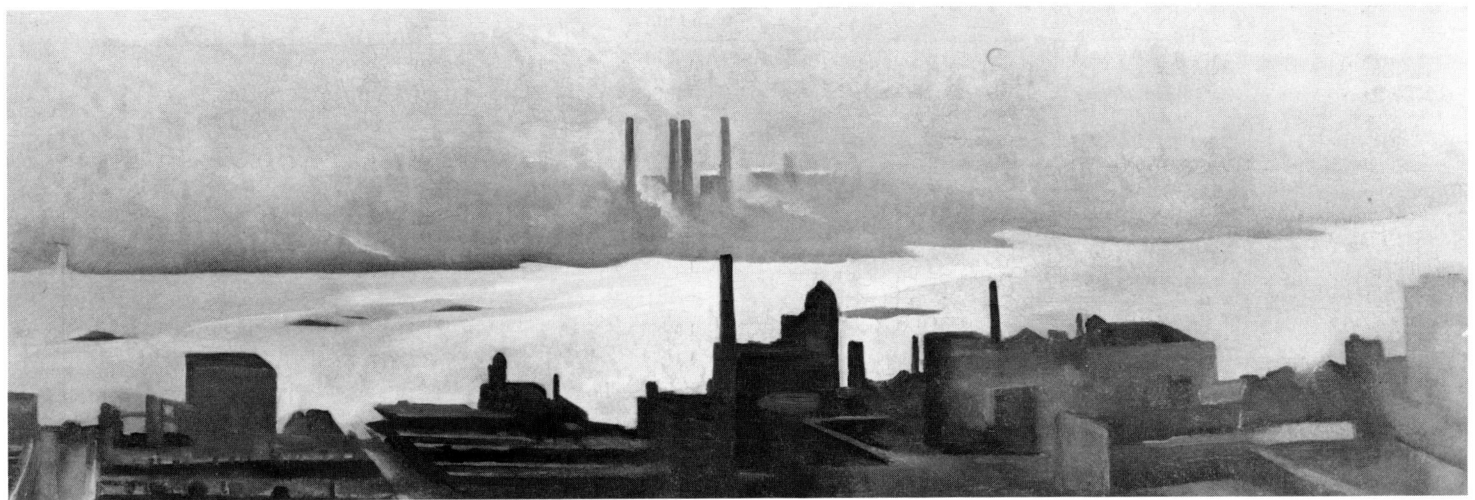

1979 Museum Purchase, Friends of the Wichita Art Museum Art Fund
(1979.35)

JOHN STORRS (1885-1956)

Ceres
Cast terracotta, nickel-plated, 1930
20¼'' h. x 5'' w. x 3³/₈'' d.

Although John Storrs spent more of his life in Europe than in America, he is recognized today as one of America's most distinguished sculptors of the period from the close of World War I until the beginning of World War II. During that period of two decades, much of the sculpture produced was closely associated with architectural projects and certainly one of Storrs' best-known works was the 31-foot-high aluminum figure of *Ceres* commissioned as a finial for the Board of Trade Building in Chicago. That building was completed in 1929 by the well-known architectural firm of Holobird and Root, but the Ceres sculpture was not installed until 1930. In the process of producing the large scale Ceres figure, Storrs executed numerous small models, one of which, seen here, is a 21-inch-high piece constructed of nickel-plated terracotta.

The work depicts the ancient agricultural goddess, Ceres, who symbolized the generative powers of nature and thus complements the grain market function of the Board of Trade. And stylistically, the work epitomizes Art Deco, one of the dominant aesthetic movements of the period, and is certainly Storrs' most significant Art Deco creation. The figure is tall and slender and stands erect. Facial features are lacking altogether. Shoulders are wide and curved but the body form tapers downwards and is fully draped. The arms are held tightly against a rigid and totally motionless body, no portion of which is revealed except the breasts and the stylized hands. What is most particularly evident are the long parallel drapery folds clearly reminiscent of the flutings of a classical architectural column. Indeed, the entire figure is geometrically conceptualized in rigid symmetrical terms but for the two slightly outstretched hands, one holding a sheaf of wheat bearing a zig-zag surface pattern, the other a bag of sample grain.

Stylistically, these aspects are highly significant and reflect clearly the aesthetic outlook of the period for the work is fully streamlined and is clearly indicative of the period's interest in elegance, machine precision and gleaming and polished surfaces. Streamlining is expressed through the interplay of straight lines and definite curves throughout the composition of the figure. And, as a design concept, streamlining was of course introduced for the purpose of increasing ease of motion and eliminating resistance to speed, yet as the Art Deco period proceeded such streamlining became more an aesthetic consideration than a functional one. Certainly it found expression both in painting and in the sculpture of the period and, more particularly, in the decorative arts from which the term ''Deco'' itself derives. However, although the Art Deco movement reached its height during the period between the two wars, with the close of World War II the style went out of fashion and only recently has experienced a considerable revival.

John Storrs was born in Chicago in 1885. He attended the Chicago University High School. In 1913, he began serious study in sculpture under Rodin in France and, in 1914, married Marguerite Chabrol in Orleans, France, where four years later his only child, Monique, was born. It was in 1929, as we have seen, that he executed the *Ceres* for the Board of Trade Building, and in 1932 and 1933, was commissioned to execute a number of sculptures, both in the round and in relief, for the Century of Progress Exhibition at the Chicago World's Fair. Storrs spent most of the remainder of his life in Orleans, France, and made his final trip to the United States in 1939. He presented numerous exhibitions throughout the Loire Valley during the 1940s and early 1950s and died at Chateau de Chantecaille in 1956 at seventy-one.

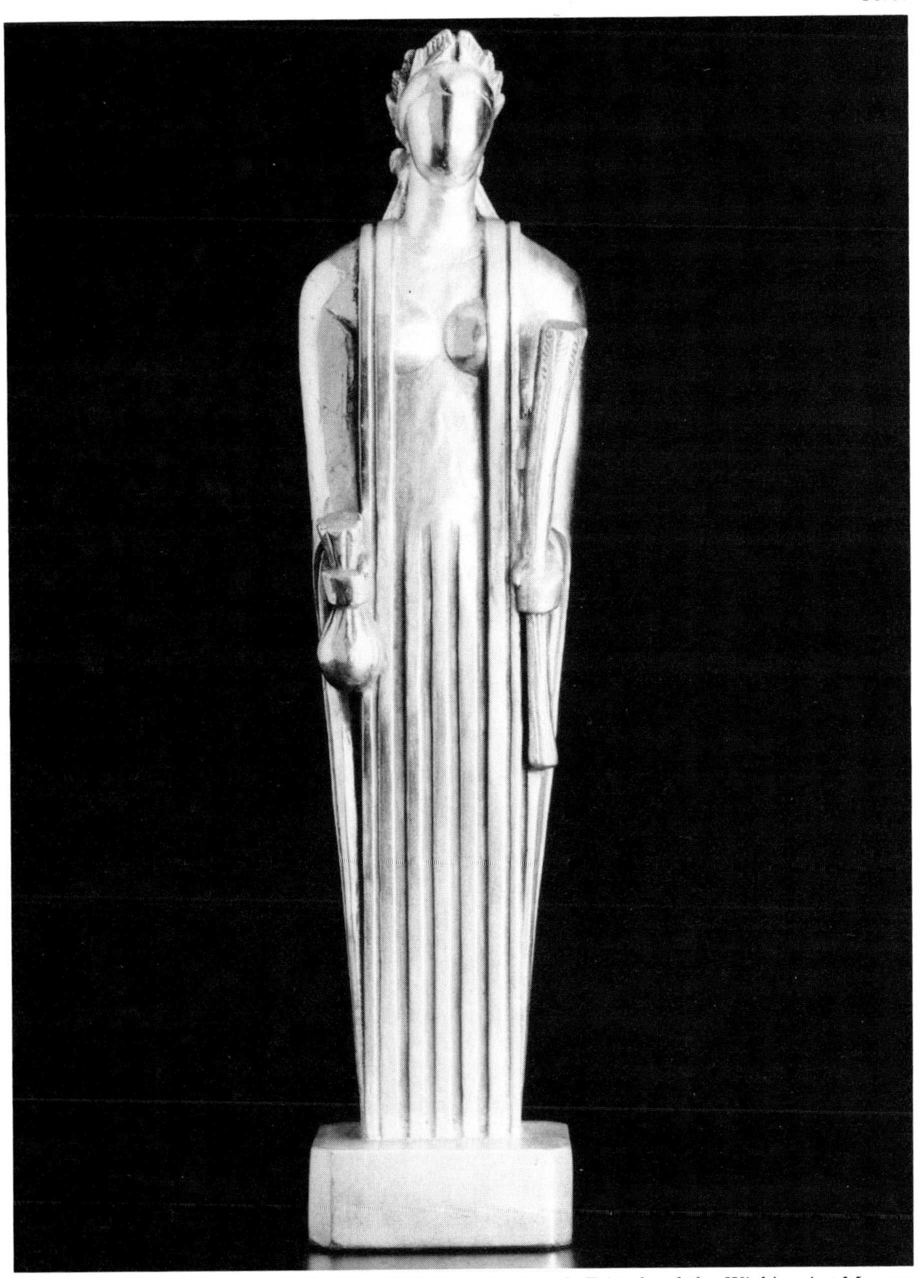

1987 Museum Purchase, Volunteer Operated Sales/Rental Gallery Art Fund, Friends of the Wichita Art Museum (1987.7)

HUGO ROBUS (1885-1964)

Girl Reading
Cast bronze, 1929/1963
15¾'' h. x 17'' l. x 15'' d.

This bronze sculpture titled *Girl Reading* by the American artist Hugo Robus was cast in 1963, just one year before the artist's death. But the work itself was modeled in 1929 and clearly captures the spirit of the Art Deco Movement that flourished during the period of the '20s and '30s both here in America and abroad.

Here a young adolescent girl is shown partially reclining and leaning on her right arm with her head tilted down toward a book which she is reading. What is immediately apparent, however, is that her book is actually not visible to us and must be supplied by our imagination, thus forcing us to participate intimately in completing the intended meaning of the composition itself. But perhaps the most striking feature of this work is found in the simplified but highly refined forms and in the organic geometry of coiling lines and interlocking masses. Moreover, the smoothly polished texture of the bronze medium produces gleaming highlights that scatter across the soft and supple surface of the body imparting a quality of sensual elegance and commanding tactility so typical of many works executed by Robus at this time.

Aesthetic coherence is achieved here by virtue of the combination of complex and rhythmic curves which flow from the lower back upward to the shoulders and around the head and face and thereafter carry across the left arm looping around the abdomen and finally along the right arm and up to the shoulder and the head. Indeed, in this work the artist uses body form as he wishes, freely introducing distortions which create a lively three-dimensional abstraction rather than a literal representation of human anatomy. At the same time, however, qualities of innocence, fresh vitality and uninhibited adolescence are convincingly communicated with great charm and visual delight.

A point of special interest is the bare head with but short tresses of hair combed at the sides and back as well as the smiling facial expression and the affectations of body gesture. These features are frequently found in works from the fashionable Art Deco period and to no small degree betray the influence of Egyptian painting and sculpture from the 18th Dynasty which had gained much popularity during the early 20th century.

In a discussion of a 1916 painting by Hugo Robus (see above, page 46) it was noted that although Robus' early interest was focused solely on painting, by about 1920 he shifted his attention and efforts entirely to sculpture for the rest of his life. Yet he was forced to wait until the early 1950s before receiving the recognition he deserved as a sculptor. In 1958 he held a one-man exhibition at the Corcoran Gallery of Art and in 1960 a major retrospective at the Whitney Museum. He died in New York City in 1964.

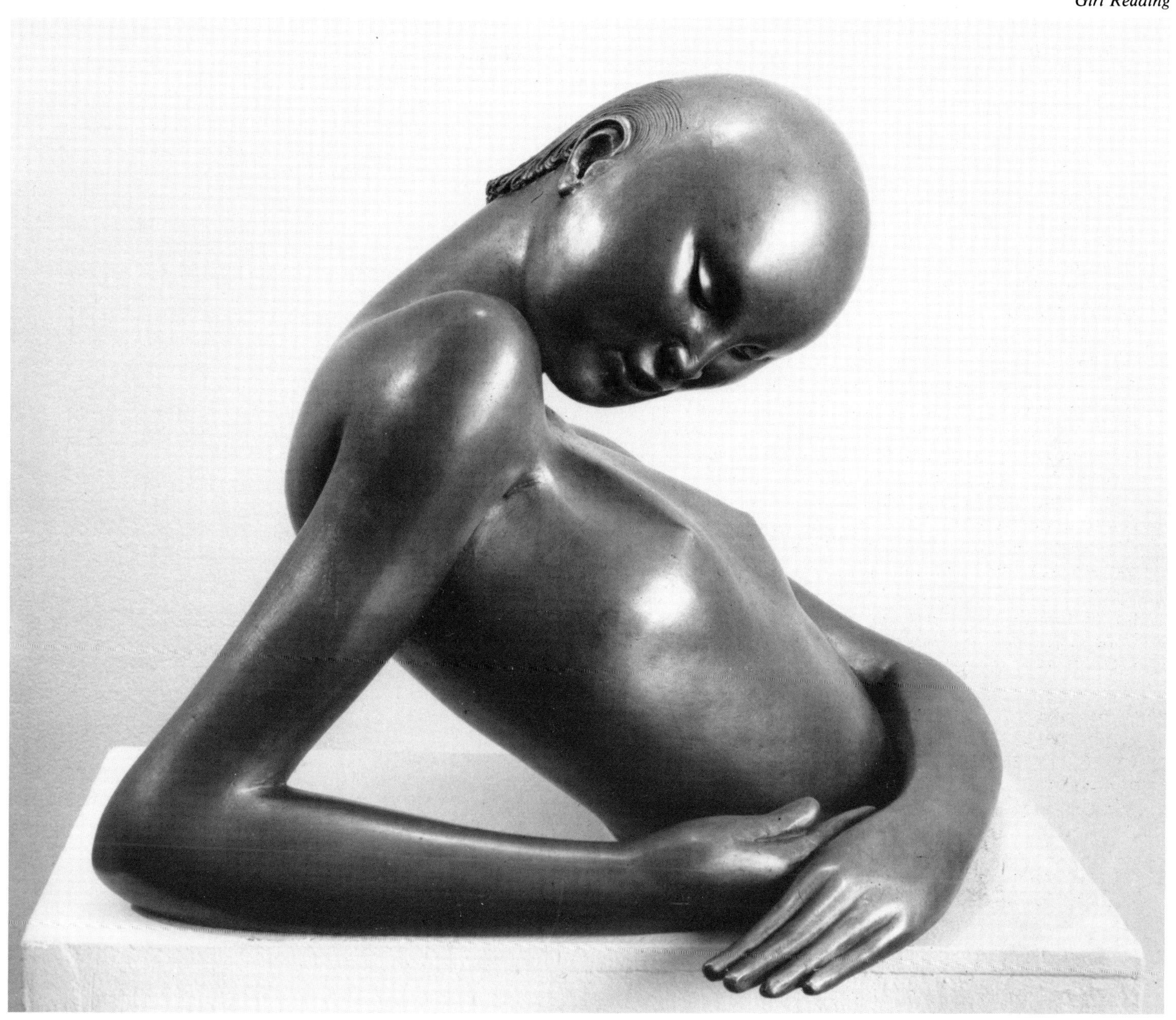

1983 Donation from Sol & Bella Fishko of New York City
(1983.74)

THEODORE ROSZAK (1907-1981)

Metaphysical Structure
Red conté crayon, gouache, ink on paper, 1933
21³/₈" x 15⁵/₈"

In the period immediately following his return in 1931 from a two-year study trip to Europe, the young American artist Theodore Roszak designed and executed his first major sculptures in plaster. One of these, titled *Metaphysical Structure* or *Musical Elements as Architectural Forms,* consisted of a combination of biomorphic mechanical and musically derived images incongruously arranged as an architectural construction. Actually, the work was more a comment on the nature of existence from the standpoint of the reality and function of the human mind than an architecturally inspired model. Regrettably, the original plaster has been destroyed, but the drawing shown here and dated 1933 is an interesting study from which the plaster itself was apparently designed.

Compositionally, this drawing is a pyramidal arrangement of forms rising from a broad base to a vertical tower-like member that terminates with three narrow cylindrical tubes at the peak of the composition. Neither the forms nor the functions are fully interpretable. Yet many do clearly suggest musical instruments as, for example, the tuba-like massing of the composition, the violin headstock, the lid of a grand piano, the pipes, tubes and valves, and the strings which appear to integrate and stabilize the compositional members and at the same time bring to mind the strings of a violin or lyre.

What is most significant, however, is the fact that this work is a highly personal statement consisting of forms which for the most part lie outside the realm of everyday experience yet, at the same time, appear vaguely familiar and, in the eye of the observer, stimulate a kind of emotional pull, an erotic appeal by virtue of the delicate color tones, the refined modeling and the soft and smooth interlocking surfaces represented.

Moreover, the strangely enchanting familiarity of both the elements and relationships invites our contemplation and brings to the conscious level of our minds the recollections of forgotten events and experiences apparently stored in our subconscious. Indeed, this work is veritably charged with mystery and magic and clearly illustrates how a work of art might lack all traditional subject matter and appear to be entirely meaningless, yet nevertheless can possess pure visual and tactile poetry as well as powerful forces of psychic suggestion.

Although with this drawing there is a sense of existence in a three-dimensional space, the net result is actually the production of an entirely new creation which does not exist in the world of everyday experience except in the form of the art object itself as brought into being by the artist. These characteristic features embody essential aspects of the system of surrealist thought which had developed by the mid-1920s and which by the early 1930s found expression in much American painting and sculpture.

Theodore Roszak was born in Poznan, Poland in 1907 and was brought to the United States by his family in 1909. He studied at Art Institute of Chicago. In 1929 he was awarded an Anna Louise Raymond Fellowship for European study. It was in Europe that he first discovered contemporary art and where he was especially influenced by the teachings of the Bauhaus. Today Roszak is best remembered for his post World War II sculptures. Yet his paintings and his constructions executed during the 1930s are among his most significant and indeed most creatively exciting works. Roszak died at his home in New York City in 1981.

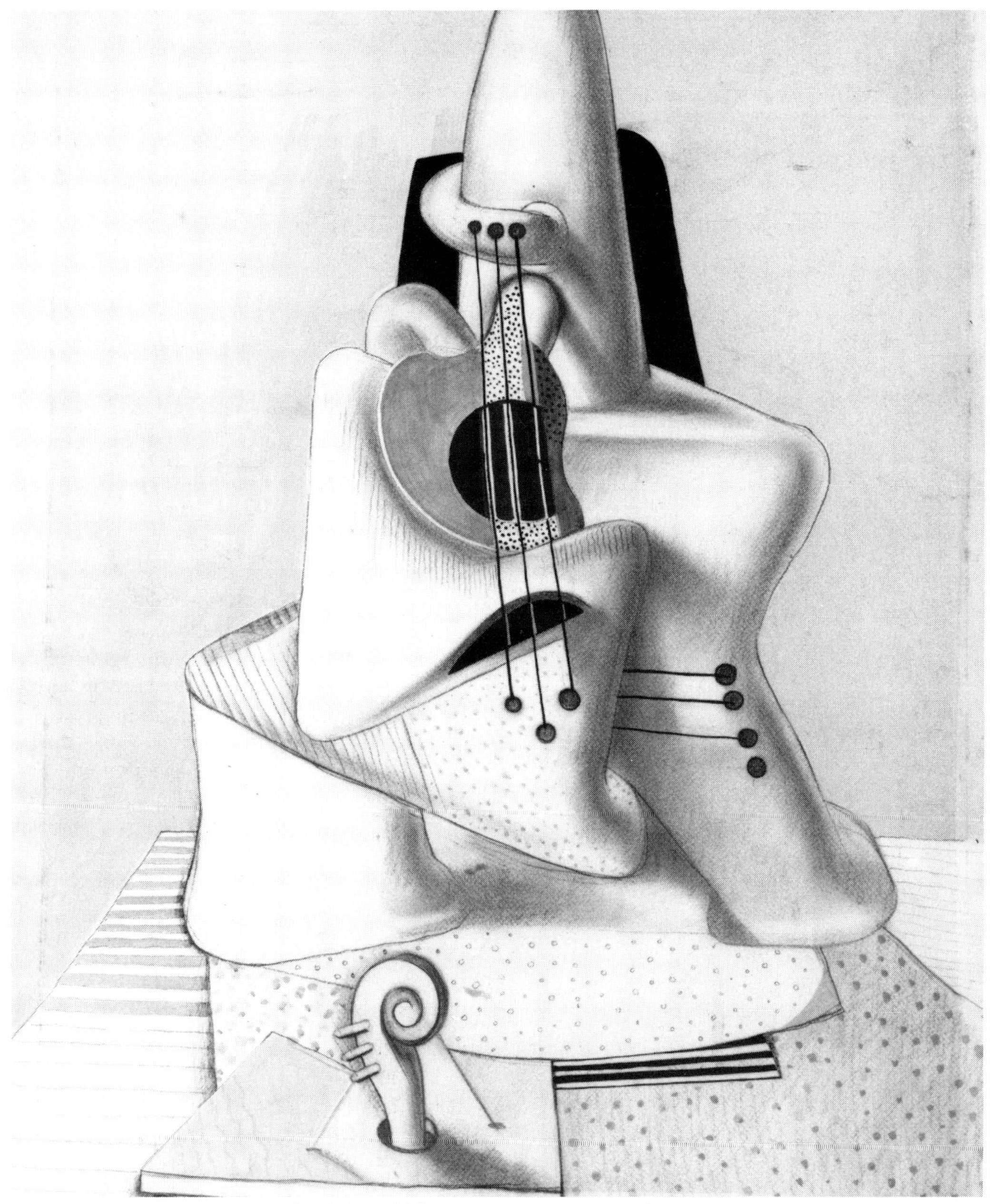

*1986 Museum Purchase, Friends of the Wichita Art Museum Art Fund
(1986.51)*

KENNETH HAYES MILLER (1876-1952)

The Singer
Oil on canvas, 1925
34" x 28"

Kenneth Hayes Miller was one of the most prominent artists and art teachers in America during the first half of the 20th century. He was a student of Robert Henri and like Henri strongly reacted against the stylizations of the genteel tradition that had typified much of late 19th century art, preferring instead unsentimental genre subjects which drew upon events and happenings of everyday life. Miller's technique reflected an enthusiasm for the High Renaissance tradition in terms of craft if not subject matter. He is often credited for having revived that tradition through his teaching at the Art Students League during the 1920s and 1930s. This is especially true in regard to his use of color and color relationships and his rendering of space, texture and three dimensional modeling as dominant considerations in painting.

In this work painted in 1925 and titled *The Singer,* Miller has accurately described the setting of an afternoon song recital presented in the parlor of a private home. In addition, however, he has clearly caught telling aspects of the times, not only in his choice of theme but also through the singer's fashionable ladies' apparel: the wide brimmed hat with rounded crown, the fox fur piece around the shoulder, the loose fitting dress with deep folds and white collar, and the long gloves appropriate for an afternoon occasion.

The compositional plan of this work constitutes one of the principal formulas employed by Miller during the late 1920s and in many instances throughout the '30s as well. Here the thematically dominant figure rendered in rounded sculpturesque masses, is placed not only in the center of the composition but also in the immediate foreground. This arrangement supplies compositional stability and at the same time assures the integrity of the picture plane without destroying the visual interest furnished by slightly blurred backdrop devices which bleed off the edges of the composition. Indeed the integrity of the picture plane was one of Miller's most consistently sought-after objectives and one which he emphatically demanded of his students.

Moreover, the foreground figure, forcefully thrust onto the frontal plane, not only strengthens compositional stability but at the same time furnishes a sense of physical presence. In mood, the scene clearly speaks for itself, for as we look at this painting, we readily sense that a quiet prevails throughout the surroundings and that the audience listens attentively while only the voice of the singer is heard.

Miller was born in Kenwood, New York in 1876. Throughout his career he was widely respected as an artist, but perhaps his greatest contributions rest upon his far-reaching influence as a teacher at the Art Students League, especially during the 1930s when his students included such notables as Edward Hopper, Isabel Bishop and others as we shall see. Miller died in New York in 1952.

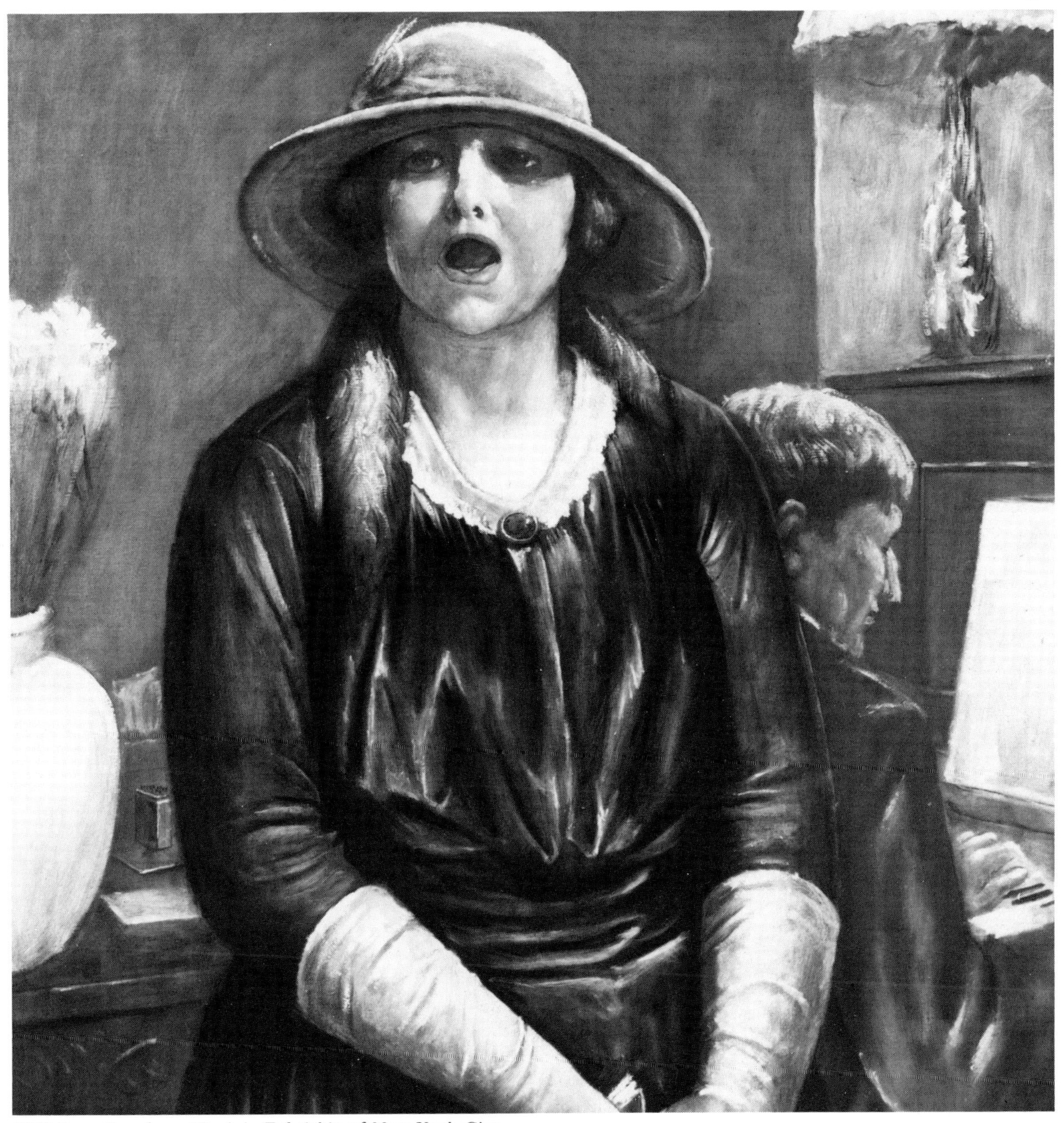

1983 Donation from Virginia Zabriskie of New York City
(1983.64)

KENNETH HAYES MILLER (1876-1952)

Show Window
Oil on canvas, 1938
27¼" x 21"

Kenneth Hayes Miller was the eldest member and, in a very real sense, the leader of a group of urban realist painters who gained wide recognition in New York throughout the 1930's and 1940's. That group is sometimes appropriately referred to as the Fourteenth Street School because the subject matter of their paintings derived from the teeming life of the crowds who populated, worked and shopped in the area along Fourteenth Street and Union Square, just north of the noted artist colony of Greenwich Village in New York's lower Manhattan.

One of the central themes of many of Miller's works is the ubiquitous bargain shopper found in the stores along Fourteenth Street. In this particular painting, titled *Show Window* and executed about 1938, Miller's statement is quite typical. In the foreground is a close-up rendering of a well-dressed shopper standing in front of a women's clothing store. In the background, the store window advertises a sale of ladies' dresses and, just outside the store entrance, three young girls stand talking. Their triadic arrangement is a feature common to many of Miller's paintings and one which he frequently likened to the Three Graces of classical mythology.

In many respects Miller's style is quite clearly classically inspired. His figures are carefully outlined and firmly structured, and his interest in dynamic space is emphasized by the alternating dark and light tiles of the pavement in front of the store entrance and by the gradually receding forms seen through the store entrance door. And, although the space of the composition is as compact and cluttered as one might expect the bargain sales counters inside to be, the compositional conception is fully integrated and the subject matter is clearly understandable. Of especial interest is the ob-

vious contrast between the carefree but relaxed figures of the three young girls standing at the store entrance and the self-conscious foreground figure, so stiff and awkward in her posed stance, and affected in the way in which she clutches her packages and holds her umbrella. Moreover, her anemic skin coloration echoes the pale color tones found in the lifeless displays in the store window behind her.

Miller's paintings are for the most part enviably competent, and as an artist he was widely respected throughout his very prolific career. Yet his fame and his significance rest upon his tremendous influence as a teacher at the New York School of Art and at the Art Students League. Among his students were such artists as Edward Hopper, Reginald Marsh, Peggy Bacon, Isabel Bishop, Yasuo Kuniyoshi, Edward Laning and a host of others. Miller was a member of the National Academy of Design and of the National Institute of the American Academy of Arts and Letters. He died in New York in 1952.

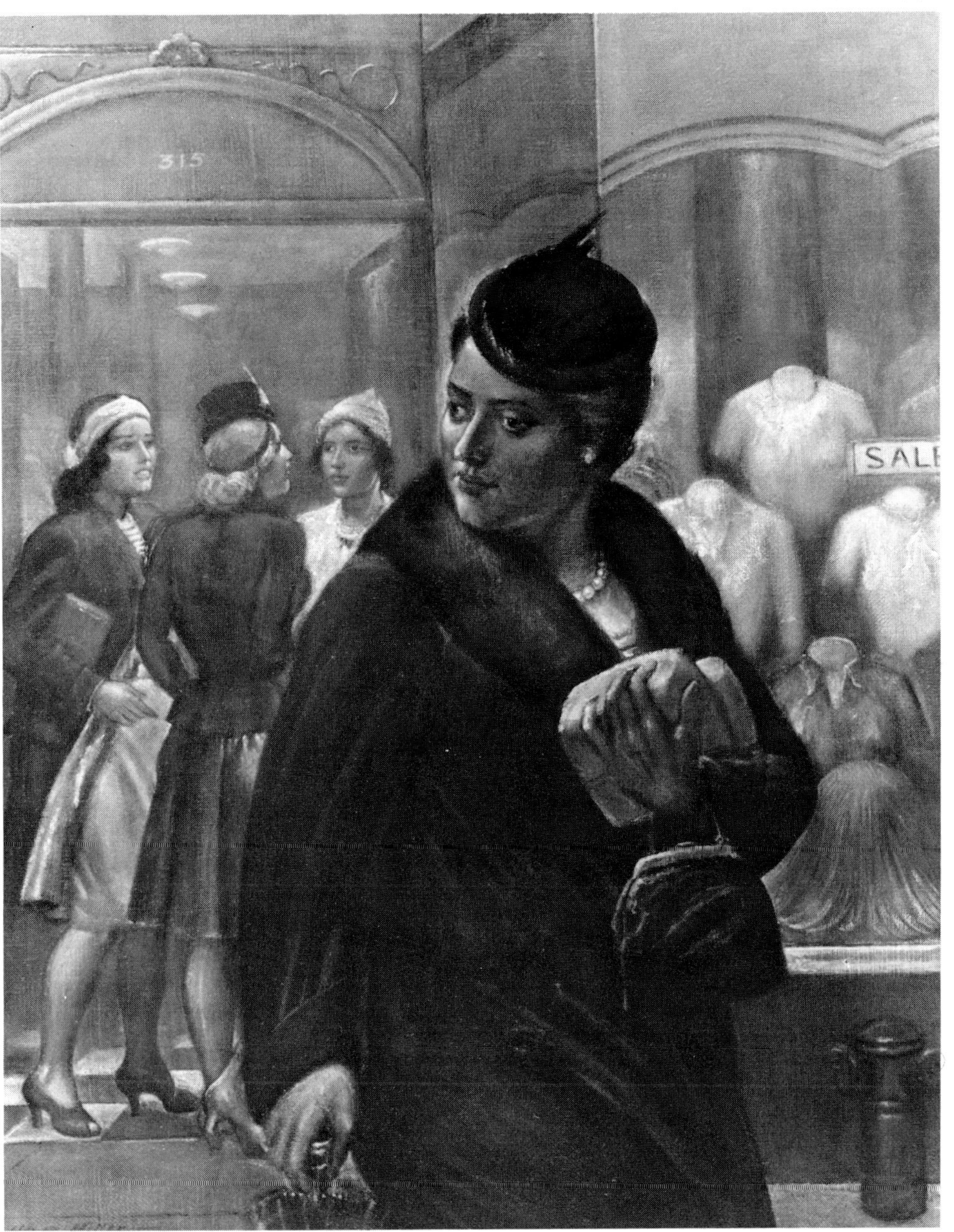

*1980 Museum Purchase, Friends of the Wichita Art Museum Art Fund
(1980.67)*

MARGIT VARGA (b.1908)

The New Moon
Oil on canvas, 1931
18" x 24"

In this painting titled *The New Moon* by Margit Varga, a combination of verticals, horizontals and sharp diagonals becomes the framework of a dynamic composition that presents the topography of one section of New York's Manhattan and at the same time proclaims the excitement of everyday hustle and bustle on the city streets. Contrasting types — fashionably dressed men and women, an old woman walking her dog, a newsboy, a man with amputated leg who leans against a lamppost and sailors on shore leave — together define the tempo of life. All of the figures appear hastily drawn in an almost caricature-like manner but with much spontaneity, infusing the painting with a lively energy and convincing sense of gaiety and light heartedness. Yet that posture masked the reality of the times, for the painting was executed in 1931, a transitional moment when America had just emerged from the boom years of the 1920s following the close of World War I, and was now in the early grips of the Great Depression.

One of the most interesting features of the composition is the abrupt shift in scale that the eye experiences as it moves from left to right or from foreground to middle ground. At the same time the artist has ably caught the distinguishing contrasts that characterize the urban setting, as for exampie the introduction of the gigantic skyscrapers, built just a year or two before this work was painted, and the old and somewhat dilapidated rows of storefronts from the past; or again, the tall and graceful turn of the century lampposts and the modern neon advertising signs. Such contrast is carried still further by the suggestion of the deafening roar of the elevated railway on the one hand and the quiet of the clear glow of the blue sky with its new moon, the feature from which the painting quite appropriately derives its title.

Margit Varga was born in New York City in 1908. She attended the Art Students League in New York and studied painting under Boardman Robinson and Robert Laurent. Her works are included in numerous private and public collections throughout the United States including the Metropolitan Museum of Art, The Pennsylvania Academy of Fine Arts, the University of Arizona Art Gallery in Tucson, and many others. In addition she has exhibited widely in such museums as the Whitney Museum of American Art, the Carnegie Institute, the Corcoran Gallery, the University of Illinois and the Art Institute of Chicago. She was art editor of *Life Magazine* from 1936-1956 and assistant art director from 1956-1960. From 1960-1970, she served as art consultant for *Time, Inc.* Her studio today is located in Bridgehampton, New York.

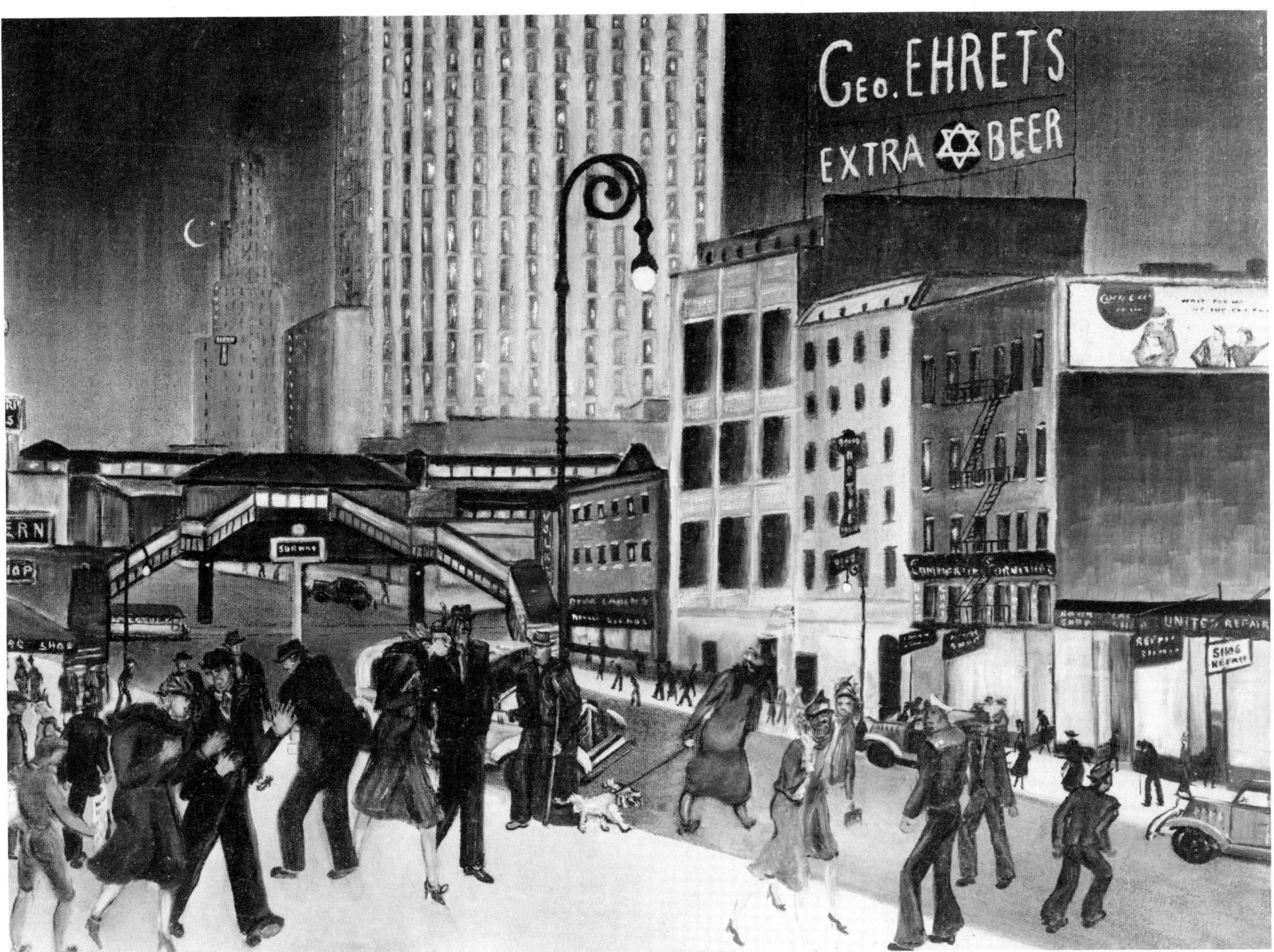

1984 Museum Purchase, Volunteer Operated Restaurant Art Fund, Friends of the Wichita Art Museum (1982.8)

N.C. WYETH (1882-1945)

The Homesteader
Oil on canvas, 1930
36³/₈'' x 40¹/₈''

Certainly one of the most widely acclaimed American illustrators during the early years of the 20th century was N.C. Wyeth. Among his most popular works were those produced to accompany such adventure stories as Robert Louis Stevenson's *Robinson Crusoe* or to illustrate short fictional tales that appeared in weekly and monthly magazines.

This painting titled *The Homesteader* was executed in 1930 and was reproduced in full color in the September, 1930 issue of the *Ladies Home Journal* as an illustration accompanying a short story titled ''Green Vigil: A Saga of the West'' by Wilbur Daniel Steele. The caption read, ''Where there had been no tree, now there was a tree. It changed the plain'', words fully appropriate for the theme shown.

An illustration differs from what we generally think of as a work of ''fine art'' in that, above all, it is more concerned with story-telling and description than with design and technique, although such formal aspects themselves can, of course, never be ignored. Secondly, a successful illustration must condense the facts needed to convey the essence of the subject depicted so that we both understand and experience its full meaning at a glance. Finally, an illustration is generally intended for reproduction; it is produced to accompany the text of the book or magazine for which it was executed.

All of these elements are fully exemplified in this painting by N.C. Wyeth where incident, facial features, gestures and character combine to create a convincing pictorial image whose meaning we grasp at once. Here, our attention is, of course, centered on the young woman posed in the foreground and standing next to a small tree. At her feet is a tiny patch of daisies and nearby an empty water bucket. The setting is the open plains, presented as a vast emptiness but for what appear to be the beginnings of farm settlement: a simple wood hut and barn, a cart, one cow and two horses grazing in the distance. The young woman *is* the homesteader, the symbol of the strength of American womanhood, courageous in staking a claim on the farm and on a new life. Indeed, the work is a compelling image of the promise of achieving the American dream so well suggested by the fertile fields and valley and the bright blue sky which shows through the heavy swollen threatening clouds. These forms, somewhat reminiscent of contemporaneous works by Thomas Hart Benton and John Steuart Curry, are of especial interest since the date of the painting coincides with the onset of the Great Depression and points forward to a decade ahead that would demand sacrifice, toil and strength in human resourcefulness for survival.

Newell Convers Wyeth was born in 1882 in Needham, Massachusetts but settled in Chadds Ford, Pennsylvania early in his career soon after he began to study with the noted illustrator Howard Pyle. He was an active member of the Society of American Illustrators and the Salmagundi Club and throughout his career was the recipient of numerous awards for his popular illustrations, as well as for easel paintings. Wyeth also executed a number of well known murals, including those at the Missouri State Capitol, the New York Public Library and elsewhere. He was the father of the noted contemporary American painter, Andrew Wyeth, who was also his student. N.C. Wyeth died in Chadds Ford in 1945.

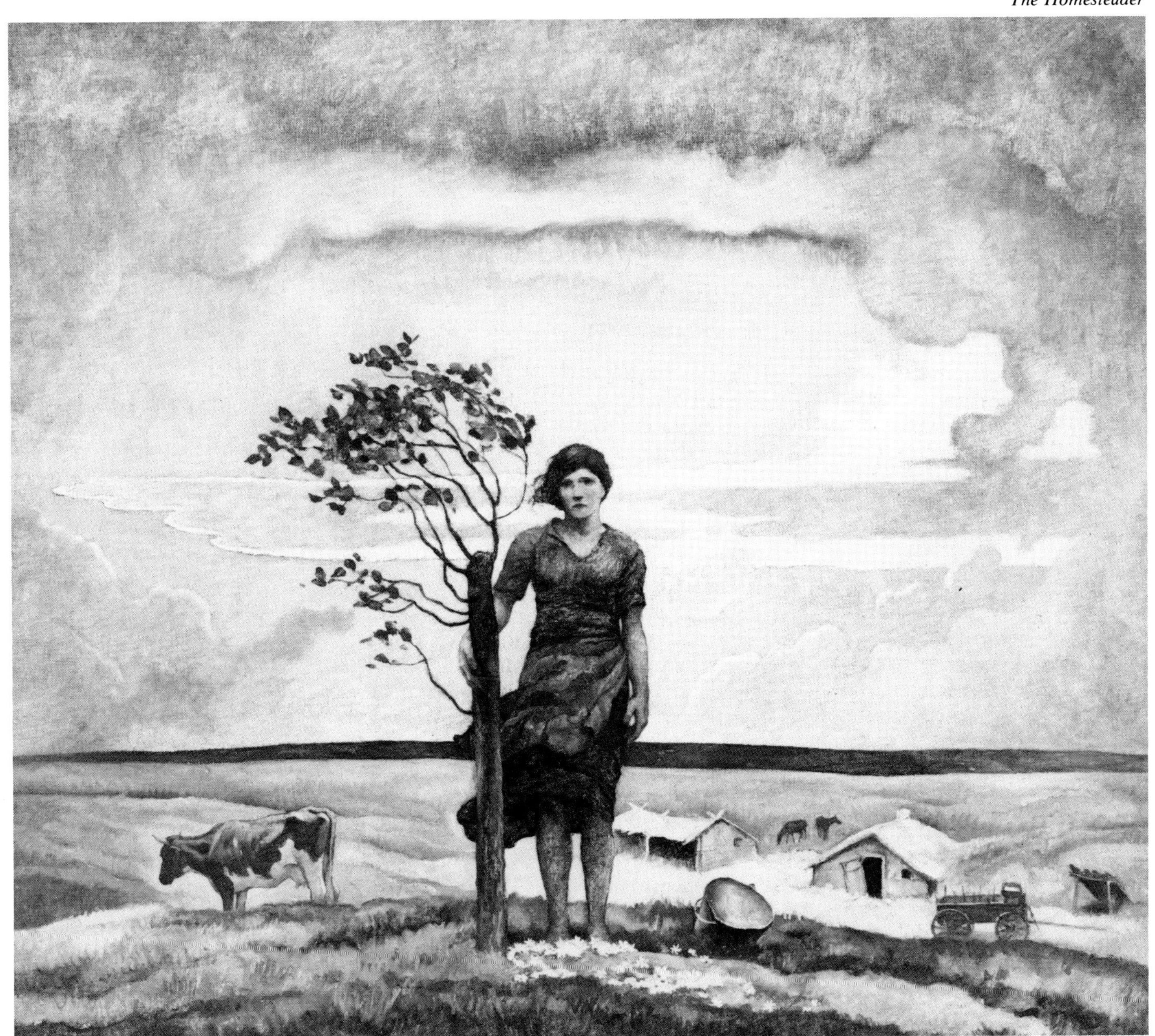

*1981 Museum Purchase, Paul Ross Charitable Foundation Fund
1981.45)*

CARL WUERMER (1900-1983)

The American Farmer
Oil on canvas, 1930
36¼'' x 36¼''

This striking painting appropriately titled *The American Farmer* was executed in 1930 by the American artist Carl Wuermer. The work is of course the portrait of an elderly farmer with tough wrinkled skin, enlarged hands and knarled fingers: physical features which together reflect a life of hard labor and courageous toil. He carries a cane and wears a hat, a knotted necktie and a three-piece suit and clearly presents an air of dignity and integrity.

A most telling aspect of this work is the fact that the figure of the farmer is in the immediate foreground, so close to the viewer as to appear to occupy our space as well as the pictorial space of the composition itself. Behind him, stretching into the background depths, is his luxuriantly green farm representing his life as both a source of struggle and a symbol of pride in past accomplishments. At the same time he stands at the threshold of the actual present and with chillingly penetrating eyes he stares into the unknown future of the Great Depression which by 1930 was just beginning. Yet it is determination and perseverance more than uncertainty that are registered on his face. And it is in this sense that the work became an icon of reassurance during a tragic and despairing moment in American history.

Indeed, in 1930, one fourth of the American population occupied the nation's six and a half million farms. And already throughout the '20s, following the close of World War I, farmers' incomes had dropped steadily at the same time that mortgage debts and taxes rose steeply. Protective tariffs were adopted but, instead of benefiting farm economy, they closed many foreign markets to United States trade. Then as now, the American farmer was suffering enormous losses which he would continue to face throughout the ensuing decade and beyond.

Carl Wuermer was born in Munich, Germany, in 1900. He came to America in 1915 and soon thereafter became an American citizen. Wuermer studied at the Art Institute of Chicago and the Art Students League and exhibited widely throughout the United States and abroad. His works are included in major collections, both private and museum, in America. He adopted Woodstock, New York, as his permanent residence and it was in Woodstock in June, 1930 that he painted *The American Farmer* using the Schutis Farm as the setting and an elderly resident named Hommel as the foreground figure. Wuermer died in Woodstock in 1983. This work has been widely exhibited during the past half-century and on several occasions was illustrated in popular magazines during the '30s.

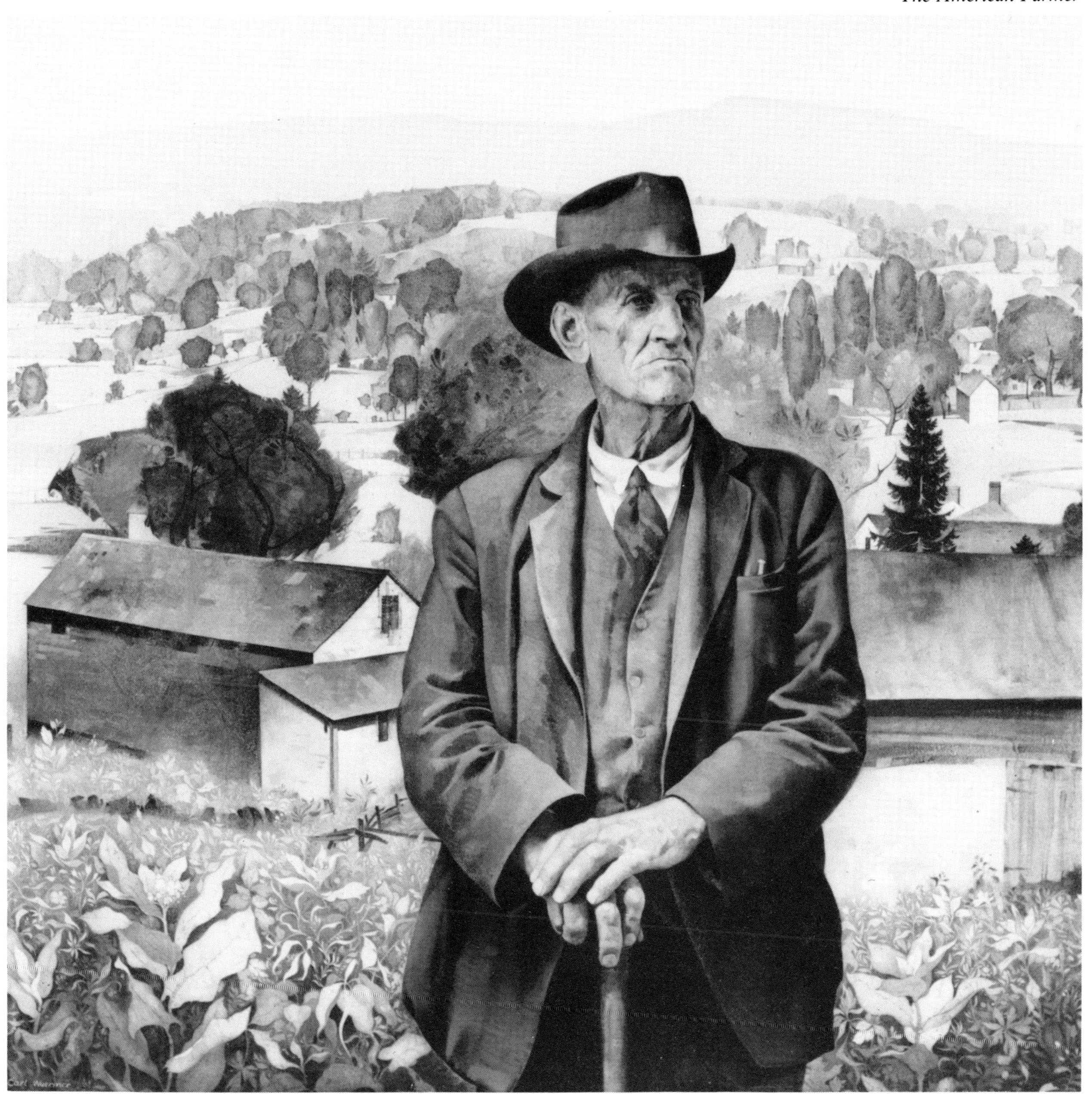

1987 Museum Purchase, Volunteer Operated Gift Shop Art Fund, Friends of the Wichita Art Museum
(1987.6)

WILLIAM PALMER (1906-1987)

August Threshing, Iowa
Tempera on canvas mounted on masonite, 1932
16'' x 20''

One of the dominant movements in American painting during the period of the Great Depression was the so-called American Scene, a movement which emphasized familiar subject matter, treated in literal terms so as to communicate clearly and widely. Economically, these were despairing times and it is understandable that a nostalgic flavor often found expression in the art of the period, a quality which — especially in the farming regions of the Midwest — celebrated the simple traditional virtues of life close to the soil.

This painting, titled *August Threshing, Iowa,* was executed in 1932 by the Iowa-born artist William Palmer and epitomizes the strong regionalist sentiment of the period. Here the subject is pictorially stated in clearly organized visual language. The land is flat, the horizon is low and the focal point of interest is at the center of the composition where a threshing machine, operated by power transmitted through belts from a steam tractor, is shown loading the separated grain kernels onto mule wagons and at the same time ejecting the chaff onto a mound seen on the left. Throughout the composition, outlines are soft and colors are subdued except for the rather vivid red used to emphasize selected parts of the threshing machine. At the same time, the arrangement of forms rising diagonally from the swollen mound at the lower left of the barn seen near the distant horizon line at the right, dramatizes the action depicted. In turn, that action is complemented by the fluid pattern of abstract forms in the sky where whirling billows of smoke and fluffy balloon-like clouds with cool-reflected color tones repeat both the forms and the colors seen in the subject below.

American Scene painting is sometimes viewed as an escapist reaction against the machine age in general and more particularly the collapse of the industrial economy of the '20s. However, that interpretation is hardly valid in a work such as this. For here man is seen not as a victim of the machine but is depicted rather as being in full control of his environment and as achieving productivity by working in harmony not only with nature but also with modern technology.

Such a progressive outlook was actually true of many American Scene painters and especially of William Palmer who throughout most of the 1930s worked actively on various New Deal art projects and came to be especially recognized for his series of murals installed in the Queens General Hospital, New York City, that depicted aspects of preventive medicine and that were used in the instruction of both hospital interns and nurses.

William Palmer was born in Des Moines, Iowa in 1906. He studied in France and from 1941 to 1973 served as Director of the Munson-Williams-Proctor Institute School of Art in Utica where he remained Director Emeritus until his death in 1987. Palmer exhibited in numerous exhibitions throughout the nation and is represented in major museum collections both in America and abroad.

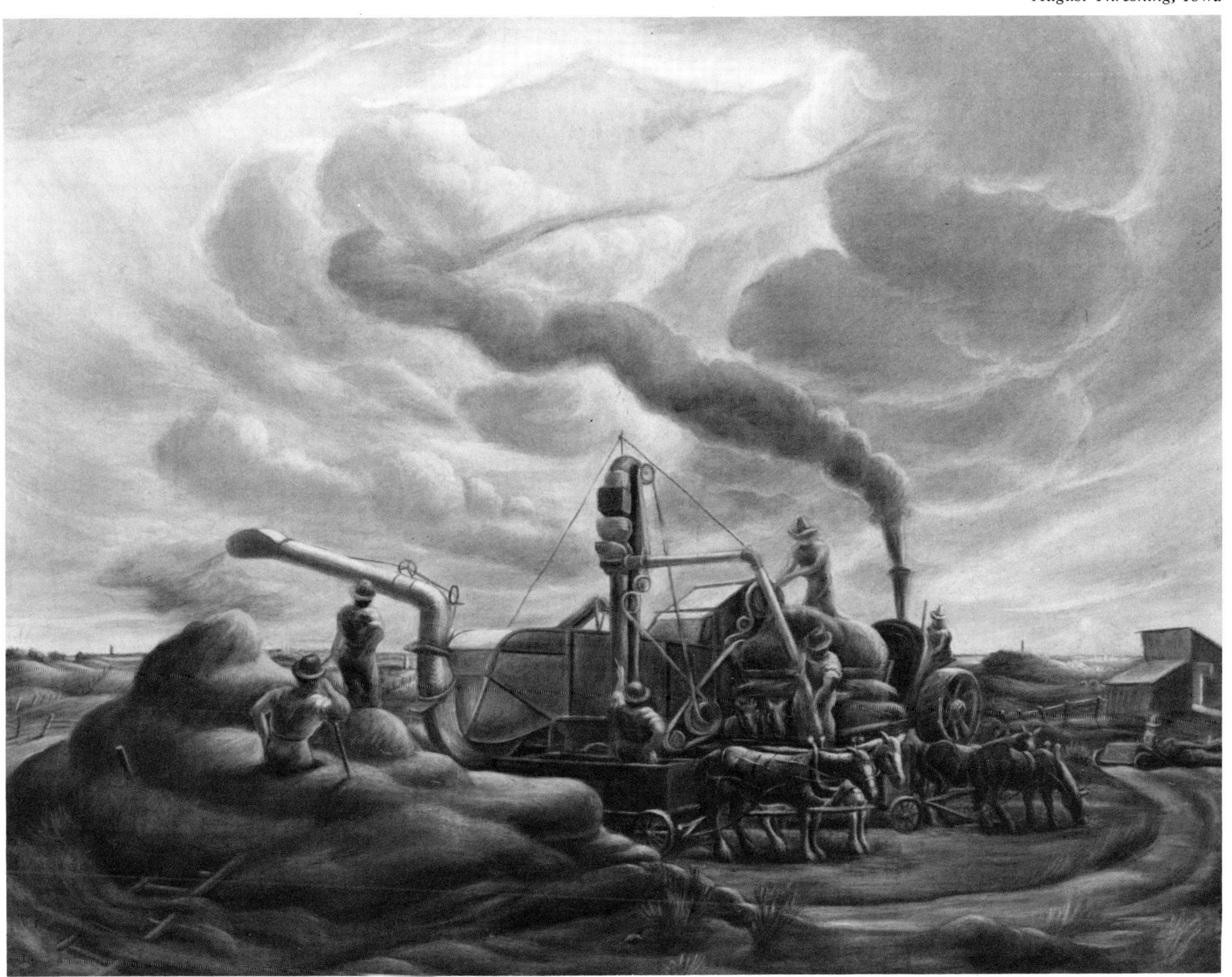

1983 Museum Purchase, Friends of the Wichita Art Museum Art Fund
(1983.24)

ETHEL MAGAFAN (b.1916)

Wheat Threshing
Tempera on masonite, 1937
17½'' x 34⁷/₈''

Strong nationalist sentiments of the tragic depression years often equated the actively productive life on the rural farms with the virtues of self-sufficiency that had characterized the pioneering spirit of America's past. For it was on the farm more than in the city where men might act in concert and at the same time reassure themselves of their own individuality and usefulness in accomplishing purposeful work. The depression years also saw the Federal Government promoting the arts through several supportive New Deal programs, one of which was the so-called Section of Fine Arts under the Treasury Department which commissioned competent artists to produce works of art for newly built Federal buildings.

This small painting, titled *Wheat Threshing* by Ethel Magafan, is a 1937 color design study which was used as the model for a large mural that she executed for the Auburn, Nebraska Post Office building under a Treasury Department commission. The purpose of the work was to dramatize the life of the farmer in America's wheat belt. Subject matter is communicated clearly and forcefully and is presented as three distinct episodes: pitching the gathered wheat shocks onto a horse team wagon, feeding the wheat onto the threshing machine hopper, and collecting the wheat grain in large bulky sacks stacked against a mounting heap of ejected chaff.

For us today, the theme is interesting, for the threshing process as depicted is no longer in use. Even more interesting is the style and compositional dynamics adopted here, especially when we remember that the artist had to take into consideration the emplacement of the final work for which this little painting was intended to serve merely as a model. For the small version was ultimately translated on a vastly more massive scale to the walls of a post office where as a mural the composi-tion would be viewed from well below the high level at which it was finally painted.

Here the visual field is shallow and compressed, forcing the forms to adhere closely to the surface plane and thus reinforce the reality of the flat wall on which the mural would appear. Actually, the only hint of deep space is found in the relatively narrow segment near the right end of the composition where a distant wheat field is glimpsed between the heap of chaff and the thresher ejector funnel. As rendered, the theme is accurate and forceful, yet there is no intention of precise photographic likeness. Instead, the forms are simplified and boldly modeled so as to be readily recognized from the viewer's distance. Excessive detail that might sacrifice impact has been avoided and the subject is, therefore, communicated through only the principal thematic essentials. Action is concentrated, for the artist has selected three episodes by which to express the theme and as a result the long horizontal format can be read as a continuous narrative, beginning at the left, moving through the center and ending at the extreme right. However, the large mural might also be viewed from a considerable distance, in which case the entire composition can be grasped at one glance. This possibility is effectively accommodated by the classical arrangement of the design which is framed by balancing groups of three figures with corresponding poses at each end, one figure facing the spectator, one in profile, and one facing diagonally into the scene and directing our attention on the central action of the thresher. At the same time, the dominant use of a warm yellow disperses a unifying light throughout the composition and appropriately defines the coloration of the farm setting and echoes the bright summer sunshine.

Ethel Magafan was born in Chicago, Illinois in 1916. She studied at the Colorado Springs Fine Arts Center under Frank Mechau and Boardman Robinson. She is a member of the National Academy of Design and has executed major murals in various locations throughout the country. Since 1950 she has maintained her residence and studio in Woodstock, New York.

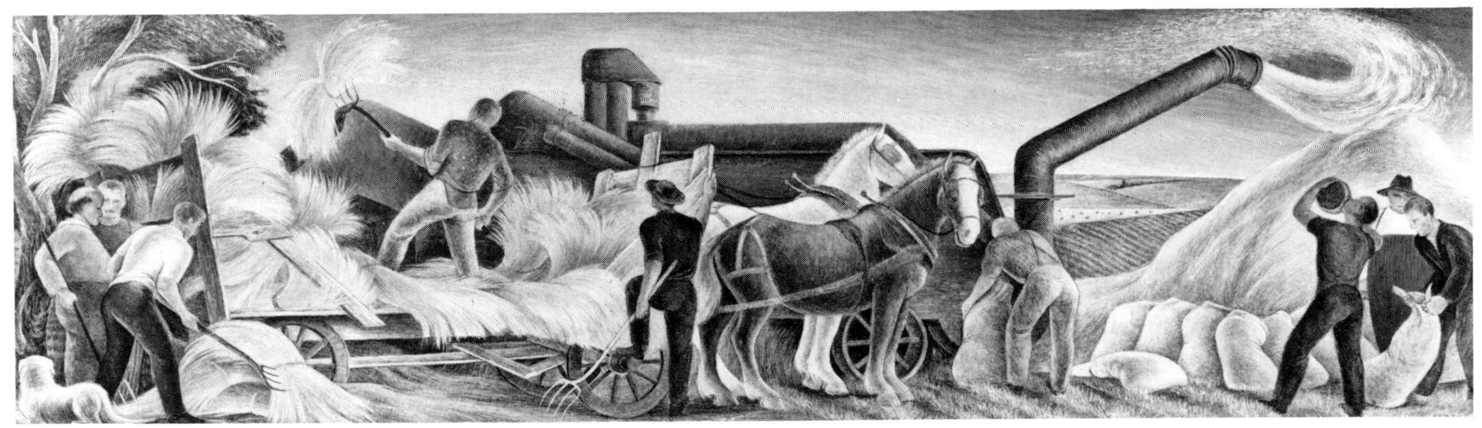

*1981 Museum Purchase, Friends of the Wichita Art Museum Art Fund
(1981.19)*

RAPHAEL SOYER (1899-1987)

The Crowd
Oil on canvas, c.1932
25⁵/₈" x 22⁵/₈"

A commonplace urban scene during the 1930s and a subject frequently depicted by artists of the period was the street orator speaking before crowds of people standing in an open square. This painting titled *The Crowd* was executed by Raphael Soyer about 1932 or so and in certain respects effectively captures the spirit of the period. Here, a close up view of only a small segment of a crowd is shown. All of the figures wear serious facial expressions, yet the young people appear anxious and perhaps discouraged but undefeated whereas the older man with the mustache at the right seems somewhat forlorn. And although the orator himself, to whom they are attentively listening, is unseen, meaning is quite clearly conveyed. Indeed, in both its descriptive content and its technical purity the work itself is monumental, for the volumes are simplified, the forms full and imagery straight forward and unpretentious. Soft surfaces and slightly blurred edges together with vigorous brush strokes and broad and scattered patches of pigment impart a strong painterly quality to the composition as a whole and correspondingly invest the figures with vitality and alertness. At the same time, a sense of dignity is implicit in the serious attentiveness of the figures, yet a mood of despondency is evoked by the subdued and sombre colors employed throughout. Disciplined but unlabored brushwork, typical of Raphael Soyer's masterful technique, further reflects the artist's genuine understanding of human form and emotion and his own tender sympathy toward his subject matter.

It is interesting to note that this work was initially a part of a somewhat larger composition in which additional figures including the orator had been shown. However, Soyer once commented that when the original work was completed he was dissatisfied with the composition as a whole but enthusiastic about this particular segment which he regarded as a complete statement in itself. It is also of interest to note that the young people portrayed here were art students in Soyer's acquaintance and that the older man at the far right is a portrait of the superintendent of the building where Soyer's studio was located at the time.

Raphael Soyer was born on December 25, 1899 in Tombov, Russia. While still a young boy, he settled in New York City when his family emigrated from Russia. He studied at Cooper Union, the National Academy of Design and the Art Students League. Although an implicit social message is inevitably conveyed in many of his works from the period of the Great Depression, unlike many of his contemporaries Soyer was never actually a social protest artist. Instead his main thematic focus was on the dignity and strength of character of the individual rather than on a conscious attack upon the capitalist system per se. Throughout his career, Soyer remained one of America's most distinguished and influential realists, dedicated always to expressing and describing the lives and times of people playing out their daily roles in life. And it is the study of individual character in facing the challenges of life that would seem to be the essential message of this painting.

Following an extended illness, Raphael Soyer died at his home in New York City at the age of 87 years in November 1987.

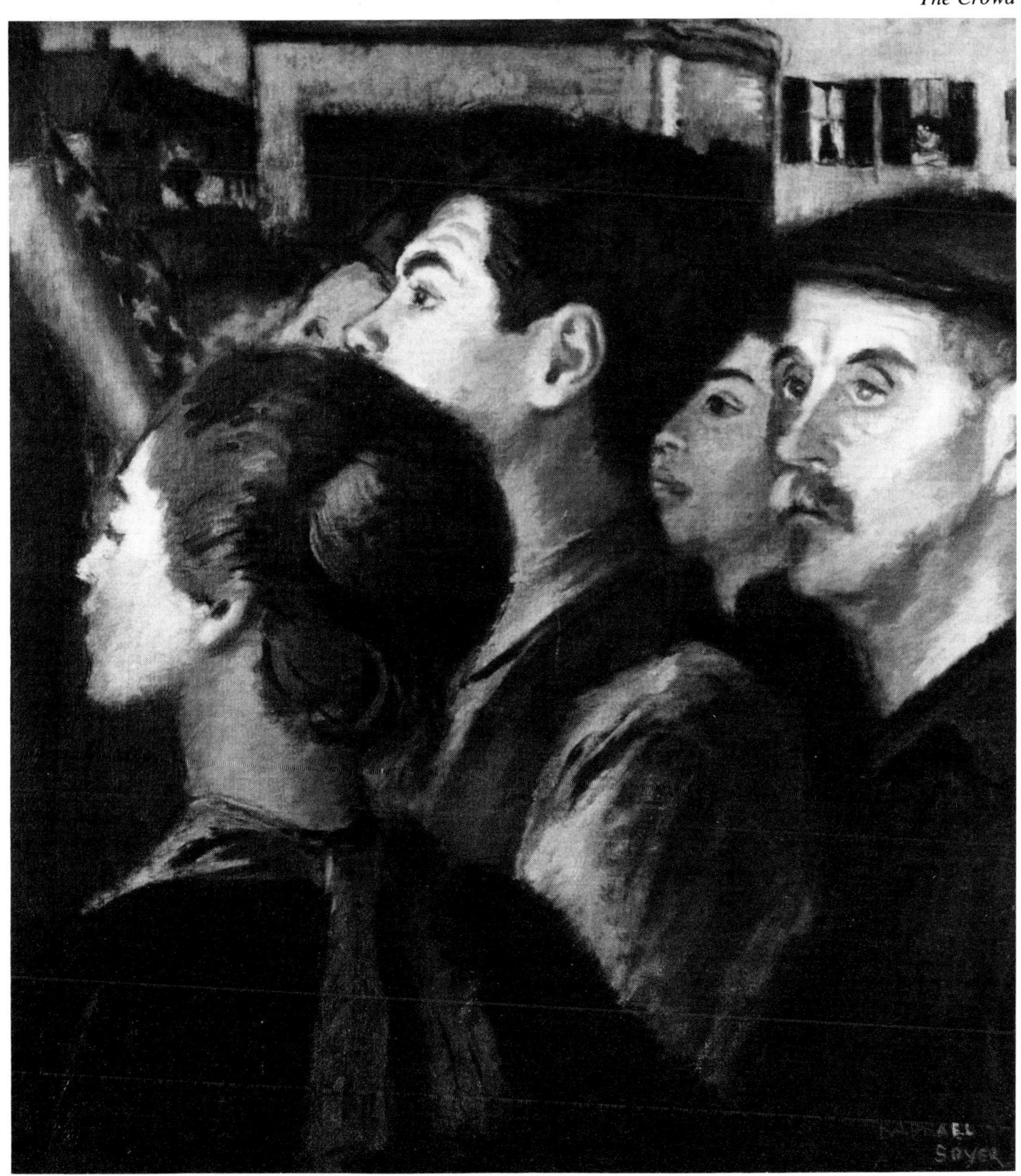

1982 Museum Purchase, Funds donated by Stockholders & Friends of KAKE-TV in honor of Martin Umansky (1982.6)

HARRY GOTTLIEB (b.1895)

Dixie Cups
Oil on canvas, 1936-37
24¼'' x 41''

Artistic interest in the theme of industrial labor during the years of the Great Depression is well exemplified by this striking oil on canvas titled *Dixie Cups* painted between 1936 and 1937 by the American artist Harry Gottlieb. Gottlieb's inspiration for this composition was the spirited action displayed by iron workers as they switched rail cars that carried "dixie cups", loaded with smoking molten iron, from the iron smelters to a foundry for casting.

Although the forms here are clearly defined with attention given only to principal thematic elements, the setting itself is dingy and the atmosphere appears to be filled with smoke from the iron smelting furnaces seen in the distance. Yet a sense of explosive energy is suggested by the sharp diagonal emphasis, the lively brushwork, and the massive and bulky forms of the laboring figures and, even more, by the strong colors and distinctive color contrasts introduced.

Gottlieb saw noble dignity and heroism expressed in the role played by the American laborer. And although his art is an art of social concern, his works are far more than pure propaganda, for powerful aesthetic qualities are readily apparent in color usage and in compositional dynamics that are independent of subject matter but that at the same time serve to effectuate the anecdotal scene depicted.

Throughout his productive career, and especially during the years of the Depression, Gottlieb vividly documented incidents in the everyday life of American laborers in the steel mill, the coal mines, the railyards, and other segments of the industrial scene and through such efforts over the years he has optimistically sought to promote public awareness and rally support in behalf of rectifying what he has often regarded as unfair labor practices.

Gottlieb was born in 1895 in Bucharest, Rumania. In 1907 he emigrated to Minneapolis and between 1915 and 1917 studied at the Minneapolis Institute of Art and thereafter spent one year in the United States Navy. In 1918, he moved to New York City and then in 1923 to the art colony of Woodstock, New York, where he remained for a period of eight years except for a one-year study tour in Europe, undertaken through a Guggenheim Fellowship. In 1935 he settled in New York City permanently, joined the Federal Arts Project of the W.P.A. and participated actively in the Artists Union, the Artists Congress and other organizations. During the late 1930s, he was one of the pioneers in the use of silk screening as an art medium. His residence and studio are in New York City where he continues to work actively at age ninety-three years.

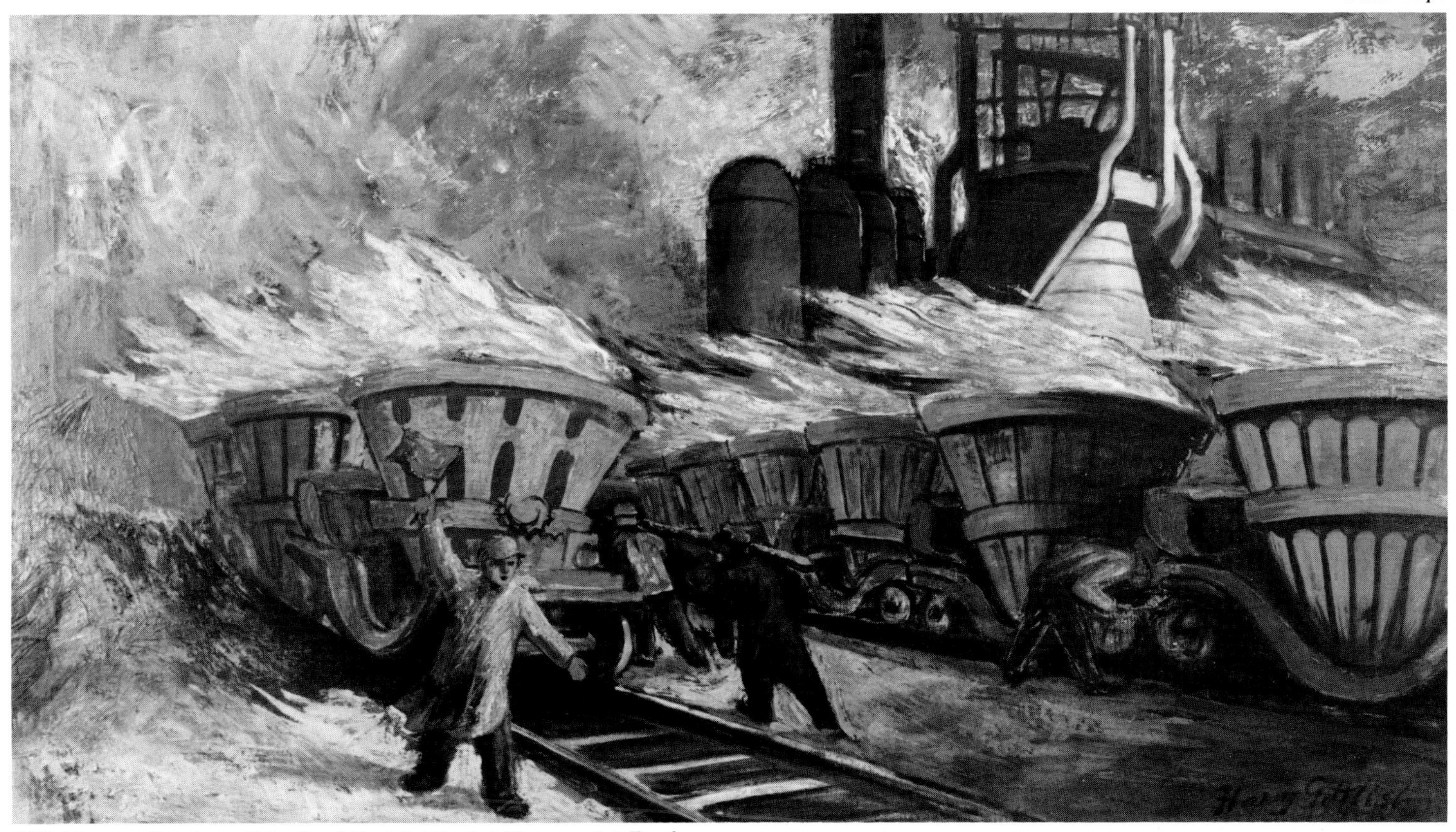

1982 Museum Purchase, Friends of the Wichita Art Museum Art Fund
(1982.42)

SAUL BAIZERMAN (1889-1957)

Road Builder
**Hammered copper, wood base, painted black, 1939
28½" h. x 13⁷/₈" w. x 7⁷/₈" d.**

Until well after the close of World War II, sculpture played at most a secondary role in the development of American art. Indeed prior to World War II, most American sculpture functioned primarily as architectural decoration or as monumental statuary generally placed in city squares and public parks. Yet independent sculpture was not entirely absent from the art scene, and in retrospect many of the sculptors of the period deserve to be considered among the major artists of America.

One of the most interesting and innovative sculptors during the 1920s and 1930s was Saul Baizerman, an artist who developed new techniques and created forms quite unlike those in the world of prevailing statuary. In this work titled *The Road Builder* and executed by Baizerman in 1939, the theme chosen reflects the artist's more universal concern in celebrating labor and the daily toils of the laboring man, a concern especially timely during the years of the Great Depression. What we see here is the depiction of a slightly stooped figure of a workman. The frontal treatment, the heavy proportions and the massive curves of the arms and shoulders, symmetrically arranged, impart a powerfully commanding presence. However, what is especially interesting is the technique employed in the production of this piece, for although the entire work is over two feet in height, it consists of but a single sheet of heavy copper hammered into the shape of the figure. Moreover, the hammering process has created a pebbled surface of tiny concave and convex shapes that produce a glittering effect under light, blurring the outline and surface and effecting a rather mystical aura across the figure. No effort is made to render either facial or body detail yet the image itself, although clumsy in overall appearance, is clearly recognizable and fully intelligible. Symbolically, the image suggests stability, determination and physical strength and at the same time the weary and heavy burden shouldered by all workmen. And of course it was that message which Baizerman sought to communicate in this work as well as in most of his other sculptures.

Saul Baizerman was born in Vitebsk, Russia in 1889 but emigrated to the United States in 1910 when he was 21 years old and settled in New York City. He studied briefly at the National Academy of Design and made numerous visits to Europe where frequent exhibitions of his work were held. In 1933 he had his first United States exhibition in New York City, but it was not until 1949 that he began to win wide acclaim, receiving awards at the Pennsylvania Academy of Fine Arts and having major American museums seek his works. In 1957 he died in New York City.

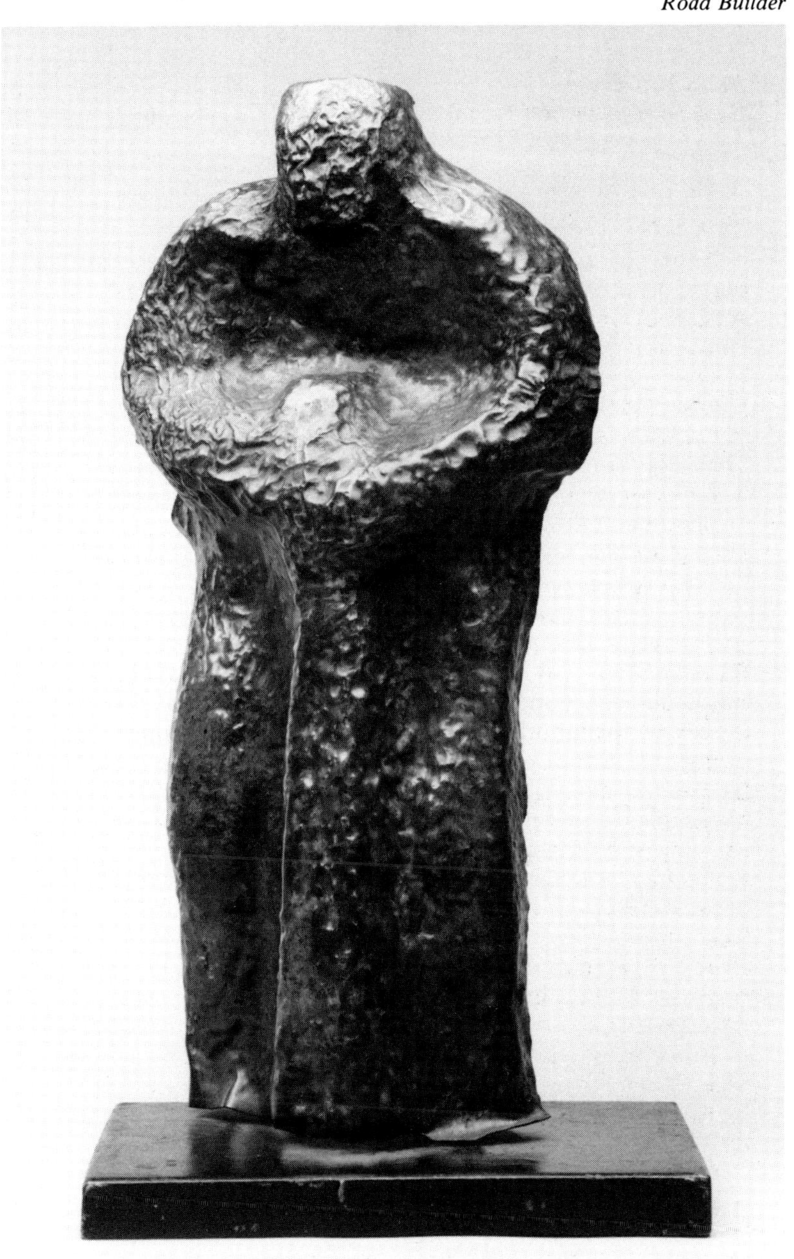

*1985 Museum Purchase, Friends of the Wichita Art Museum Art Fund
(1985.47)*

EDWARD LANING (1906-1981)

Camp Meeting
Oil on canvas, 1937
$32^7/_8$'' x $48^1/_8$''

Many paintings executed by American realist artists during the 1930s served to report aspects of everyday life of the period. In this work, titled *Camp Meeting* and executed in 1937 by Edward Laning, the subject is a revival meeting such as frequently took place throughout the country, most typically in the south and midwest. Here Laning effectively documented the physical frenzy that accompanied a mass spiritual ritual held in an open barn on a late summer evening in the artist's hometown of Petersburg, Illinois.

The drama enacted here would seem to be a crusade against adultery as suggested by the headline of the newspaper tossed casually on the straw covered floor at the extreme left. In the upper right, the preacher devoutly prays for the rescue of courageous sinners who, possessed of shame and in the presence of witnesses, have penitently confessed their sins and are experiencing the ecstacy of spiritual restoration. Particularly interesting are the participants' attitudes, all convincingly portrayed, including supplication, wailing, rejoicing, prostration, forgiveness, scorn and simply curiosity. Yet it is the moment of illumination, of a profound spiritual conversion, which holds our attention and which is so expressively caught by the vigorous brushstrokes, the mood of urgency and the sense of surrender implicit in the volatile physical gestures accomplished by a network of interlocking masses in conflicting directional movement.

As a social phenomenon, the religious revival certainly goes back to early antiquity and for a time was widespread throughout America, especially during the post Civil War period. Its popularity during the Great Depression as depicted in this painting is sometimes explained as a reflection of economic and social malaise that blighted American life, generating fear, disillusion and despair which in turn found compensatory release in spiritual revelation.

Edward Laning was born in Petersburg, Illinois in 1906. He studied at the Art Students League, especially under the noted teacher Kenneth Hayes Miller. Like many artists of the so-called lost generation following World War I, Laning lived and worked briefly in Paris, but with the onset of the Depression was forced to return home and settled in New York City. In 1931, he held his first New York exhibition and during the late 1930s he painted a series of murals for the New York Public Library. However, with the coming of World War II and the growing national interest in avant garde art, he like other realists was soon overshadowed by abstraction. Laning nevertheless continued to work in the realist manner and as recently as 1980, he was commissioned to produce a second major series of murals for the New York Public Library. Preliminary work on these murals was underway when he died suddenly in May, 1981.

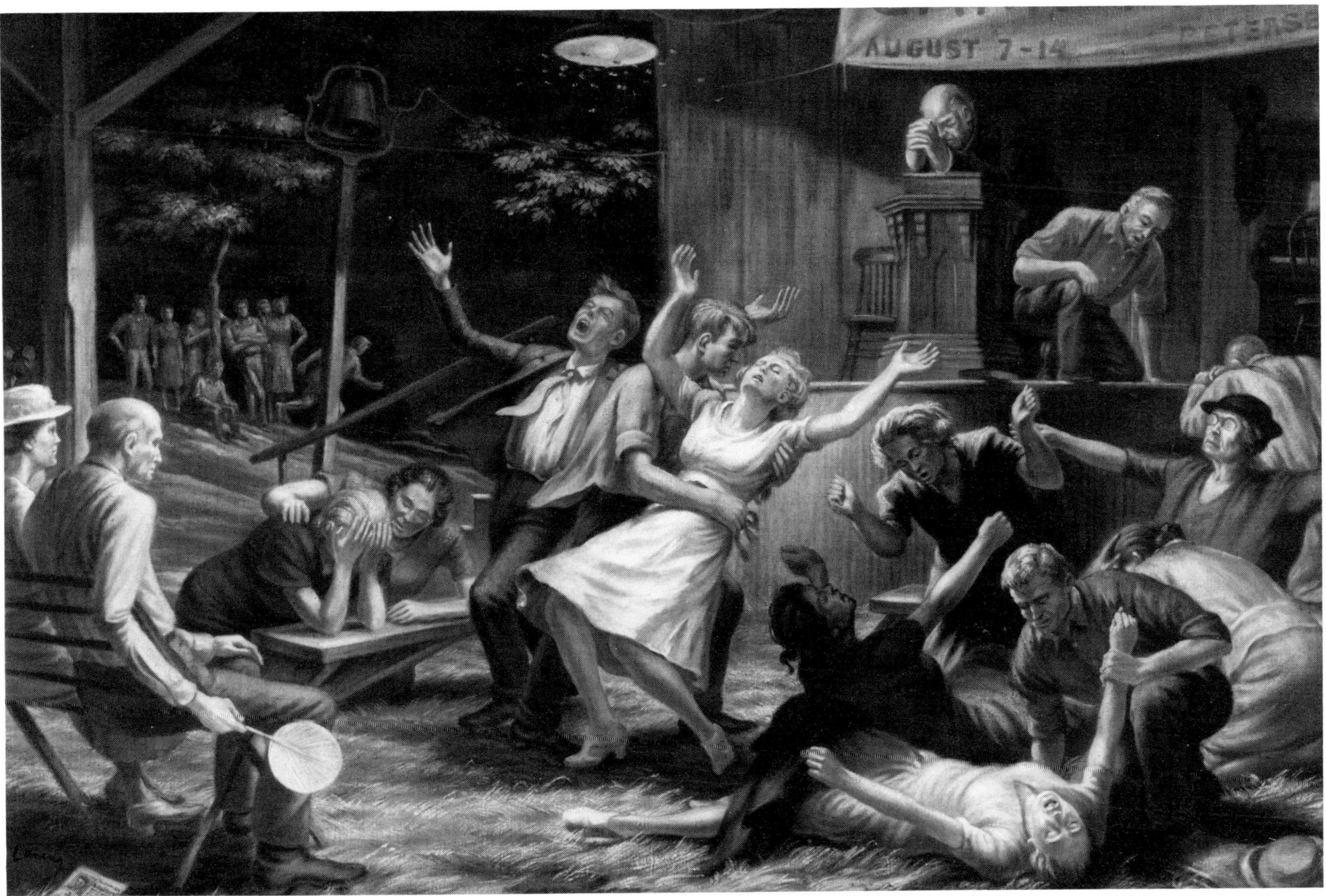

1981 Museum Purchase, Volunteer Operated Gift Shop Art Fund, Friends of the Wichita Art Museum
(1981.10)

PAUL LANTZ (b.1908)

Storm over New Mexico
Oil on canvas, 1938
24" x 32$^{1}/_{8}$"

Much of the realist painting executed in America during the 1930s and early 1940s was concerned with recording familiar scenes and events in everyday contemporary life. But just as the mode of life differed in the many regions of the nation, so the styles and idioms employed differed throughout the various regions. As a result, many of the artists — especially those in the more rural sections of the midwest — were often known as regionalist painters of the American scene.

This was the period between the crash of 1929 and America's entry into World War II in 1941, a period marked by economic depression and in many instances by a spirited nationalism. It was one which searched for an answer to the question "What is America?", and it produced an art with a social purpose, generally opposed to contemporary currents from abroad. This was also a period when a whole generation of young American artists — many influenced by such notables as Thomas Hart Benton, Grant Wood and John Steuart Curry — reached professional maturity just at the outbreak of war. Many entered the armed services. But once the war was over, the popularity of the American Scene had waned, for advancing internationalism accompanied by a growing interest in the more abstract avant garde movements rendered the nationalist focus of the 1930s provincial and out-dated. Many of the artists of the 1930s generation then turned to teaching, or to commercial art and book illustrating, and many others entered new and unrelated careers. Today, most of their works have been forgotten entirely.

One of those artists was Paul Lantz who painted primarily in New Mexico. *Storm over New Mexico,* executed in 1938, was one of his well known works. The scene of course, is a panoramic view of a New Mexico ranch located at the foothills of the Rocky Mountains.

Here a bolt of lightning brightens the clouds and accents the rugged mountain slopes and various features of the dark landscape below. And a gusty wind blows violently across the lowlands and through the trees. Forms are stylized but highly expressive and demonstrate a primitive quality which reflects the growing nationalist interest during the 1930s in early American primitives. One interesting feature is the emphasis on the neatly cultivated strip of green farm land, centrally placed in the composition and serving as a comment on the high esteem for the American farm during a period that had experienced deprivation and the need for farm relief and which lived with bitter memories of the dust bowl days.

Paul Lantz was born in 1908 in Stromburg, Nebraska. At the age of 15 he enrolled as a student in the Kansas City Art Institute. In 1925, he travelled to New York and studied at the National Academy of Design and the Art Students League. When the depression came in 1929, he was forced to leave New York and settled in Santa Fe where he eventually gained recognition as a painter of murals. In 1940, he returned to New York and staged a successful one-man show at the 460 Park Avenue Gallery. In 1942, he enlisted in the U.S. Army. Following the war, he taught briefly in Kansas City and San Francisco but finally settled on a ranch in Springer, New Mexico.

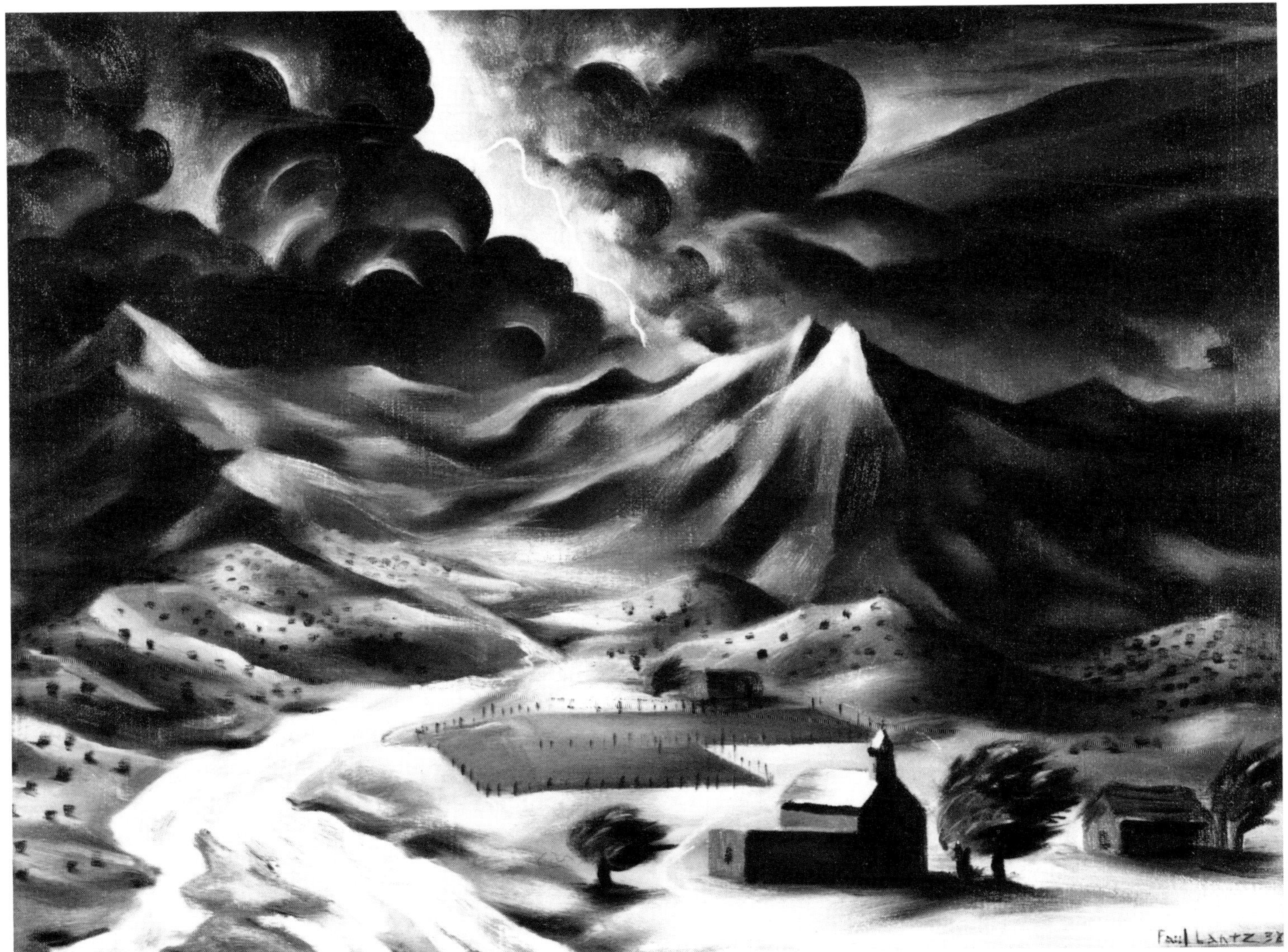

*1980 Museum Purchase, Friends of the Wichita Art Museum Art Fund
(1980.66)*

JOSEPH SOLMAN (b.1909)

42nd Street Shuttle
Oil on canvas, 1937
24" x 35"

Beneath New York City's well known 42nd Street, one short section of subway operates to connect two of the main branches of the extensive New York subway system. The underground station there is dingy and drab and late at night it is almost entirely deserted. One wonders why such a subject would be chosen as the theme for a work of art. Yet it is the artist who has the unique capability of finding beauty and mystery in the most unexpected places. This explains why the American artist Joseph Solman executed this 1937 painting, *42nd Street Shuttle.*

What we see here is a view of the underground platform and an emergency train bumper with a red stop signal marking the end of the shuttle line. Nearby stand two men, one a subway workman and the other perhaps a passenger waiting for the shuttle to arrive. In the upper left is seen a passenger descending the stairs leading down from ground level.

In no sense, however, is this a literal representation of the underground, for the forms depicted — all heavily outlined in black — are expressively suggested rather than accurately described, thus allowing the viewer's imagination to come into play and complete the scene. Moreover, although such traditional spatial cues as receding lines and receding masses are clearly in evidence, Solman has intentionally distorted the overall space encompassed here by exaggerating the tilt of the platform floor as it extends into the distance, thereby charging the composition with a dynamic quality that echoes the nature of the setting itself.

But such energy derives even more from Solman's use of rich and boldly contrasting colors. Solman has always been a strong colorist and in this work, by means of color control and the use of modulated saturations of red, he has created a vibrant and lively space, totally independent of subject matter. And that sense of aliveness achieved by color usage is further intensified by the radiant glow emanating from many of the forms edged with a narrow fringe of green or turquoise blue.

What is especially significant about this work is that Solman has produced the equivalent of an abstract expressionist painting a full decade before the abstract expressionist movement came to dominate the American art scene, but without abandoning identifiable forms. At the same time, the strong flat geometric shapes appearing throughout the composition, and in particular such signs and emblems as the circular stop light and the arrow on the long diagonal red band, suggest features of what will later be assimilated as image-types used by Pop and Photo-Realist artists.

Solman was born in 1909 in Vitebsk, Russia but settled with his family in 1912 in Jamaica, Long Island. He attended night classes at the National Academy. During the Depression, he worked on the WPA and served as editor of the Artist's Union publication *Art Front.* Currently he resides in New York where he continues to paint and to present quite frequent solo exhibitions of his works.

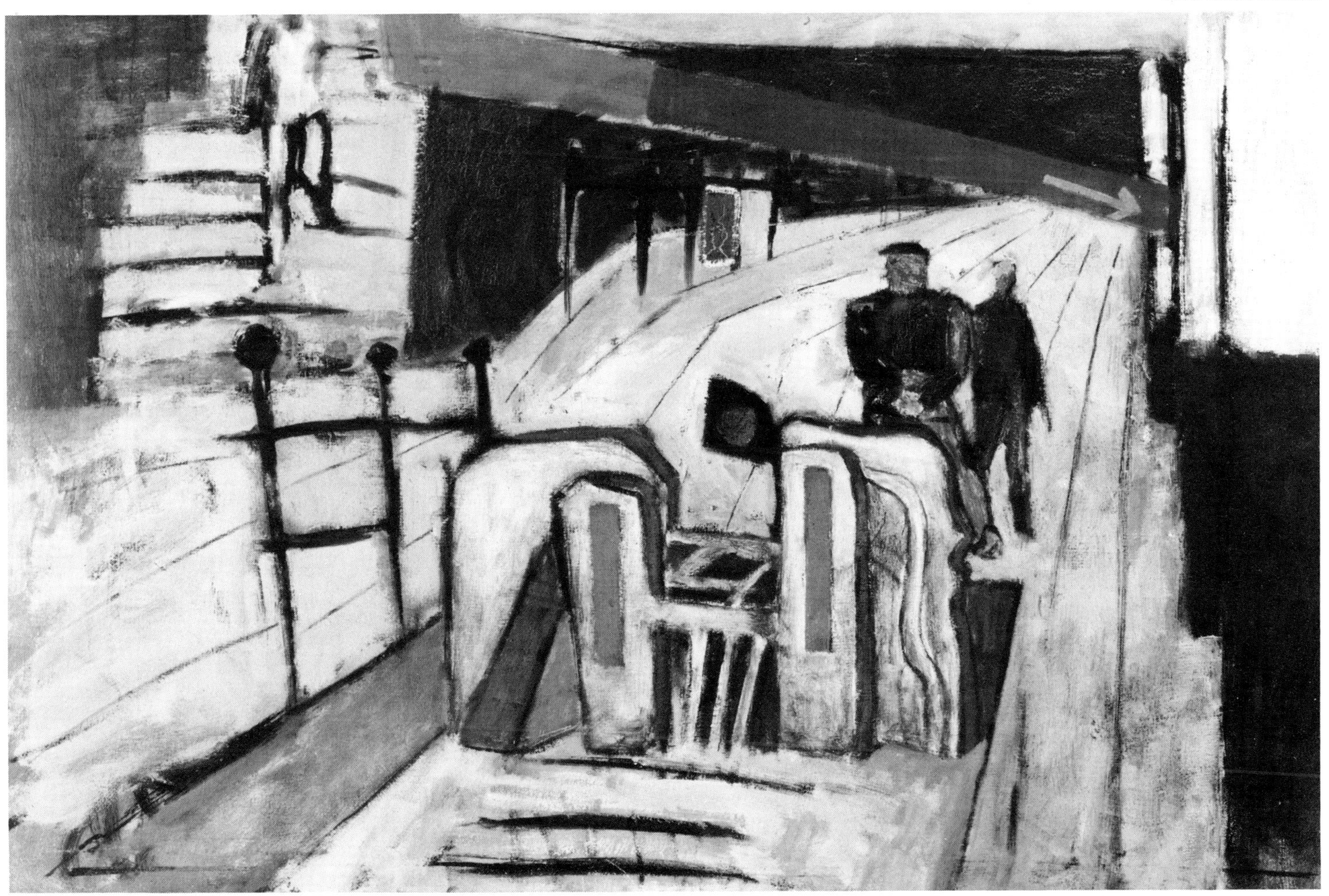

1983 Museum Purchase, Friends of the Wichita Art Museum Art Fund
(1983.16)

LAWRENCE BEALL SMITH (b.1909)

Ring Around the Chimney
Oil on canvas, 1939
25" x 30¼"

This 1939 oil painting titled *Ring around the Chimney* was executed by the contemporary American, Lawrence Beall Smith, in the closing years of the Great Depression. Here our attention is focused on an intimate human incident taking place on adjacent roof tops of what would seem to be tenement dwellings. In the immediate foreground, a woman seated by the face of a red brick chimney and wearing a loose fitting pink house dress and bedroom slippers, stretches forward slightly to keep an attentive watch over a small child who crawls around the chimney. On the adjacent roof a second woman, hanging up her clean wash on a clothes line, looks with a smile of amusement over her left shoulder at the tiny child. The chimney is thus the pivotal element in the composition, not only by virtue of its central placement and its comparatively large size, but also because it defines the locus of the child's action upon which the attention of the two women is directed.

Smith's painterly technique and his thematic emphasis on one isolated commonplace urban incident together point up the lingering influence of the ash can tradition that had flourished during the early decades of the 20th century. However, on another level of expression and of considerably more interest is the social comment made. For like many other paintings executed during the Depression, this work reflects the period's awareness of the rapidly changing ecological character of the city. Indeed the tall smoke stacks of a factory seen in the left background belch heavy clouds of thick black soot into the atmosphere, clearly intruding upon the quality of life as lived in the industrialized American city. And although human adaptabiliy to an unfavorable condition is acknowledged by the fact that life itself obviously does carry on, the artist symbolically confronts the situational reality by the contrast cunningly introduced between two polar opposites, namely the white laundered clothing on the one hand and the surrounding pollution on the other.

Lawrence Beall Smith was born in Washington, D.C. in 1909. He graduated from the University of Chicago and studied at the Art Institute of Chicago and at the Boston School of Fine Arts. His works are included in numerous major collections, both public and private, throughout the country. Smith currently resides in Cross River, New York.

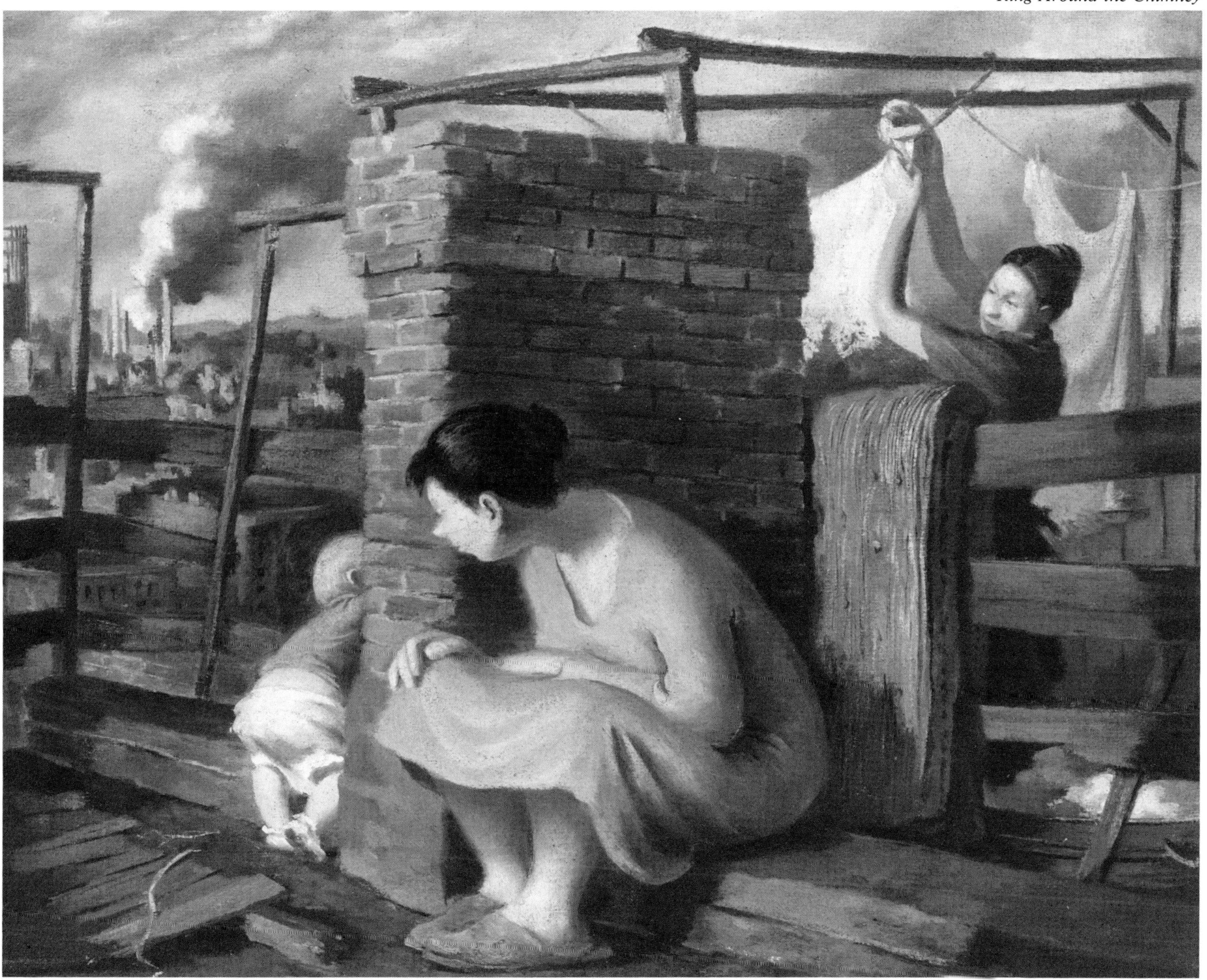

1981 Museum Purchase, Friends of the Wichita Art Museum Art Fund
(1981.20)

JOSEPH WOLINS (b.1915)

The End of Scammel Street
Oil on canvas board, 1939
23⁷/₈" x 30"

This painting titled *The End of Scammel Street* was executed in 1939 by the American artist Joseph Wolins. The setting is a small enclosed park on a narrow run-down street known as Scammel Street situated on the lower east side of Manhattan in New York City. Today, the park is covered with concrete, but during the Depression years it served as a playground for the near destitute children of the neighborhood.

Wolins chose this site as the subject of an extended series of paintings that he executed during the late 1930s while working under the Federal Arts Project of the WPA. He lived nearby and was fully acquainted with the dilapidated state of the neighborhood with its old 19th century row houses as seen in the background. And it was the shabbiness of the location, especially on a gloomy winter day when slush and dirty snow had accumulated on sidewalks and in the park, that so clearly echoed the depressive mood of the times. That mood is skillfully caught here but at the same time is balanced by the active play of children who run, chase and throw snowballs in the park.

Particularly striking are the strong compositional geometry and the interesting style which Wolins has adopted. Lines and masses are so arranged that the eye is forcefully pulled across the park to a sharp arrow-like point at the far left. In turn that pull is balanced by the line of the broad, deserted street at the right as well as by the exaggerated tilt of the large apartment dwelling situated at the right corner of the house row seen in the background. Human figures are treated as silhouettes clearly resembling cardboard cut-outs. And the row of houses with its irregular roofline and dingy facades, black windows and dark and uninviting doorways seem mournfully forbiding. Moreover, that house row sags at each corner and appears about to tumble. Yet this work commands attention, for the energetic flow of pigment, the simplified and expressive forms and the muted color tones employed throughout combine to effectively communicate a sense of spirited optimism and aliveness in a setting which is otherwise grim and foreboding.

Wolins' apparent interest in specifically conveying these opposing qualities rather typifies the attitudes of many Depression artists. For contrary to what we might expect, at the heart of American Depression painting, a note of optimism and hope is frequently widely experienced throughout the period.

Joseph Wolins was born in Atlantic City, New Jersey in 1915. He studied at the National Academy of Design from 1931 to 1935 and worked under the WPA Art Project from 1935 until 1941. He has exhibited widely throughout the United States and his works are in such collections as the Metropolitan Museum, the Butler Institute and elsewhere. He has been the recipient of numerous awards including the Mark Rothko Award which he won in 1971. Wolins currently lives and paints in his studios in New York City.

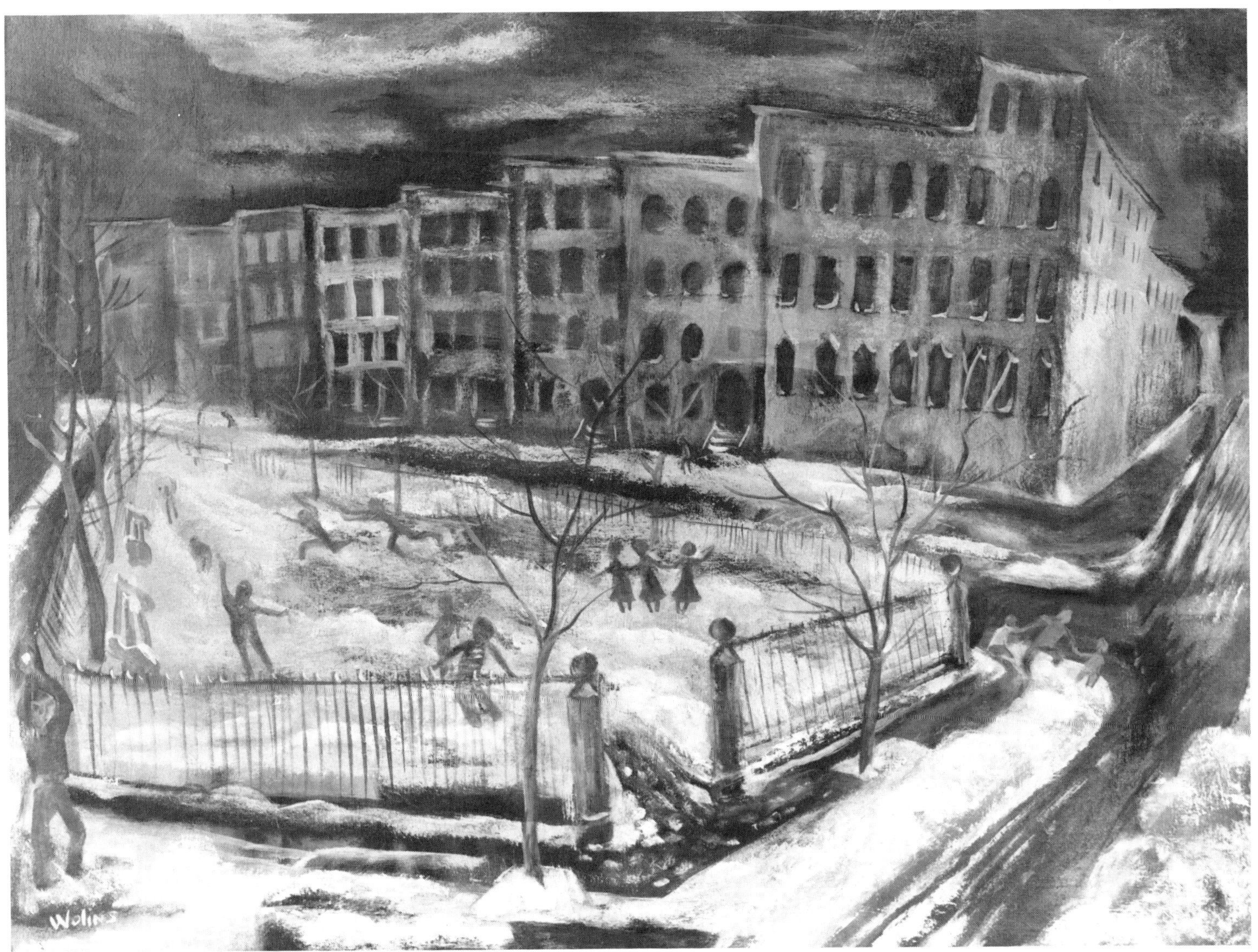

1982 Museum Purchase, Friends of the Wichita Art Museum Art Fund
(1982.9)

PAUL R. MELTSNER (1905-1966)

Martha Graham Dance Class
Oil on canvas, c.1939
28" x 36"

One of the many highly creative and superbly competent but now largely forgotten artists of the 1930s was Paul Meltsner. Like other artists of the depression years, Meltsner spent much of his early career executing murals for public buildings. Subsequently he turned to still life painting and then to subjects which typically glorified the labor theme so popular during the Great Depression. By the mid and late '30s he produced numerous portraits of Broadway celebrities including Carmen Miranda, Gertrude Lawrence, Lynn Fontanne, John Barrymore and others. But his favorite portrait subject was Martha Graham whom he painted on many occasions.

In an era when artists were eagerly searching for ways to celebrate the American spirit and vitality in order to compensate for the self doubt which so widely prevailed during the depression years, Martha Graham was understandably an appropriate subject. For like Meltsner himself as well as many other American artists of the time, Martha Graham actively sought to introduce a genuinely American component into the spirit of her own art and as early as 1930 participated in the formation of New York's Dance Repertory Theatre which she saw as one means of making ballet distinctly American rather than an imitative production of European performance.

In this particular painting titled *Martha Graham Dance Class,* the foreground figure is a portrait of Martha Graham herself. Here, the design is intricate but direct and the forms are decisive yet highly simplified with little concern for detail. All of the figures are classically sculpturesque and although perhaps somewhat dramatic are nevertheless rendered with composure and grace. Of particular interest is the sense of balance and compositional coherence produced by the rhythmic interplay between body forms and other features in the setting. This is evident, for example, with the figure toward the left seen in profile with upraised arms and whose back curve closely repeats the curvature of the elevated piano lid. Similarly, the upraised and enclosing arms of the foreground figure echo the overlapping structural arches in the background. At the same time, the rich colors beautifully harmonize, thus adding to the unity and structural strength of the composition as a whole.

Paul Raphael Meltsner was born in New York City in 1905. He studied at the National Academy of Design and was a member of the Society of Independent Artists. Even in his early career, his paintings reflected the tremendous impact of the "modernistic" or Art Deco movement which flourished throughout both America and Europe during the 1930s. Meltsner was strongly nationalistic in his point of view and devotedly supported the labor movement throughout the Depression. In 1945, near the close of World War II, he donated eight of his paintings for sale in the Fifth War Bond Drive which when sold raised nearly $3 million in War Bonds. During the 1930s his works were acquired by leading museums across the country and in Mexico, Europe and the Soviet Union. He ultimately settled in Woodstock, New York where he died at the age of sixty-one in 1966.

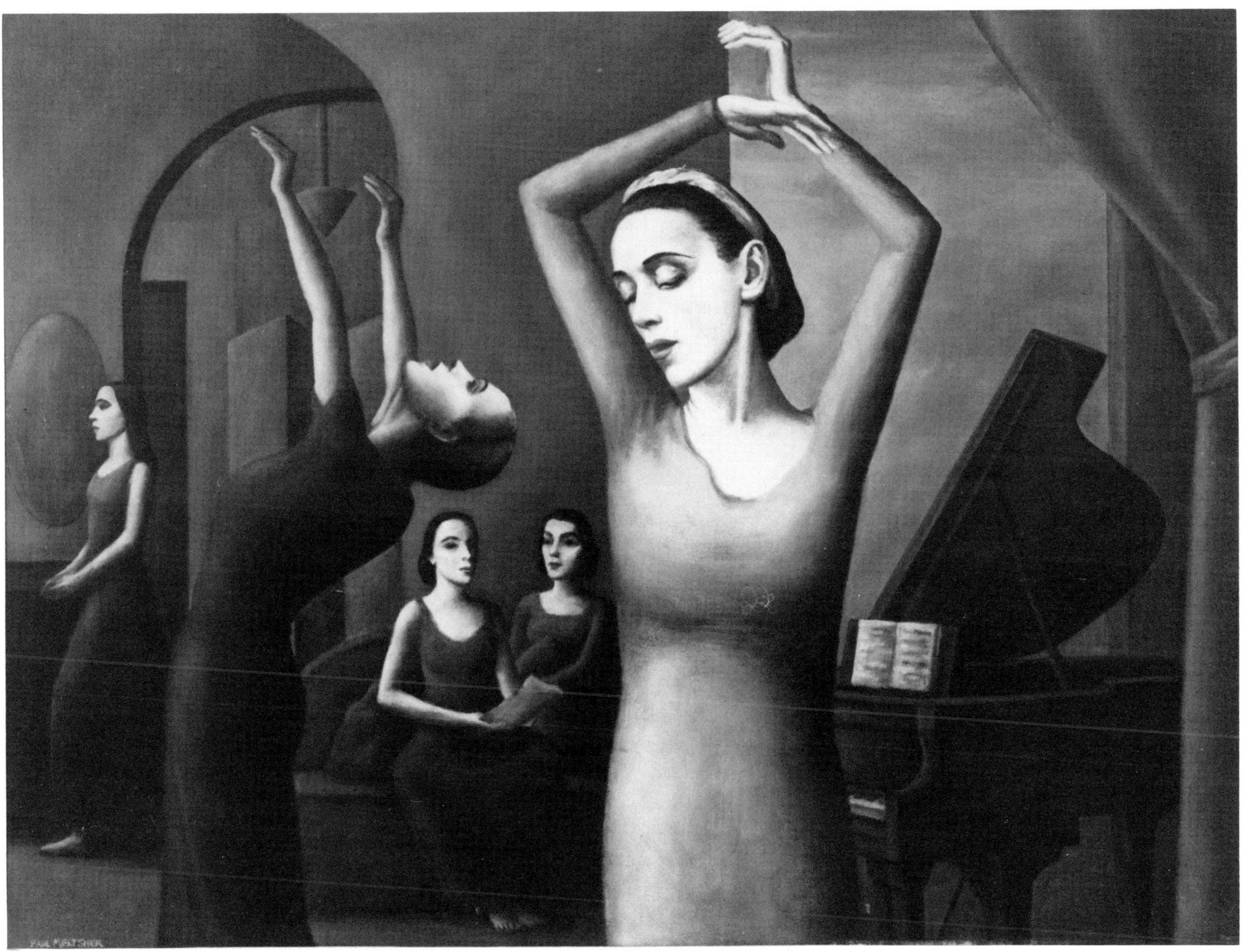

1981 Museum Purchase, Friends of the Wichita Art Museum Art Fund
(1981.9)

NIC MAYNE (1899-1947)

Psyche and Cupid
Oil on board, 1940
29⁷/₈'' x 19⁷/₈''

Ancient peoples instinctually possessed profound understandings of human personality and couched their explanations in what to us today may seem to be childishly naive fables. One of the most persistently charming is the tale of Psyche and Cupid, the theme of this 1940 painting by the Nebraska-born artist Nic Mayne. The story tells of a young maiden named Psyche or *soul* whose beauty incurred the jealousy of Venus, Goddess of Love. Venus dispatched her son Cupid with instructions to shame Psyche by making her fall in love with a monster. Instead Psyche and Cupid fell in love with one another. But Cupid warned Psyche that she must never see him in the light. Nevertheless one night Psyche's overwhelming curiosity led her to steal upon Cupid while he slept, and holding a small globular oil lamp over him, she accidently spilled a tiny drop of oil on his face. The hot oil promptly awakened him and he leaped from his bed. It is this moment that is depicted in this painting. The story goes on to tell how Cupid, angered by Psyche's broken promise, fled and how the remorseful Psyche searched the earth for her lover throughout her life. Only many years later was she reunited with him in heaven. The deeper meaning therefore symbolizes the tormented soul's eternal search for human love.

But Mayne's fascination with ancient thought went beyond mere interest in a classical theme. For here he has used soft color tones — blue-gray, ivory, green and brown — quite similar to those found on archeological remains from ancient painting. Moreover, his treatment of the standing profile figure of Psyche, with her large almond shaped eye, long tresses, delicate ivory flesh tones and sharp linear outline, is strongly reminiscent of Minoan fresco painting which during the 1920s and 1930s was beginning to be widely publicized in popular literature throughout the world. Also important here is the formal balance of strong geometric shapes by which the moment depicted is so effectively expressed, for Psyche is silhouetted against the dark background drapery while a contrastingly bright funnel-shaped shaft of light dominates the right, illuminating the figure of Cupid who draws his left arm across his face, avoiding the light and obscuring his identity.

Although Mayne was widely recognized during his career, little is known today of his life. He was born in Nebraska about 1899 and settled in New York in 1923 where he studied at art schools as well as under the direct instruction of George Luks with whom he shared a studio. In the years immediately prior to his death, Mayne was apparently a recluse and in 1947 was found dead in his studio loft.

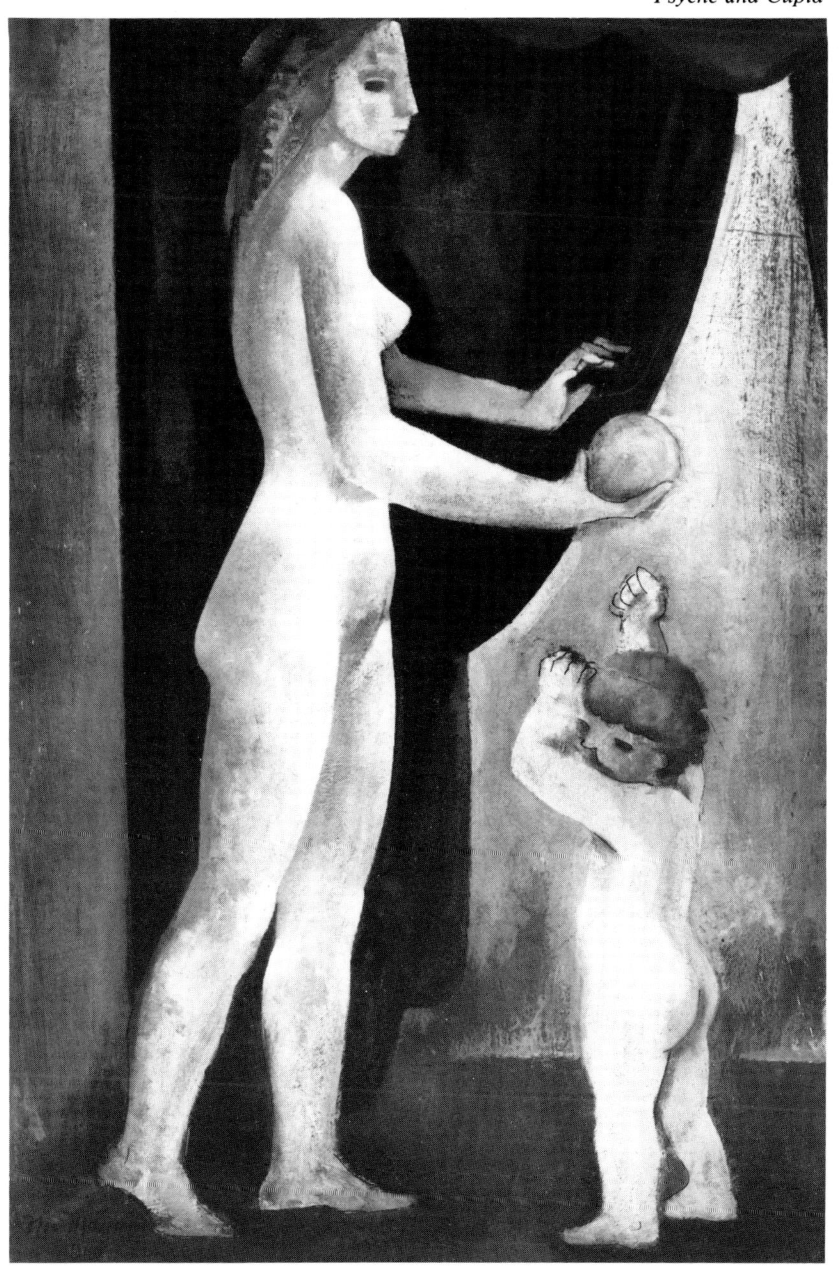

1983 Donation from Mr. & Mrs. Joseph Wolins, New York City
(1983.25)

ANDREE RUELLEN (b.1905)

River Men
Oil on canvas, 1940
18" x 24"

This oil on canvas titled River Men was painted about 1940 at a site along the Savannah River in Georgia by the American artist Andree Ruellan.

Thematically the work clearly represents the continuation into the 20th century of the anecdotal genre tradition established by such artists as William Sidney Mount, George Caleb Bingham and Richard Caton Woodville and which was popular in America during the decades preceding the Civil War.

Here, located in the foreground of the composition is a small wooden cabin situated at the edge of the wide river running parallel to the picture plane. To the right is a casually arranged group of five men informally chatting, while inside the cabin is a seated woman, barely visible through the small open door. Patches of blue sky, a swollen river with its blue-green water and leafless but brightly illuminated trees on the far side of the river impart clarity to the composition. At the same time they suggest a late winter setting.

All of the forms are tightly drawn and precisely outlined. Otherwise, brushstrokes are freely applied in small but broad intersecting daubs, thus imparting a strong faceted statuesque effect to the figures throughout the composition. Indeed, the artist is obviously more interested here in defining volumetric form than in furnishing meticulous details, a fact which quite possibly reflects her study of sculpture on one hand and the influence of training under Robert Henri on the other.

A point of special interest is the attention given by the artist to the use of black subjects throughout the composition. This is easily explained in part by her own longstanding sympathy for the plight of black Americans. More significant, however, is the fact that the work was executed in 1940 when the issue of racial inequities had begun to emerge from the social climate of the Great Depression and was already engaging the attention of some Americans prior to the outbreak of World War II.

Ruellan was born in 1905 in New York City. At an extremely young age she embarked upon a career in art. She was a child prodigy, participating before she was 9 years old in New York Exhibitions with such notables as Henri and George Bellows. At age 15 she studied sculpture with Leo Lentelli and drawing with Maurice Sterne at the Art Students League in New York.

In 1922 she won a one-year scholarship for study in Rome, after which she spent five years in Paris where she met and married the artist John W. Taylor. When she and her husband returned to the States in 1929 they settled in Woodstock, New York. John Taylor died in 1984 but Andree Ruellan continues to reside in Woodstock. Her works are included in major museum collections throughout America.

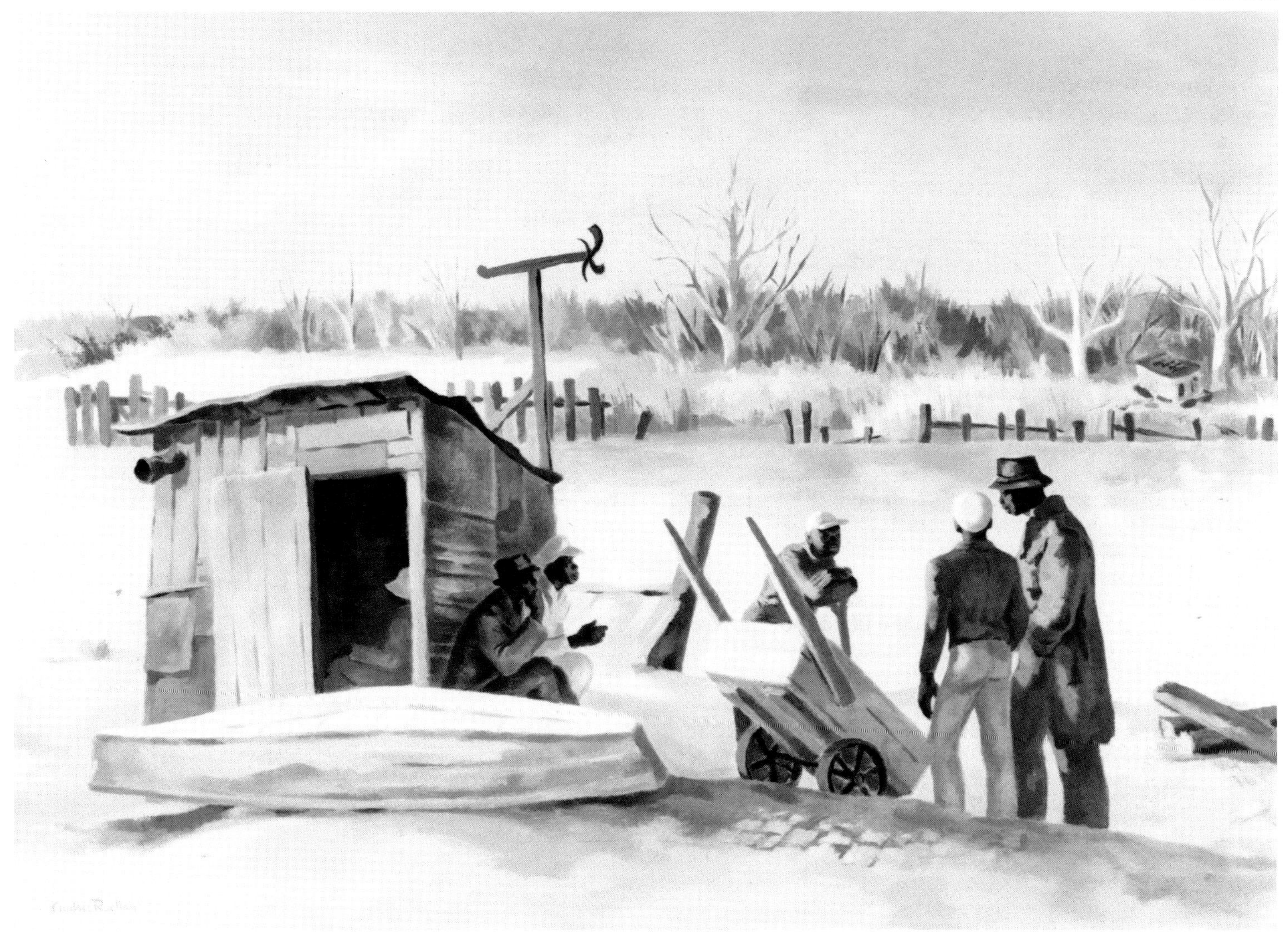

1987 Museum Purchase, Volunteer Operated Gift Shop Art Fund, Friends of the Wichita Art Museum (1987.33)

KARL FORTESS (b.1907)

Landscape in Winter
Oil on canvas, 1940
20¹/₈'' x 40³/₈''

For centuries, nature and the changing moods of the seasonal cycle have been among the principal themes for painting throughout Western culture. In this impressive work titled *Landscape in Winter* executed in 1940 by the American painter Karl Fortess, a barren setting at the height of a bleak winter is convincingly depicted. The ground is blanketed with snow, trees are leafless, the icy roadway is deserted and the pervasive mood is one of gloom. Nowhere can the human image be found.

Yet if we look closely, the composition seems to come to life, for forms and spaces dynamically interpenetrate, and a restless pattern of alternating dark and light areas is spread across the entire surface of the canvas. Indeed, the naked tree branches that reach upward and the powerful geometry of such interesting masses as the small section of wall at the left, the sweeping roadway that ascends from the lower foreground together carry the eye toward a narrow streak of delicate blue that glows through the otherwise cloud-filled sky. Moreover, swollen forms in the distant terrain coupled with occasional patches of muted green, russet and yellow that punctuate the desolate landscape convey a sense of latent vitality and the promise of renewal and therefore of hope for the future. Spring will follow winter; the cycle of life will go on and beauty will once again be reborn.

But there is another aspect of the painting which cannot be ignored. This work was painted in early 1940. War in Europe was already underway and news of the Hitler-Stalin Non-Aggression Pact, signed just a few months before, was particularly shocking to artists throughout the nation. That America would eventually become involved seemed inevitable.

Like a dream, a painting is sometimes an unconsciously expressed wish fulfillment. And it is therefore not surprising to find hope combined with despair in such a work as this executed in a moment when the political and psychological climate was so fearfully threatening. And in this instance, it was nature — a source of consolation and of beauty and truth — that Fortess apparently found the appropriate symbolic outlet for transforming his deepest concerns.

Karl Fortess was born in Antwerp, Belgium in 1907 but settled in America while still a youth and became a U.S. citizen in 1923. He studied at the Art Institute of Chicago, the Art Students League in New York and — with Yasuo Kuniyoshi — at the Woodstock School of Painting. Throughout his prolific career he has been the recipient of numerous awards including a Childe Hassam Purchase Award, a Guggenheim Fellowship and a Salmagundi Prize through the National Academy of Design. In 1940 he was awarded First Honorable Mention in the Carnegie International competition for *Landscape in Winter*. His works are included in such major collections as the Museum of Modern Art, the Brooklyn Museum, the National Collection of Fine Arts and numerous others. For many years Fortess was a professor in the School of Fine Arts at Boston University. Currently he resides in Woodstock, New York where he works actively as a painter and printmaker.

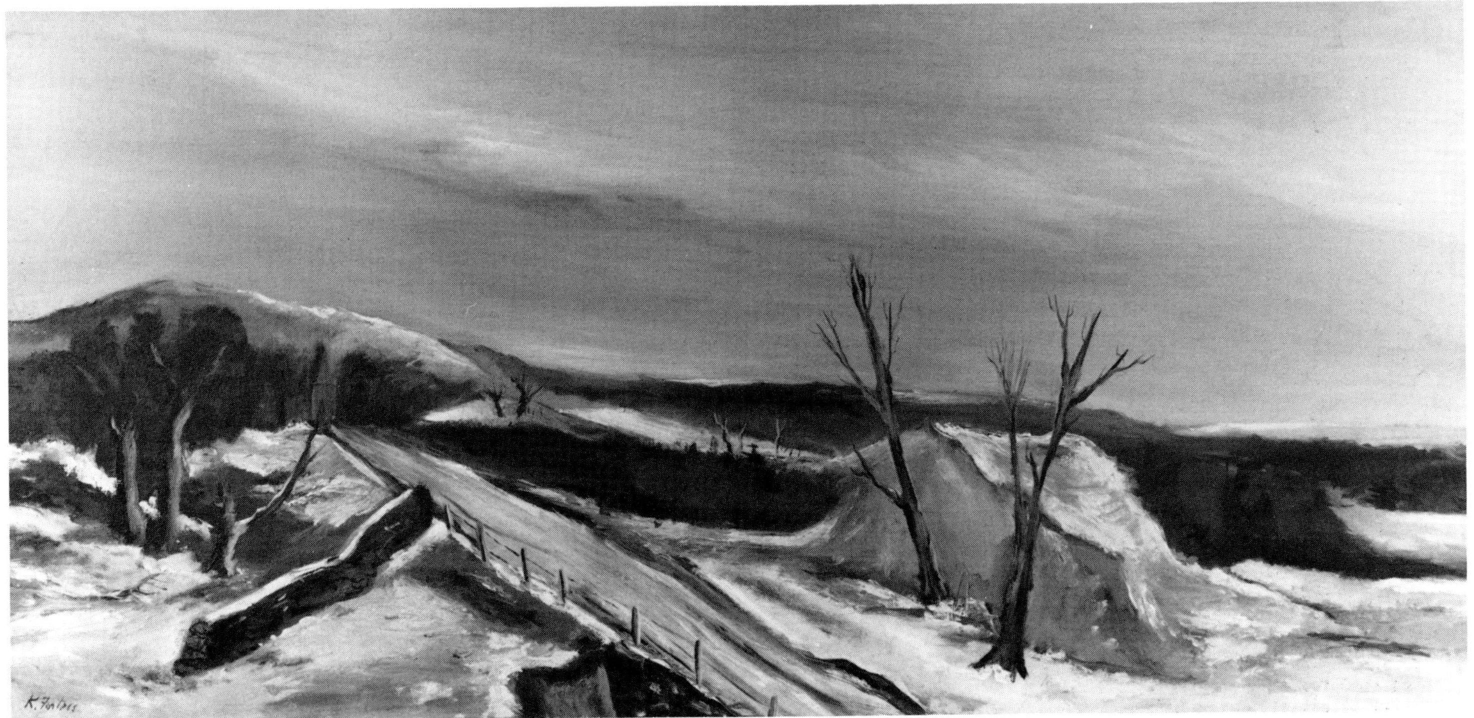

1982 Museum Purchase, Friends of the Wichita Art Museum Art Fund
(1982.44)

JEAN XCERON (1890-1967)

Untitled
Oil on canvas, c.1939
40¹/₈'' x 30¹/₈''

This untitled abstraction was executed c.1939 by the American painter Jean Xceron. Here the artist has created a completely non-objective statement where simple geometric planes coupled with contrasting horizontals and verticals are harmoniously unified within a structured grid pattern. All of the forms cling tightly to the surface of the canvas thus producing an entirely flat composition. Fundamentally, this work is an abstract system in which interactive unity of diverse elements is emphasized and where purity of form and color is a dominant feature.

That a work such as this may be categorized as *dehumanized* by virtue of its total lack of any human reference goes almost without saying. Yet such a statement might also be viewed as entirely prophetic of an age when human values and human existence are highly threatened. And it was the rise of totalitarianism which had emerged following World War I and throughout the ensuing 1920s and 1930s that culminated in 1939 in the outbreak of World War II in Europe and the horrifying spectre of America's imminent involvement. Moreover, the powerfully abstract character of this painting suggests a well-known generalization often stated by critics that when the artist perceives social conditions as terrifying, his art becomes increasingly abstract.

But there is far more here than either a hidden social comment or merely a structured pattern of fine colors and simplified geometric forms. Indeed, conceptually this work arises out of a long humanistic tradition in Western thought that refers back to ancient Platonic philosophy which stressed the existence of simple geometric forms as the underlying bases of reality and which proclaimed that the particularistic three-dimensional appearances of natural objects and relationships are but corrupted reflections of a pure and perfect universal reality. Understandingly therefore in this work only elemental essentials are seen and any illusion of representational reality is completely avoided. To Xceron and other artists who worked in accord with such an idealistic outlook, it is the artist's mission to seek that universal reality and to give it plastic form in the work of art itself.

Jean Xceron was born in 1890 in Isari, Greece but settled in the United States in 1904. He attended the Corcoran School of Art in Washington from 1910 to 1916 and thereafter studied in New York. He resided in Paris from 1927 to 1937 during which time he participated actively in numerous exhibitions and at the same time served as an art reviewer for American Newspapers. His first one-man show was held in New York in 1935. In 1938, he settled permanently in New York and like many other American artists, he worked under the W.P.A. during the late 1930s and early 1940s. Shortly after the war he was employed as a member of the staff of the Guggenheim Museum where he remained until his death in 1967.

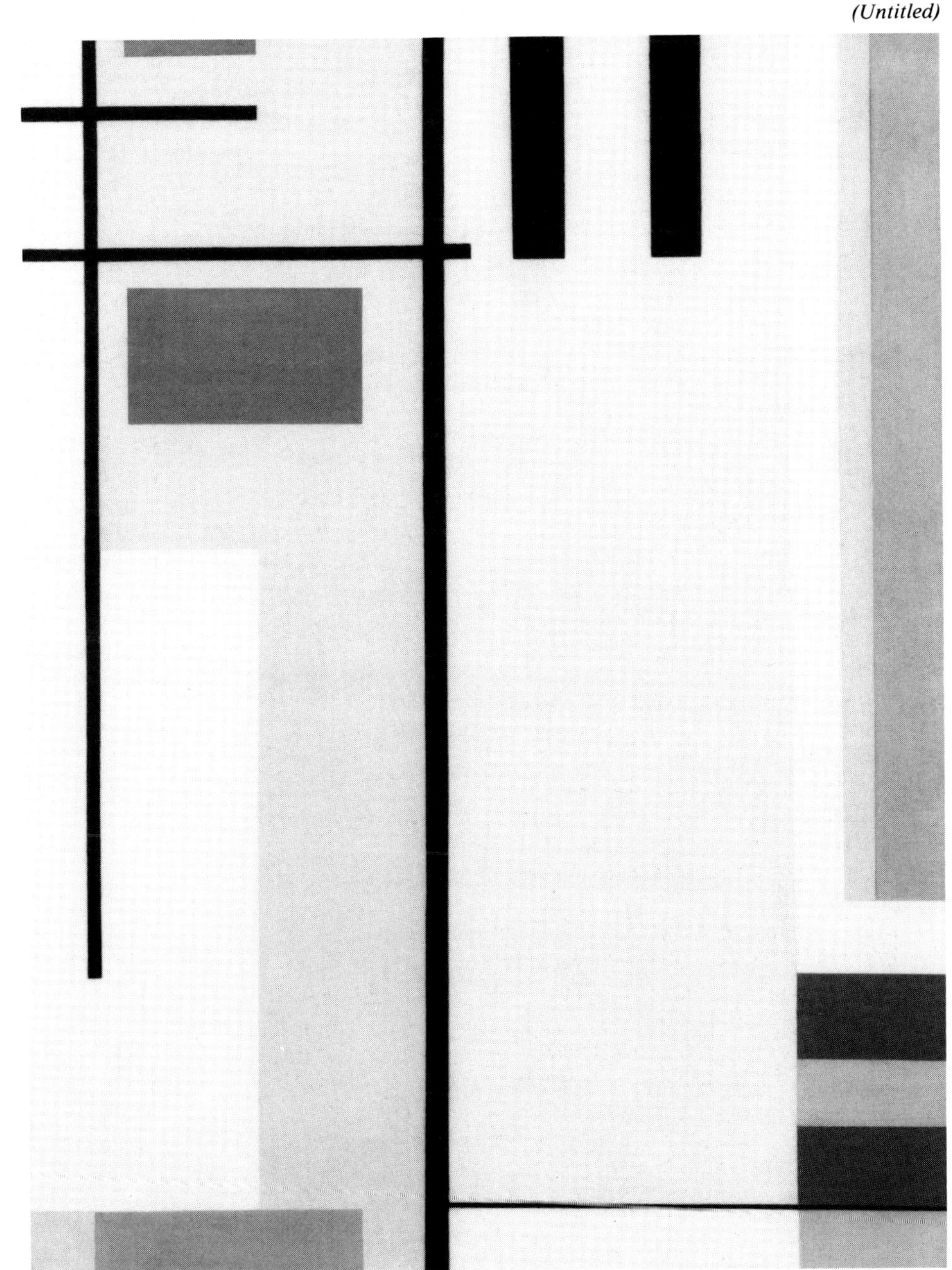

1984 Museum Purchase, Volunteer Operated Gift Shop Art Fund, Friends of the Wichita Art Museum (1984.31)

WILLIAM THON (b.1906)

Sea Gulls and Ferryboat
Oil on canvas, 1943
20'' x 30''

The artist's sensitivity to the spirit of the times is a trait which in many respects distinguishes the artistic personality from all others. And it is this sensitivity which finds concrete, though not neccessarily literal, expression in true art in contrast with illustration or imitative mannerism.

Certainly this quality is notably documented in this painting titled *Sea Gulls and Ferryboat* executed in 1943 by the American artist William Thon. Here the objective setting appears at first somewhat ambiguous. But clearly in the foreground is seen the end of a ferryboat with a snow-covered floor during the depth of winter. Across the railing and through a precarious opening, protected only by a rather flimsy folding metal gate, is a chilling view of the dark gray winter sea and the infinitely deep cloud-filled sky out of which a flock of sea gulls approaches the ferryboat. The absence of all human figures, the presence of long gloomy gray shadows and the use of sombre neutral tones rather than vivid colors together evoke a mood of eeriness and disquietude that is further heightened by the predatory gulls hovering around the boat. In a very real sense this mood coincides with the tragic moment when the work itself was painted. The year was 1943, a year when the free world was deeply engaged in a contest for survival during World War II.

How beautifully this sense of threat and anxiety is expressed and how effectively these feelings allude to the troubled times. Yet no form in this work visually depicts any familiar representation of war *per se*. For what we see before us are not the literal signs of war but instead are symbols of the feelings associated with war. This is the language of the artist who speaks at a level of awareness far deeper than the eye alone sees. And during the early war years, William Thon was one of the most versatile American artists in the command of that language.

William Thon was born in New York in 1906. He studied at the Art Students League in 1924 and 1925 and has been the recipient of numerous awards both in America and in Europe. His works are included in both public and private collections throughout the world. Today at the age of eighty-two he continues to paint actively in his studio and in Maine and exhibits quite frequently in New York.

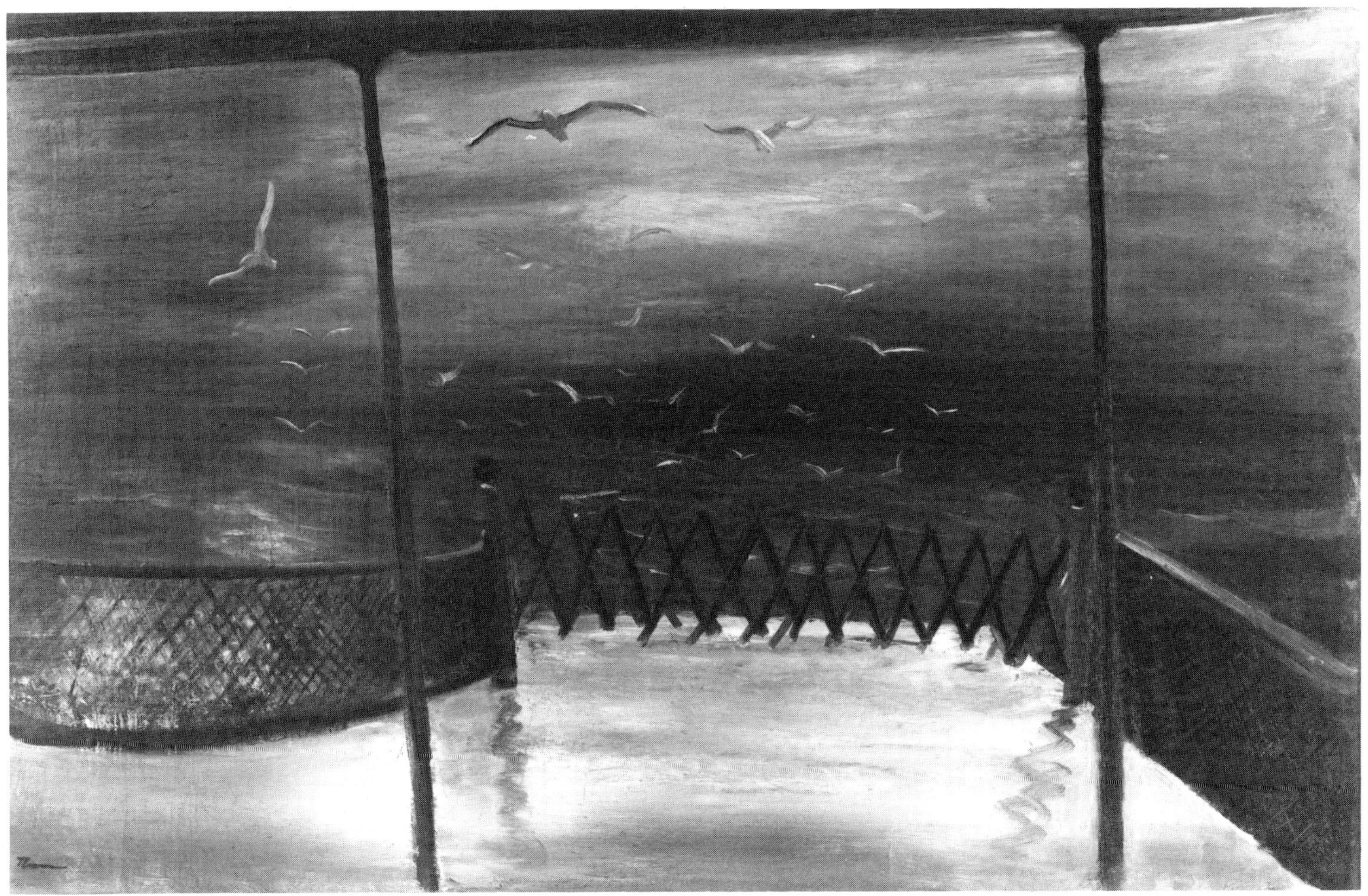

1982 Museum Purchase, Director's Discretionary Fund, Friends of the Wichita Art Museum (1982.29)

ANDREW WYETH (b.1917)

This engaging watercolor painting by the noted American artist, Andrew Wyeth, was painted in 1965 and is titled *After the Chase*. The work portrays a gentle hunting dog quietly resting at the foot of a tall tree which stands in a shallow open clearing. In the background at the edge of a wood, a fallen tree leans toward a small stone farm building. The scene is quiet and restful and reflects Wyeth's dedication and sensitive response to nature. Yet it is the predominance of green tones as much as the subject matter itself that is responsible for the freshness and cool tranquility suggested here. And, despite the loose technique and the varied forms used, the eye moves rhythmically across the surface by virtue of the continuity of texture, absorbing the entire composition at a glance and pausing only on the dog and the farm building which stand out boldly in bright color tones against the dark green surroundings.

Of particular interest is the strong geometry which Wyeth employs in constructing the design. For the bold cylindrical shape of the towering tree in the foreground anchors the composition securely and in turn is balanced by the cluster of three forms — a small stone building and the two interesecting trees — clearly in evidence in the upper right. Moreover, throughout the design, sharp acute angles are introduced as, for example, between the dog's back and the base of the slightly leaning tree where he sits — or, again, in both the roof gable and the roof stoop of the little stone building, between the two intersecting trees nearby and, even more important, between the foreground tree and the line of the fallen tree in the background. This illustrates an important principle of design, for the repeated use of any one geometric form throughout a composition causes the various parts to echo one another and thus tends to bind diverse segments together. And, although such repetition might not be readily noticed, it nevertheless constitutes a device to which the eye unconsciously responds and one used by artists throughout the ages to impart compositional unity.

Andrew Wyeth was born in Chadds Ford, Pennsylvania, in 1917. Much of his training in painting came through his father, the well-known American illustrator N.C. Wyeth. Like his father, Andrew Wyeth has painted in a realist tradition throughout his prolific career and during the past several decades has been recognized as one of America's most distinguished living artists. All of his paintings demonstrate masterful craftsmanship and a meticulous control of medium. Moreover, his subject matter is never controversial and, instead, expresses a love of nature, a sensitivity to the traditions of American life and a respect for recognizable imagery which together have enabled him to communicate in readily understandable artistic language and to produce widely admired paintings with which almost all people can identify. Chadds Ford today remains the place of Wyeth's residence and studio.

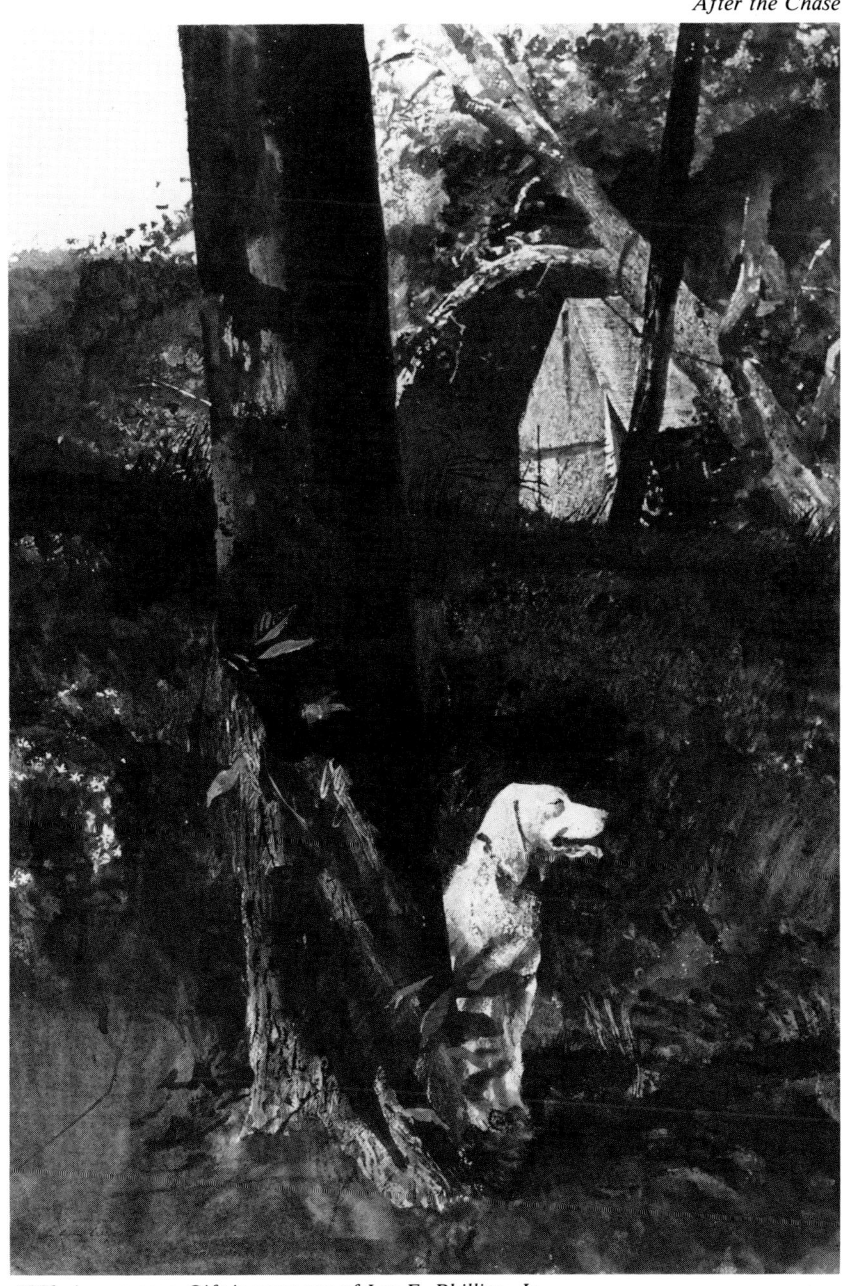

1979 Anonymous Gift in memory of Lee E. Phillips, Jr.
(1979.54)

MOSES SOYER (1899-1974)

Girl Wearing Roses
Oil on canvas, n.d.
25" x 20"

In painting a portrait of a human being, the artist is never satisfied with pure imitation. Of course, he must have reverence for his subject but he must also probe deeply into his subject's personality and emotional state. And his end product, the finished portrait, must certainly exceed simple photographic likeness, for the artist's mission regardless of what he paints is to discover and reveal humanity beneath the surface.

This was certainly the objective of Moses Soyer when he executed this very refined portrait, an oil on canvas titled *Girl Wearing Roses*. Here a beautiful young woman with dark brown hair and wearing a white gown with a blue-green sash is shown silhouetted against a gray background as she sits on a Windsor chair with her arms folded across her lap. Her red lips echo the full red roses that she wears at the neckline of her gown and in her hair. In his rendering of the delicate facial features — the slightly parted lips, the slender nasal ridge, the dreamy but alert eyes — Soyer has sympathetically and with great subtlety captured the glowing innocence of youth in this painting.

Yet like any true work of art, this painting is not a pure imitation. Instead it has a life of its own, largely independent of subject matter. Compositionally, the wide dark vertical bar at the far left defines the spatial depth of the setting and serves to balance the more dominant form of the sitter who occupies the center and right foreground. The heavy outlines of the hands and arms emphasize the contrasting delicacy of the face. And although the mood of the young sitter is peaceful and tranquil, the overall bravura of the brushwork effectively imparts an energetic vitality both to the sitter and to the composition as a whole.

Moses Soyer was born in Tombov, Russia in 1899. In 1912, he with his twin brother, Raphael Soyer, emigrated to New York City. He studied at the Cooper Union Art School and the National Academy of Design as well as with Robert Henri and George Bellows, and was forced to support himself by performing various jobs including factory work and selling newspapers. Throughout the '20s and '30s he was clearly associated with the so-called "Fourteenth Street School" of New York painters whose chosen subject matter was the everyday life of the poor laboring classes who lived and worked in and around Union Square. However Soyer also deeply admired the art of Degas and in many instances was enormously influenced by Degas' ballet dancers, and it is perhaps that interest which is suggested in *Girl Wearing Roses*. Major exhibitions of Soyer's works have been held in numerous museums across the country and his paintings are included in the Metropolitan Museum, the Whitney Museum, the Museum of Modern Art, the Brooklyn Museum and many others. Soyer died in New York City in 1974.

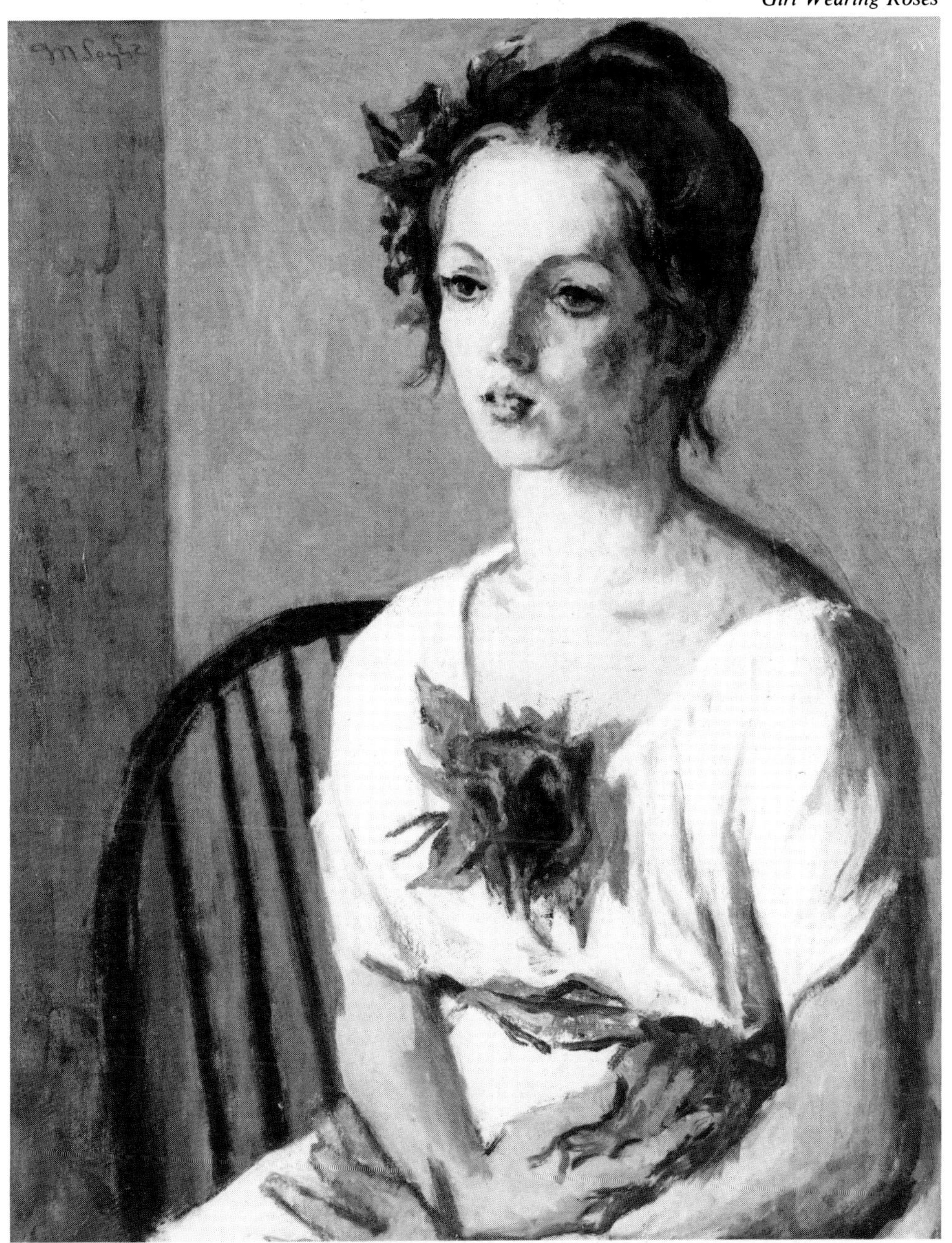

1985 Gift from Mr. David Soyer, New York City
(1985.73)

IVAN ALBRIGHT (1897-1983)

Quivering Trees of Aspen
Oil on masonite, 1964
14" x 18"

Quivering Trees of Aspen, a 1964 oil on panel by the American aritst Ivan Albright, quite typifies Albright's work of the 1950s and 1960s. Here, at the foot of a steep mountain backdrop, two intersecting streets are shown lined with small 19th century domestic structures completely surrounded by a low picket fence. Remnants of snowfall are seen on the rooftops and on the rugged mountain slopes while heavy accumulations remain in lumpy piles along the streets where several human figures dressed in brightly-colored clothes are walking or standing. In the foreground, tall twisted and leafless trees reach upward toward the sky creating a screen that partially obscures the views of both the background mountains and the nearby houses. And at scattered locations, long spear-like icicles hang threateningly above the houses.

In many respects, this work is simply another landscape scene which in its use of excessive detail is stylistically reminiscent of many American primitive paintings. When we look beyond the superficialities of the subject itself, a disturbing quality is clearly evoked. For the old houses seem structurally unstable and the dense tangle of tree branches forms an intricate web which, coupled with the splatter of minute and nondescript forms, clutter the surface of the composition creating a *horror vacui* effect that disperses compositional focus and diminishes visual clarity of definition. Moreover, disconcerting conflicts repeatedly appear, for the trees are barren, yet life-like shoots would seem to be sprouting from the extremities of dead branches. And at the same time a warm glow of yellow light sweeps down from the dark and gloomy sky, enlivening the tree branches and unifying the fragmented composition.

Indeed the scene is mournful and simultaneously reassuring for it presents a sense of new life and renewed vitality within the context of death and imminent decay. And such vitality is further intensified by the lively but insignificantly small human figure seen in the otherwise desolate foregound setting. Albright has effectively orchestrated color and form in such a way as to impart a haunting mood to the subject by focusing attention on winter; death and decay on the one hand, and life, vitality and the promise of renewal and rebirth on the other. This pattern of co-existent opposites is of course the actuality of the life process and is the dominant mystical feature implicit in all of Albright's works executed throughout his long and productive career. This painting is thus to be interpreted far more as a psychic landscape than a physical landscape; its poetry is visible to the mind rather than to the eye.

Ivan Albright was born in North Harvey, Illinois, in 1897 and studied at various centers in the United States and in Europe. He held three Ph.D. degrees as well as several honorary doctorates and exhibited widely here and abroad. Throughout his career he remained a realist but, unlike many other realists of his generation, he introduced mystery and magic into his paintings and today his works are recognized as outstanding examples of of "the Magic Realist manner". Albright died in 1983 at the age of 86 years.

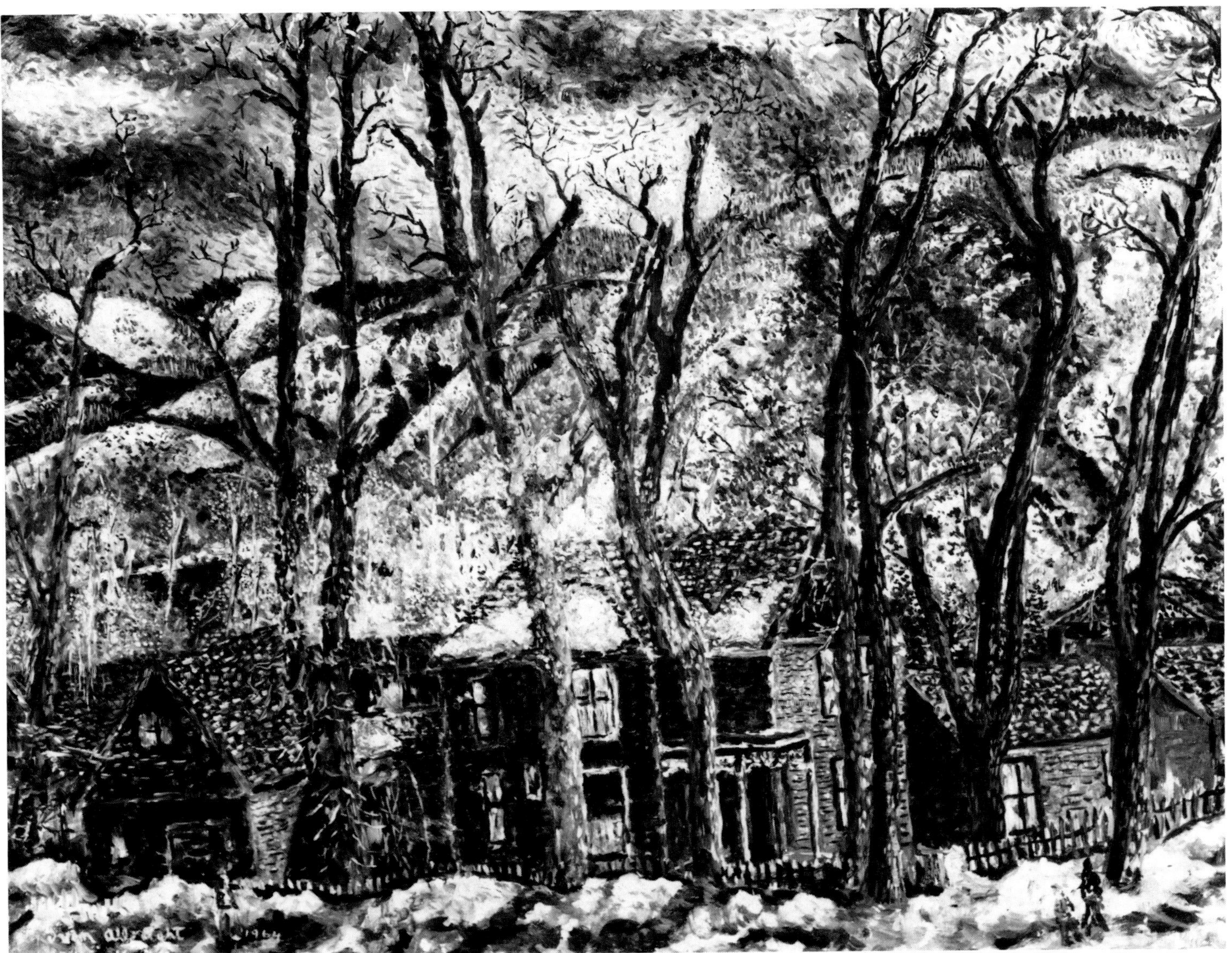

1987 Museum Purchase, Volunteer Operated Sales Rental Gallery Art Fund, Friends of the Wichita Art Museum (1987.62)

ALEX KATZ (b.1927)

Man and Woman in City at Night
Oil on linen, c.1964
49⁷/₈'' x 57⁷/₈''

This painting titled *Man and Woman in City at Night* was executed about 1964 by the contemporary American artist Alex Katz. Here, two figures, quite enormous in scale, are placed in the close-up foreground of the composition. Indeed, by cutting-off parts of the heads, arms and shoulders of both figures, Katz creates the impression that they exist partly in the space of the painting and partly in our own space. Yet, like cardboard cut-outs, the figures themselves are essentially flat and lifeless, with little or no emphasis on modeling by traditional light-shadow tone treatment.

In general, attention is given to precise drawing, although certain forms — such as the hand — show fuzzy contour lines that by intention are loosely drawn. This, coupled with the clearly visible brush strokes across the flat surfaces, emphasizes the reality of the paint itself. As a result, when we look at this work, we are forced to acknowledge that it is a painting — an object of reality in itself — and that it possesses the character primarily of pigment applied to a canvas, rather than being a make-believe view seen through a window into the world of actual existence. Yet, Katz is neither a pop artist nor a photo-realist and his works have aptly been described as "realism without reality".

One of the most interesting features here and in many of Katz's works is the evident influence of the visual media, in particular cartoon-comics and advertising placards. In addition, Katz seems to be making a strong social statement about the psychological quality of life in the present. For while the two foreground figures are obviously linked to one another by means of such formal devices as their close physical proximity, the presence of the woman's hand resting on the man's shoulder, the v-shaped neck lines, and the unifying blue background, there is nevertheless little feeling of psychological empathy between the two. Instead, the pale flesh tones and the vacant facial expressions suggest emotional solitude and resignation, and the figures seem more like manikins than they do full-blooded and warm human bodies.

Alex Katz was born in 1927 in New York City. He studied at the Cooper Union Art School and at the Skowhegan School of Painting and Sculpture and in 1972 was awarded a Guggenheim Grant in painting. In the same year he received the Cooper Union Professional Achievement Citation. Katz is represented in major museum collections throughout the United States and Europe including The Art Institute of Chicago, The Metropolitan Museum, The Museum of Modern Art, The Whitney Museum, The Hirshhorn Collection and others. Currently he resides in New York City.

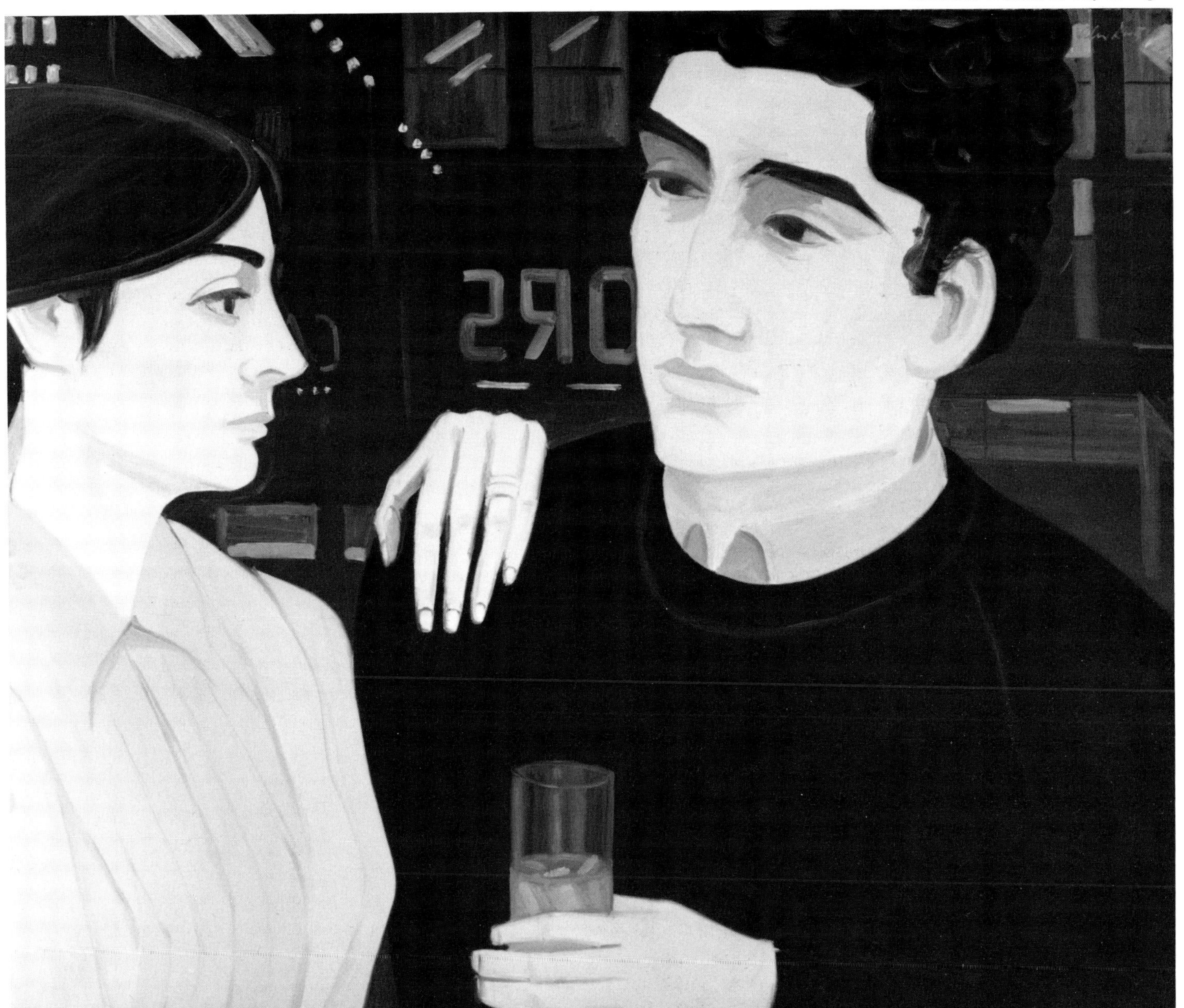

1978 Museum Purchase, Funds from National Endowment for the Arts
(1978.61)

WILL BARNET (b.1911)

Chess Game
Oil on canvas, 1973
43¼" x 33"

For over half a century, Will Barnet has been actively engaged as both a printmaker and a painter of considerable renown. And throughout his long career, he has been one of America's most progressive artists. He devoted the early years of his professional life to the production of works consisting of representational images that strongly comment on the tragedies of the Great Depression years. But during the 1940s and 1950s, he turned to non-figurative abstraction.

Barnet's abstract period was an experimental period, for it was during this time that his compositional interests were focused largely on the integration of shapes which stretch vertically and horizontally across a frontal plane, thereby markedly reinforcing the flat two-dimensional character of the picture surface itself. This was a vitally signficant period in Barnet's career, for the result of his abstractions culminated in a return to the representational rendering of fully recognizable figures by the early 1960s and thereafter. But his style then and now in no way resembles realism as we tend to think of the term. Instead, Barnet has established a new realism of tremendous aesthetic significance, and one of his finest achievements in his new realist manner is this 1973 oil on canvas titled *Chess Game*.

Here the subject is fully understandable: a young girl seen at the left concentrates on the move of her competitor, unseen but for his extended hand at the right, as the two engage in a serious chess game. Above, resting on the rail of a window, is a black cat which looks more directly at us as spectators than at the game taking place below. But the subject is of relatively little significance in comparison with the formal dynamics of the painting itself. Indeed, here Barnet's statement is his declaration of an aesthetic truth: that the most fundamental and characteristic reality of a painting is the physical flatness of its surface. In this work, the entire composition constitutes the avoidance of any deception of depth. All figures adhere tightly to the surface plane, for little modeling exists and colors are evenly applied and unarticulated. The reality of the surface is reinforced by virtue of Barnet's allowing the dominant figure to bleed off the left edge and by introducing the form of an arm and hand which stretches onto the surface from outside the composition. Moreover, although by tradition the spectator's eye is conditioned to interpret spatial depth, the use of advancing warm red-orange color in the central area of composition, including the tall window and the sky above, forces that area back onto the surface, thus avoiding spatial illusion.

This work then is exciting by virtue of the implicit truth of the reality of the flatness of any painting. In addition, the work is a return to the basic belief and stylistic usage found in both Egyptian and early Greek drawing, formal echoes of which we see in the strong linear treatment and, more particularly, in the profile head of the beautiful young chess player.

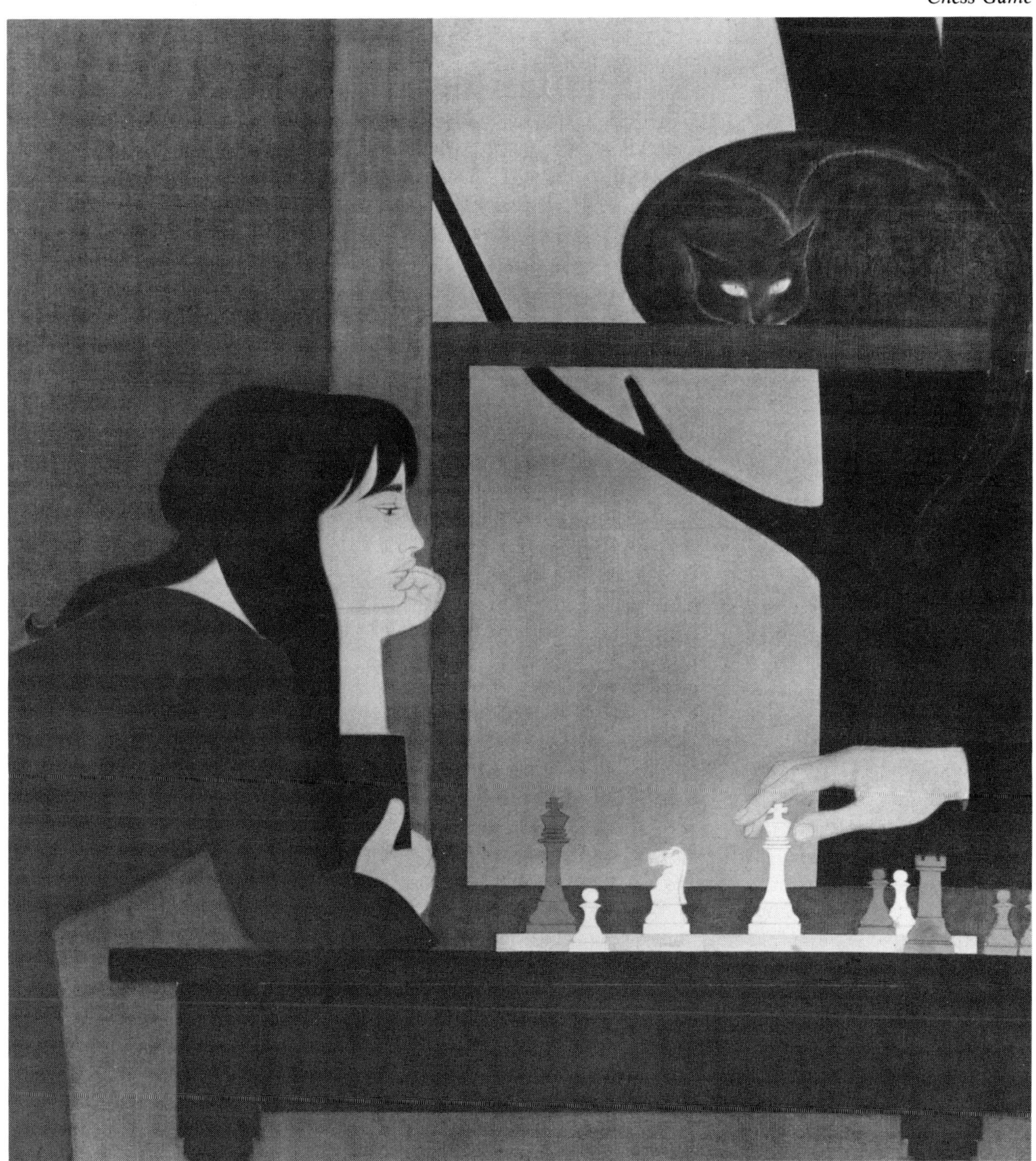

1983 Museum Purchase, Friends of the Wichita Art Museum Art Fund
(1983.4)

CHUCK FORSMAN (b.1944)

Glenwood
Oil on masonite, 1978
48" x 71¾"

A winter sports resort area in Colorado is the setting for this oil painting titled *Glenwood,* executed in 1978 by the contemporary American artist Chuck Forsman. What is shown is a close-up view of distant snow-covered mountain slopes seen by looking over a broad horizontal parapet-like band of architectural forms including panelled walls and a store front together extending across the entire width of the scene. Of especial interest are the spatial concepts in play and the sharp focus of all forms rendered. Of equal compositional significance are the familiar advertising signs shown — most offered in fragmentary form only — the snapshot-like manner by which the scene is presented, and the teasing uncertainty of what is actually taking place in the immediate, partially revealed foreground.

Muted colors are employed throughout. Yet a brisk vigor, echoing the lively mood of a resort town, is achieved by the thumb-size daubs of thick pigment applied rather uniformly across the entire surface, thus creating a decorative tapestry-like quality and serving to emphasize the physical actuality of the surface itself. The surface is further strengthened by the dominant verticals and horizontals in the foreground. And although a sense of distant space is formally created by the zigzag roadways and long stretches of evergreen trees that define steep mountain slopes of the background, sharp-focus detail is not diminished with the distance suggested. As a result, all forms tend to cling to the surface, thereby further imparting a flat, two-dimensional quality to the composition as a whole. Yet, while the eye dwells on the surface it is at the same time drawn into the distance, experiencing visual tension and in turn a marked degree of ambiguity.

But ambiguity is a reality of existence and is skillfully and deliberately introduced into this painting as an effective device for engaging attention and inviting active paricipation on the part of the viewer. Such ambiguity is further experienced by virtue of the incomplete identity and uncertain arrangement of forms in the immediate foreground. Moreover our own space is pulled into the composition by the reflections that we see in the glass store window at the lower left and by the fact that, like a close-up snapshot, the scene is deliberately chopped-off along all sides, thus creating a dynamic interplay between the viewer's space and that of the picture. Indeed, the entire scene is a cutout, a kind of suspended segment of familiar space containing fragments of commonplace objects and familiar banal images. But though the fragmentation of these images momentarily introduces uncertainty in interpretation, interest cannot be dismissed, for appropriate cues are supplied which stimulate our recall and our own creative impulses, forcing us to complete the meanings and thus to participate actively in the life of the painting.

Chuck Forsman is undoubtedly one of the most promising young realists in America today. He was born in Nampa, Idaho in 1944 and studied at Skowhegan School of Painting and Sculpture, Skowhegan, Maine, and at the University of California in Davis where he received the Master of Fine Arts degree in 1971. Since then, he has been a member of the Art teaching faculty of the University of Colorado. Forsman has held numerous solo exhibitions and has participated in many group shows. His works are included in major public and corporate collections throughout the country.

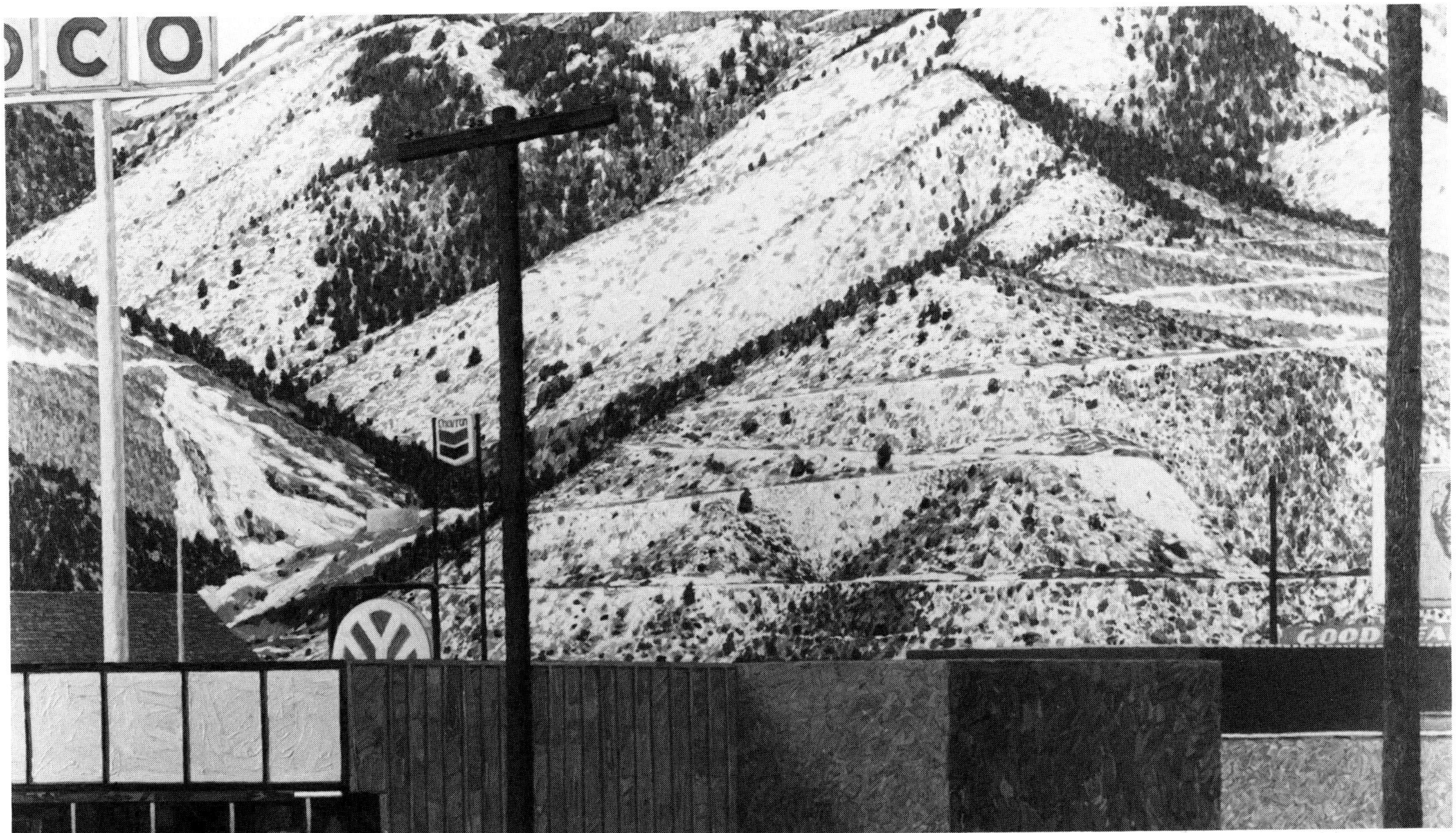

1980 Donation from the American Academy & Institute of Arts & Letters, Hassam & Speicher Purchase Funds, New York City (1979.56)

CHUCK FORSMAN (b.1944)

Denver Nights II
Oil on masonite, 1975
24" x 33¾"

A long and straight city street with neatly paved sidewalks lined with storefronts, street lights and parking meters, diagonally sweeps into the distance in this 1975 composition titled *Denver Nights II* by the American realist Chuck Forsman.

This composition is exciting by virtue of the intensity of realism in the rendering of such features as the high powered electric street lights, the neon signs, the automobiles, the chrome-framed window panels and the texture of the sidewalks. It is also fascinating in that it is filled with intriguing puzzles which compel careful and close viewing if we are to disentangle the compositional ambiguities and more fully understand the content and aesthetic significance.

Structurally, the work is divided into three vertical segments. One consists of the right edge with the angled narrow glass panel from which a street behind us with a motor sales lot and a display of lined-up autos is reflected. A second segment is the stretch of glass windows along the sidewalk, reflecting the opposite side of the street at the left. The third is the left side of the street itself. It is the interplay between these three sections that supplies the ambiguities and captures our interest. Moreover, as we view the painting, we are allowed to see what is in front of us as well as what is behind us and we are, therefore, thrust into the world of the painting and brought into direct contact with the realism of the setting itself.

But the real excitement derived from this painting is the vivid illusion of reality which Forsman furnishes us, for he has treated each component with meticulous care and objective precision — so much so that our vision is intensified and we are made to see many features of the scene that would normally remain unnoticed by our subjectively selective eye. Indeed, through the artist's interest in his subject, those features are not ignored but instead become deeply etched into our consciousness. In actuality then the illusion of reality found here as in many works of the new generation of realists, rivals the reality itself and we may certainly conclude that the image presented is in one sense more real than the reality itself. It is in that respect that the new realism differs significantly from the realism of the past, and that although the influence of the camera and of color film is evident, a work such as this can never be mistaken for a photograph.

But there is another aspect of this painting which must be considered. It is interesting that the composition itself seems as objectively impersonal as the technique is objectively precise. No part is more important than any other part. The streets are clean; there is no debris. The typically standardized icons of 20th century urban life are much in evidence but no human beings are shown and we, the unseen viewers, are the only participants. Indeed a numb stillness pervades the setting as though time had come to a halt evoking a lonely and eerie mood that is much intensified by the surface reflections and the soft hazy glow of light against the deep blue cloudless night sky.

It is always tempting to read meaning into a work of art even though such meaning may never have been intended. But art always interprets life, and it would appear certain that this work is a profound comment on the American consciousness, and perhaps on the question of how the individual fits into the total scheme of a mechanized life style which openly glorifies banality. Whatever the meaning, we can be reasonably confident that the statement is the product of a keenly sensitive and probing mind that is pointing up issues, the significance of which we are perhaps not able or yet ready to fully accept.

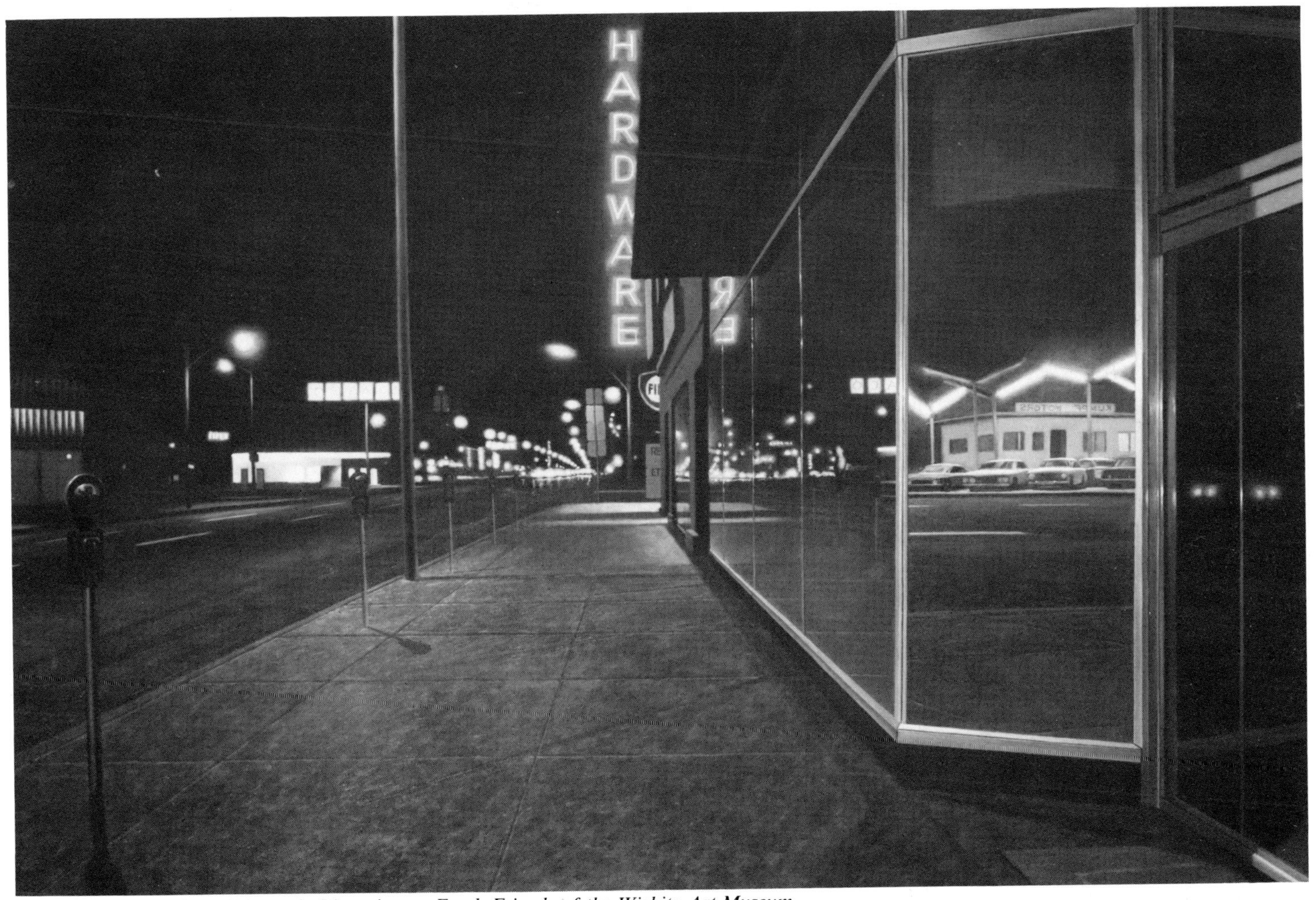

1979 Museum Purchase, Director's Discretionary Fund, Friends of the Wichita Art Museum
(1979.33)

BILLY MORROW JACKSON (b.1926)

Reading
Oil on masonite, 1980
47¼" x 71¼"

Billy Morrow Jackson is a master of contemporary American realism. He was born in Kansas City, Missouri in 1926, studied at Washington University, the University of Illinois and in Mexico, and beginning in 1954 he was on the teaching faculty of the University of Illinois as professor of art until his recent retirement in 1987. His works have been exhibited widely in the United States and abroad, and he is represented in major public and private collections throughout the country.

This work, titled *Reading,* was executed in 1980 and is unquestionably one of Jackson's most accomplished paintings. What we see here is essentially the poetry of light, for the painting is virtually flooded with brightness and with life; understandably one might figuratively assert that it was painted with colored light rather than with oil pigments.

In concept *Reading* is essentially symmetrical and at first glance would appear to be a self-contained and tranquil composition portraying a teenage girl comfortably enclosed within an architectural space where she sits alone quietly and undisturbed on a stairway step reading a book. Closer observation, however, reveals an extremely complex composition in which certain visual ambiguities are deliberately introduced that arouse our curiosity and divert our attention from the literally stated subject to the abstract qualities of the painting itself. Examples are the greatly exaggerated depth of the central hallway and the landscape view beyond, the open door near the end of the hallway, the massive hall staircase which carries the eye upward, and the threshold in the extreme left foreground through which we gain a glimpse of still another stairway, this time leading downward. Yet the composition is completely unified by virtue of an all-pervasive light, flooding the space and appearing in broad areas of brightness as well as in flickering patterns of multiple and overlapping reflections that vary in shape, size, color and intensity. Of special interest are delicate tonal nuances of cool light reflected on the ceiling above the hallway and originating from the open hallway window. Equally noteworthy are the exquisite reflections of warm yellow light on the wall in the upper right hand corner of the painting. Indeed those warm reflections echo the light that penetrates the stair windows above the young girl, and the encompassing glow effectively links areas of the composition that are passive with those that are more active, establishing an emphatic unity within the total composition.

An interesting aspect of this work is its title, *Reading.* For not only does the term *reading* apply to the portrayed subject who is shown reading the language of the book held on her lap but also to the spectator who must "read" the formal language of the painting itself in order to derive aesthetic appreciation from that painting.

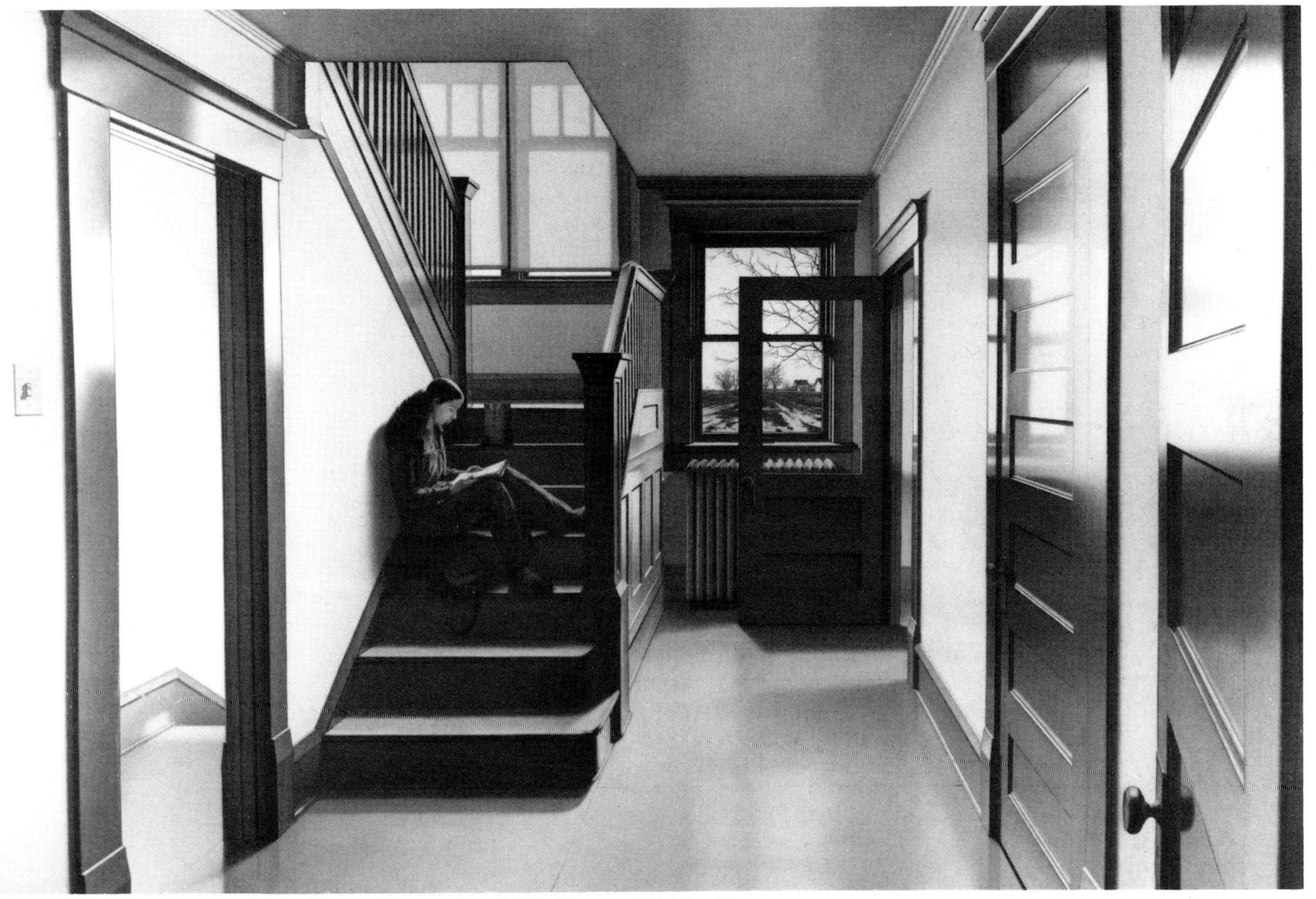

*1981 Museum Purchase, Funds donated by Mr. & Mrs. Donald C. Slawson, Wichita, Kansas
(1981.2)*

BILLY MORROW JACKSON (b.1926)

Champaign
Oil on masonite, 1984
23¾" x 31¾"

This painting is an oil on masonite titled *Champaign* and executed in October, 1984, by the contemporary American realist, Billy Morrow Jackson. The work offers a familiar view of the American prairie landscape. At a glance the painting evokes the appropriate physical sensations of the early autumn season depicted and of a variety of natural textures shown, as for example the wood siding of the red barns, the ruts in the muddy roadway, the crispy white frost that has settled on the foreground weeds and on the rooftops, and the yellowing tree leaves of early fall. The relatively low horizon is accompanied by a vast area of open and all-embracing colored sky with tonal gradations ranging from a radiant yellow-orange glow at the right of the composition to a delicate and cool pale blue at the left.

What is so especially fascinating about this painting is that we experience many surprises as we explore the scene presented. For, while the artist has quite obviously demonstrated an interest in methodically furnishing a meticulously accurate rendering of a prairie landscape, his even greater concern has been in focusing attention on the component details so harmoniously interlocked in reality, yet more often than not totally overlooked as we casually cast our eyes across the world of actual reality in which we live.

It is in pursuing this approach in painting that the artist intensifies our vision by making us more keenly aware of the minutiae of nature and at the same time promptly reminding us of the immensity of creation and its many and varying dimensions.

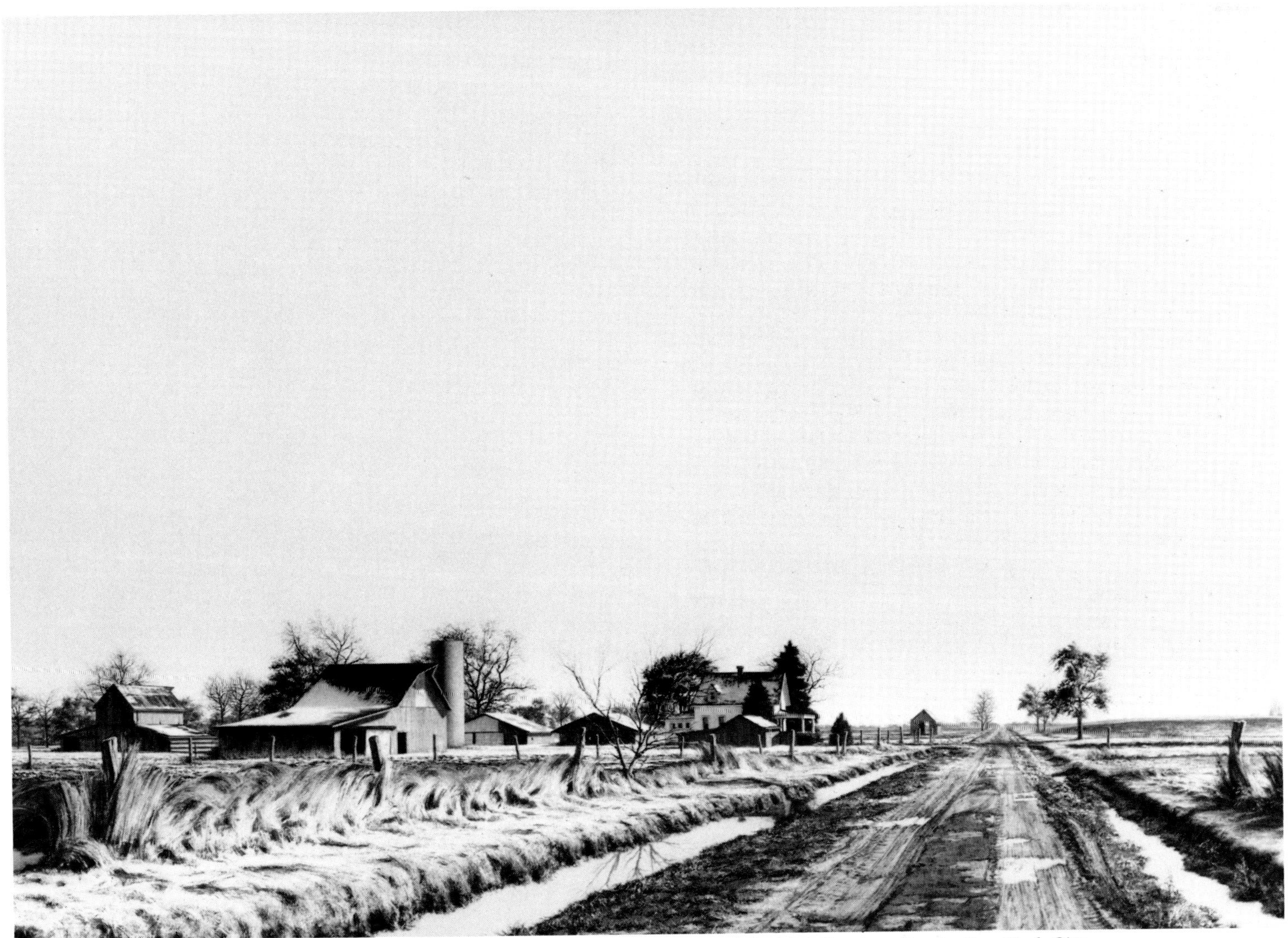

1986 Donation from the American Academy & Institute of Arts & Letters, Hassam and Speicher Purchase Funds, New York City
(1986.85)

ALFRED LESLIE (b.1927)

Television Moon
Oil on canvas, 1978-79
72¹/₈" x 84¼"

The American realist Alfred Leslie executed this still life painting titled *Television Moon* in 1978-79. Quite appropriately the central feature of the composition is a life-size color TV set from the screen of which is projected a tranquilly soothing image of a crescent moon shining high above a serene tropical sandy seashore. Casually arranged around the TV set is a clutter of everyday objects often found in the typical American home and including a telephone, a large flat china serving dish, tennis shoes, a folding metal chair, a pair of leather sandals and a wide floor brush without its handle. Realistic impact is heightened by the masterfully handled textural differences and the *trompe l'oeill* treatment of occasional imperfections such as the chips in the rim of the plate, the scars along the upper edge of the TV cabinet and the bit of masking tape stuck to the end of the metal chair seat.

This is a thought-provoking statement and one which penetrates to the very heart of the dominant focus of the American life style: the unswerving reverence for the mechanized experience furnished by TV. Indeed the TV set is endowed here with a powerfully commanding personality of its own, first by virtue of the massive scale of the composition and the enormous space occupied by the TV set in that composition, and second because the fortuitous grouping of secondary objects completes a convincingly authentic setting without detracting or claiming prolonged independent attention.

But perhaps the principal "new realist" aspect of this painting is the fact that although no human forms are present and that emphasis is placed upon contemporary banality, the intensity of the statement furnishes us a kind of reassuring confirmation of the reality of human existence in an era marked by fear, uncertainty and doubt about the meaning of our own existence.

Alfred Leslie was born in New York City in 1927 and studied at New York University and at the Art Students League. Although he worked as an abstractionist at the beginning of his career, he turned to realism quite early and at a time when most other American painters were still working in an abstract expressionist idiom. Today he is regarded as one of America's most successful members of the new realist school and has held solo exhibitions in such centers as the Hirshhorn Museum and the Boston Museum of Fine Arts. His works are in major collections throughout the United States. Currently, Leslie resides in New York City.

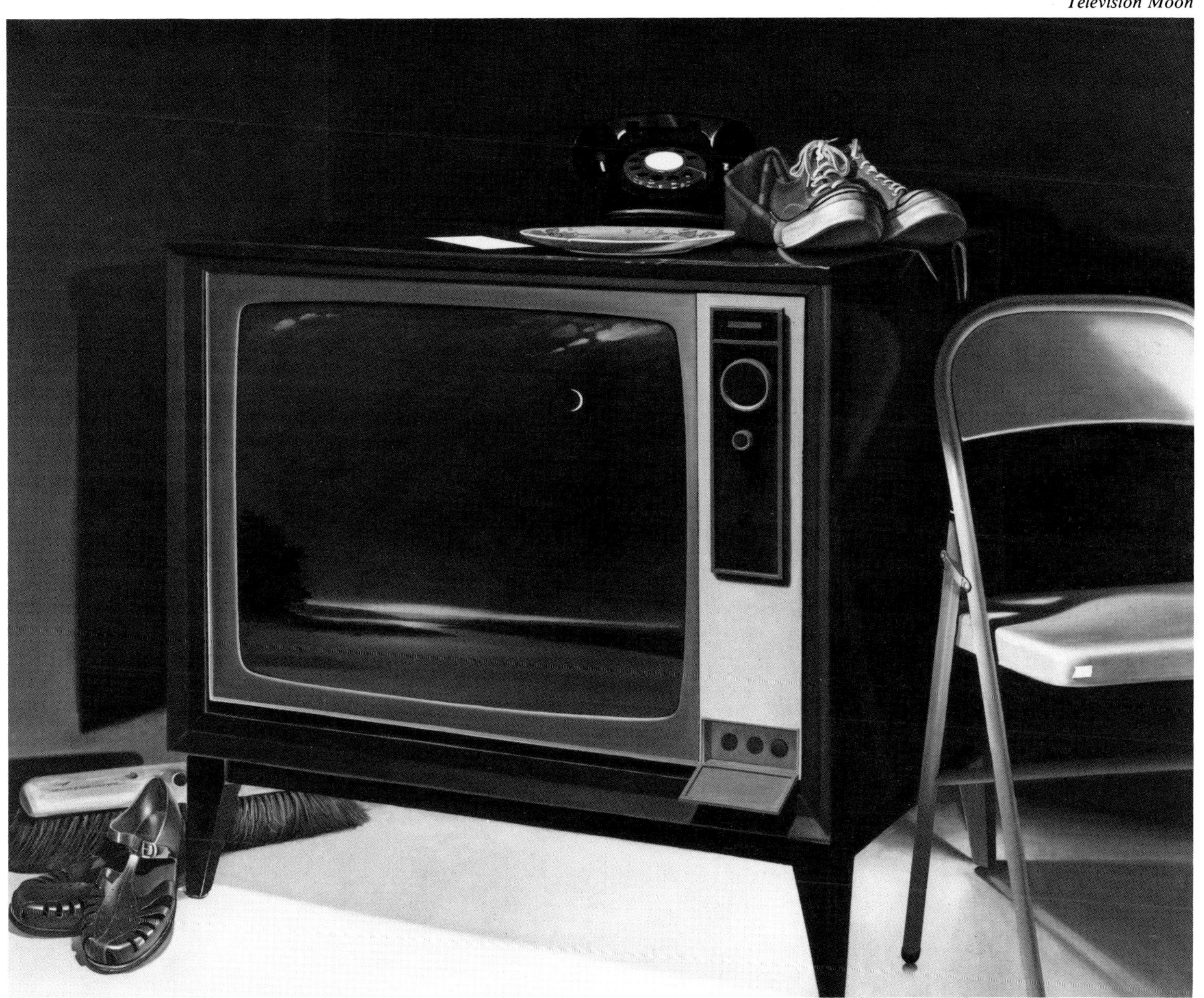

1981 Museum Purchase, Virginia & George Ablah Art Purchase Fund
(1981.54)

COLLEEN BROWNING (b.1929)

Ghost Women of Essaouira
Oil on canvas, 1983
40½'' x 48³/₈''

This painting, titled *Ghost Women of Essaouira I,* was executed in 1983 by the American realist Colleen Browning. The work simply depicts three figures — two women heavily cloaked in traditional Eastern dress and one male in western garb seen in the far distance — who are walking along a narrow, alley-like street in Morocco. But the primary interest of this painting stems not from the theme but from the powerful formal dynamics of the composition itself. Indeed, the arrangement of line, shapes and colors is geometrically planned to draw the eye to a cental focal point. For the vast stretches of wall surface that border the narrow street are punctuated by the bright blue and yellow windows and doors that cluster near the center of the composition and hold the viewer's attention. At the same time, the eye travels along the narrow street into the compositional depths where it halts as the street bends to the right in a murky atmosphere of ominous shadows. It is there that visibility ends and imagination takes over.

Another aspect of enormous interest relates to the sensorial responses vicariously experienced as the result of the artist's treatment of the scene. For the attentive viewer readily becomes aware of the stench of stale air trapped in the narrow street, the reverberating clack of the footsteps in an otherwise silent setting, and the unsightly stains both on the walls and on the street. Moreover, the marked variations in the thickness of pigment applied by the artist to the canvas accent the impression of crumbling stucco and patched wall surfaces so commonly found on actual house walls in the Mediterranean region.

One other point of much interest is found in the marked contrast between the social reality of the past in confrontation with present-day activities. This, of course, is effectively accomplished by the introduction of such anachronistic elements as the bicycle, the electric wiring, the high heeled shoes worn by the cloaked woman in the foreground and the steel manhole cover set into the street near the center of the composition. Indeed, the technique of compressing time in a composition of this type is a feature that justifies the use of the term *new realism* as a valid description of much contemporary work.

Colleen Browning is of Celtic ancestry and was born in County Cork, Ireland, in 1929. She studied art at the Slade School of Art in London. In 1949, she immigrated to America and settled in Rochester, New York. She is a resident of New York City but, at the same time, has a studio on the Caribbean Island of Granada, where she spends many months each year. She has exhibited in major museums throughout the United States and Europe and is today regarded as one of America's most prominent contemporary New Realists.

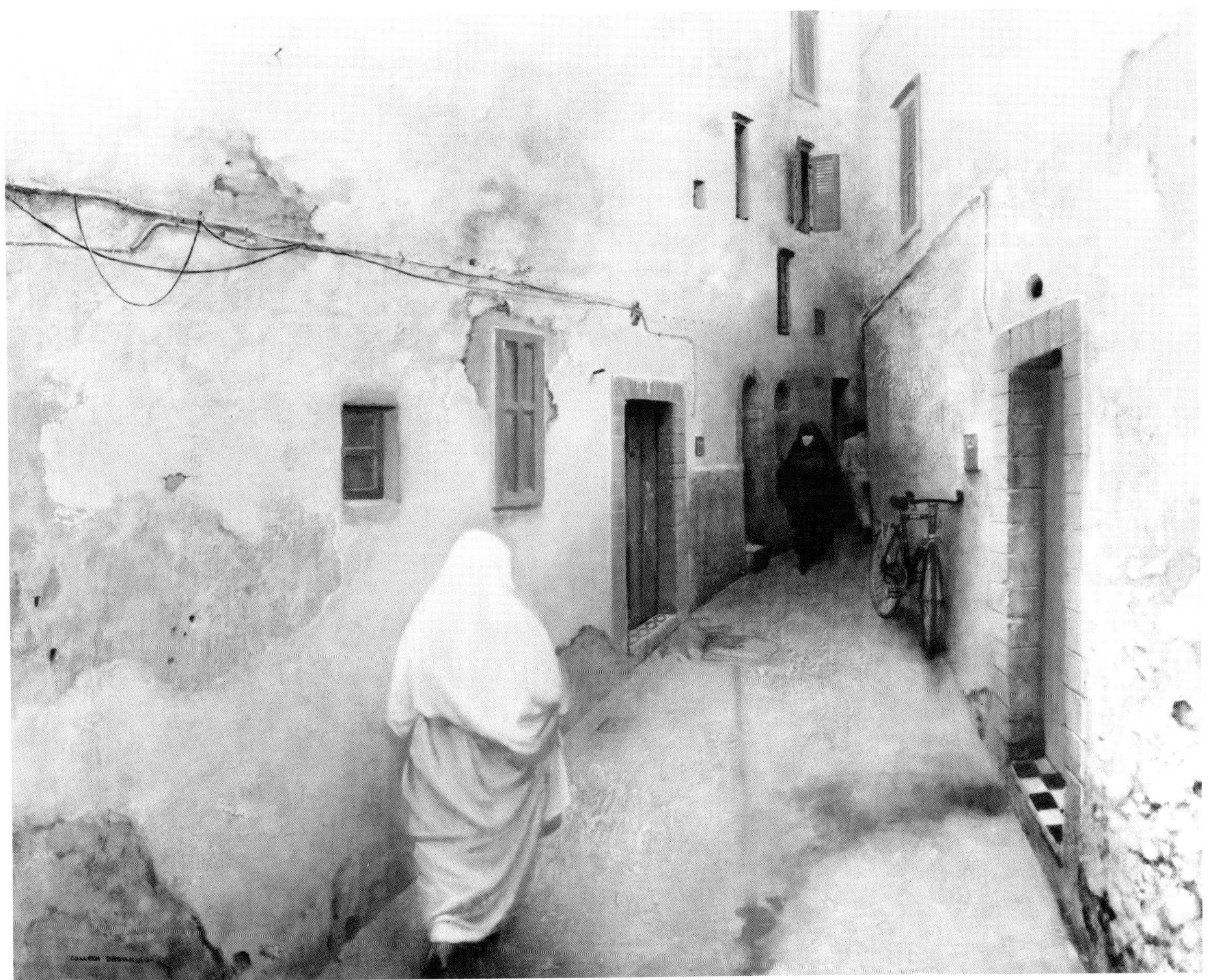

*1986 Museum Purchase, Lulu & Kenneth Brasted, Sr. Memorial Fund
(1986.83)*

HERMAN MARIL (1908-1986)

Still Life with Cattails
Oil on canvas, 1970
60¼'' x 40¹/₈''

For well over 40 years before his death in 1986, the American painter Herman Maril produced compositions in which the manipulation of delicate color and refined form created a strange sense of space that compels close attention and active involvement of the observer. In this work, an oil on canvas executed by Maril in 1970 and titled *Still Life with Cattails,* the composition consists of a carefully planned arrangement of rectangular color areas with a table top sharply tilted forward and on which rest a large circular platter and a cluster of tall and slender cattails. Here, balanced design and compositional unity are quite masterly accomplished through the coordination of varied but simple geometric shapes and soft muted colors.

As one views this work it becomes quite evident that the artist has not intended to present a photographic resemblance here. Moreover, what is at first so puzzling is that the mind and the eye compete with one another. For, out of the dominant rectangular divisions of the composition, the mind attempts to structure a framework that would create the illusion of depth and thus accommodate the table and its contents. Yet the eye resists that interpretation since the table does *not* appear to recede, nor does the relationship of form and color tone support the conventional illusion of spatial depth. Instead objects and space seem to become one, for the irregular and ragged edges of pigmental areas cause us to interpret space as flowing into the objects depicted and at the same time to see the objects themselves dissolving into the encompassing space. In addition, scattered dashes of mixed color applied unevenly across flat areas of the composition seem to energize the otherwise quiet surfaces thereby further tending to pull space and form together and strengthening the reality of the flat picture plane itself.

This painting is thus a composition into which are built strong dynamic tensions that are effectively resolved by the harmonious play of colors and shapes. As a result, the work of art becomes one which is not only pleasing to the eye but also one which forces the observer to look closely and thereby become increasingly participative in the life of the painting itself. And it is, of course, through such active participation that intimacy is generated and visual pleasure intensified.

Herman Maril was born in Baltimore, Maryland in October 1908 and over the years achieved an international reputation in the world of art. He studied painting at the Maryland Institute of Fine Arts and subsequently experimented with various aesthetic movements that America was absorbing from Europe. By 1934, he was employed by the first United States government sponsored art project when he was commissioned to execute an American Scene painting titled *Baltimore Waterfront.* It was after World War II that his works became increasingly expressive and more and more abstract, and it was during the postwar period that he earned his greatest fame. In 1947 he was appointed professor of painting at the University of Maryland, a post he retained until his death in 1986. Maril exhibited in major exhibitions throughout his career and in 1967 a retrospective of his work was presented by the Baltimore Museum of Art. His paintings are included in numerous collections, both private and public, throughout the United States including the Whitney Museum, the Metropolitan, the National Museum of American Art and others.

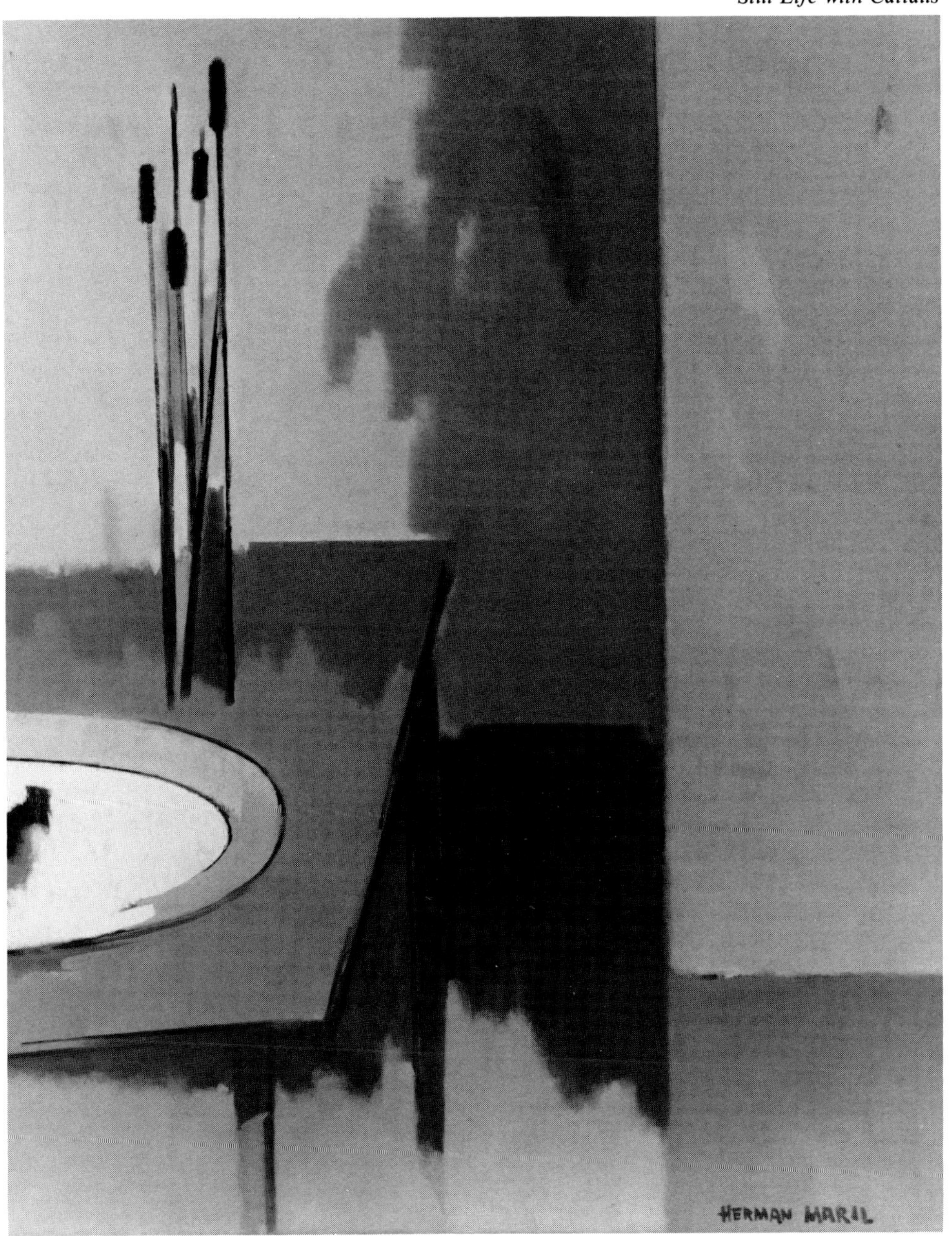

1982 Donation from Mr. Ronald Becker of Alexandria, Virginia
(1982.59)

JOHN SILK DECKARD (b. 1938)

Knife Man
Cast bronze, 1976-77
9'8" h.

John Silk Deckard's *Knife Man,* a nude male cast bronze sculpture nearly 10 feet in height, was commissioned in 1976 for permanent installation on the sculpture deck of the new Wichita Art Museum. Actually the image has repeatedly appeared in a somewhat modified form in many of Deckard's prints and drawings during the past 25 years. And indeed essentially the same image appeared in antiquity as the bound mythological figure of Marsyas and again in the 15th century Italian Renaissance, often in a social and political propagandizing context.

In the instance of *Knife Man,* Deckard's original objective was to design a bronze figure approximating the elementary geometric form of a knife blade or sword. To accomplish this, the modeled figure was necessarily elongated and the complete body form flattened in a stretched-out position. What we see therefore is a figure which stands erect, balanced on the toes of its extended feet with ankles brought together and with both arms raised together in a vertical position high above the shoulders so that hands and wrists are linked as if bound. The head is thrown back and cradled between the upraised shoulders and arms, obscuring the face but emphasizing the long neck. The body thus assumes the stance of a diver and displays the potential of piercing just as a knife or sword pierces when forcefully thrust into an object. At the same time, the stretched elongation of the body has caused the rib-cage to project prominently while the abdomen sinks deeply into the body creating heavy dark shadows that contrast sharply with the glossy highlights that play across the adjacent exaggeratedly knotty muscles. Clearly the impression of a tortured being experiencing physical agony is expressed. And it is of course the combination of these elements — the erect posture of the figure, the suggestion of physical suffering, and the knife metaphor — that clearly associates this work both in form and in symbolic meaning with ancient renderings of the mythological figure of Marsyas about to be flayed by Apollo as punishment for insolence.

A most distinguishing aspect of this work is the fact that man is represented here as a weapon that serves as the instrument of his own destruction, or in Marshall McLuhan's terms, a weapon that is actually an extension of himself. Yet this figure has a particularly commanding presence and as we view it we see not only the mournfully dreary image of death and destruction but also a sense of upward thrust, of uplift traditionally associated with the creative life force. And this notion is especially significant here inasmuch as the same figure which suggests self-destructive impulses concomitantly suggests a re-awakening and revival. Thus both the idea of death and that of rebirth combine in a single artistic statement convincingly communicating the human urge toward a balanced state between life and death, the two opposing poles of being.

John Silk Deckard was born in Erie, Pennsylvania in 1938. He studied formally at several noted art schools including the Pennsylvania Academy of Fine Arts and the Pratt Graphic Art Center. Throughout the 1950s and the 1960s he successfully established himself as a highly skilled printmaker and has produced well over 150 individual drypoint engravings. Since the early '70s his interest has shifted from the print medium to cast bronze sculptures. Certainly one of his most significant works is *Knife Man.* Another is a massive exterior sculpture titled *Soul Survivor* which stands before the entrance of the Erie Art Museum. Other large sculptures are included in major public and private collections across the United States. Deckard maintains both his studio and his residence in Erie, Pennsylvania.

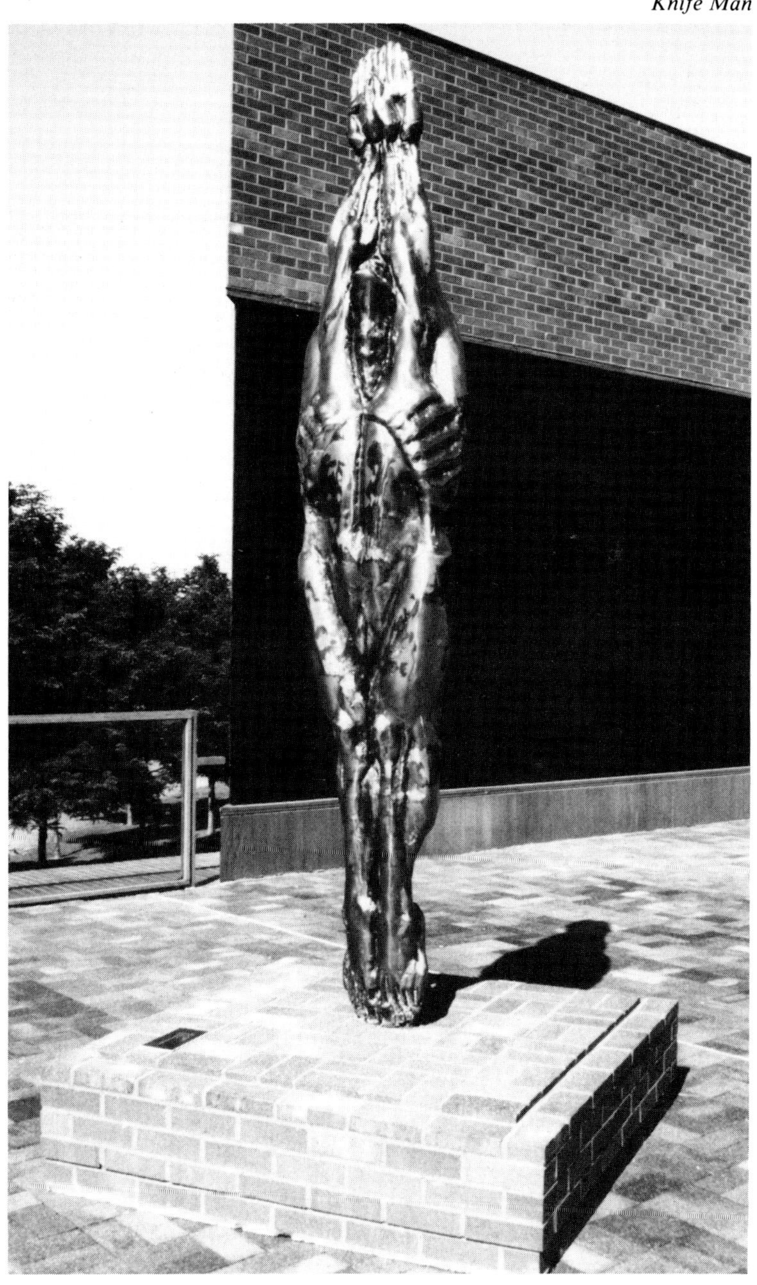

1977 Purchase, Funds donated by Volunteer Alliance
(1977.75)

SIDNEY GOODMAN (b.1936)

Daydream
Oil on canvas, 1986/87
90¼" x 67¼"

Throughout the history of art, from early Egyptian and Babylonian times down to the present, the theme of the Mother and Child has appeared repeatedly. The image itself has timeless appeal and has found expression in both religious and secular subject matter, traditionally portraying the mother, seated or standing, holding the child either in her arms or on her lap.

An unusual variation of the traditional types is seen in this most charming work titled *Daydream* and painted in 1986-87 by Sidney Goodman. Here what is depicted is a living experience, for the mother and child are actually portraits of the artist's wife and infant son.

The mother, snugly wrapped in a heavy blanket, lies in bed with her head resting gently on a deep yellow embroidered pillow. She smiles admiringly at her infant son who is lying on a nearby quilt, laughing happily and with his arms raised. Brightly colored stuffed animals, rattles and teething rings are scattered about the bed.

The mother's right hand extends toward the infant, while in her left hand she holds what is clearly a magazine open to a page showing a large photographic reproduction of a human embryo. She is the source of life and the perpetuator of civilization and, at the same time, the symbol of protection, patience and strength, all of which is reinforced by the sense of confident spontaneity expressed in the tender human relationship seen in this work.

Over and above the subject matter itself, what is especially interesting here is the harmonious combination of realism on the one hand and pure abstraction on the other. For, while the modeling of forms and the sensuous rendering of flesh tones are accomplished with meticulous precision, the left edge and upper left corner of the composition are an undefined blue and gray vaporous abstraction within which the subject of the composition appears to float. In a very real sense, the effect emphasizes the eternal and other-worldly significance of the subject which is so humanely and sensitively treated by the artist.

Sidney Goodman was born in Philadelphia in 1936. He studied at the Philadelphia College of Art beginning in 1954 and took a teaching position there in 1960 which he continued to hold for the ensuing 20 years. However, in 1964, he traveled throughout the nation on a Guggenheim Fellowship, studying American society and American social behavior, a fact that has undoubtedly contributed to his interest in representational realism.

Currently, he teaches part-time at the Pennsylvania Academy of Fine Arts, reserving the major portion of his time for painting in his Philadelphia studio. Today, he is one of the most noted artists among the contemporary realist painters in America.

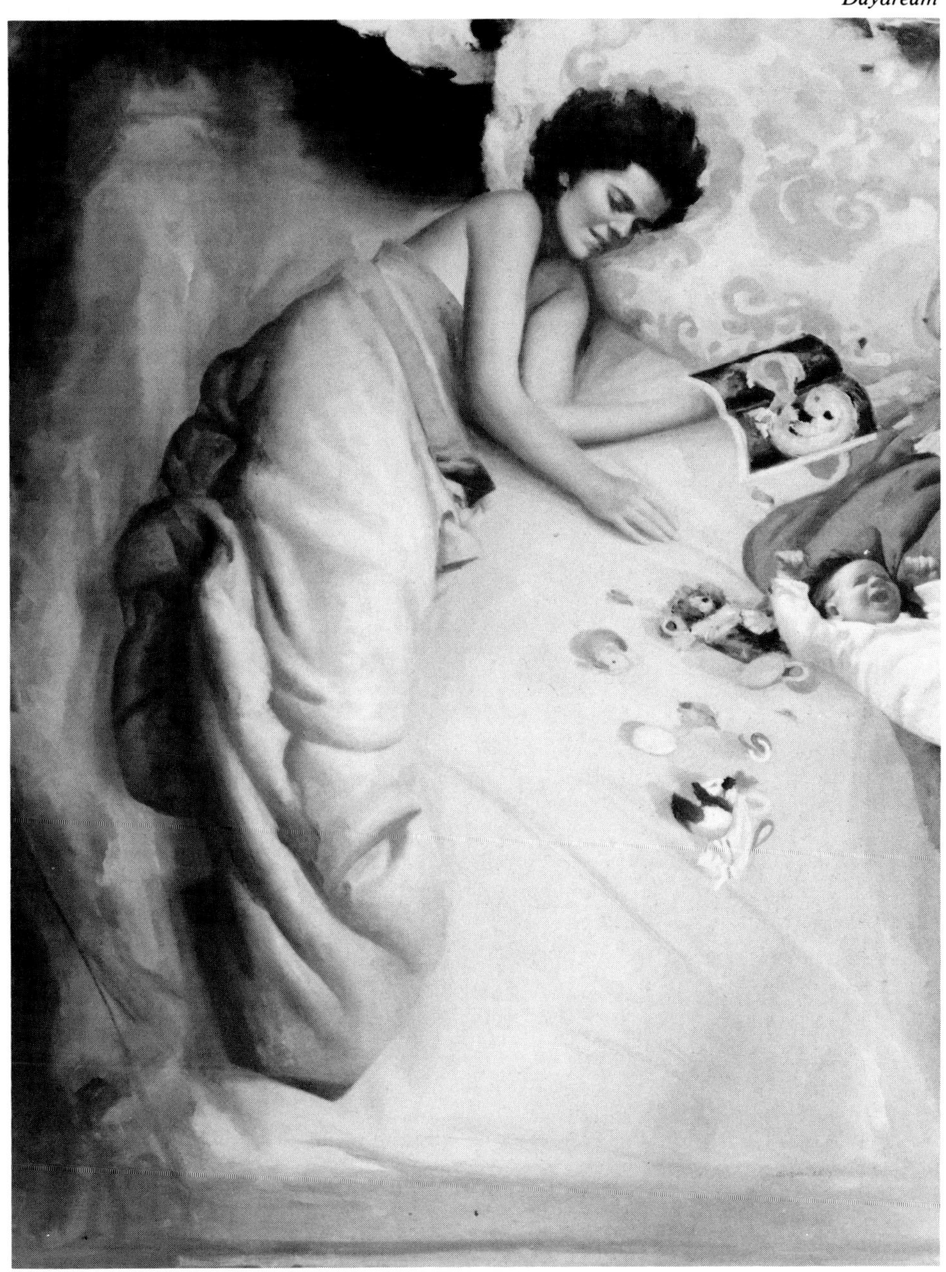

1987 Museum Purchase, Friends of Wichita Art Museum Art Fund
(1987.36)

LEONARD BASKIN (b.1922)

Medea
Cast bronze, 1980
42³/₈" h. x 16¼" w. x 18½" d.

Throughout the ages, artists have looked to ancient Greek mythology as a source of fascination, inspiration and moral teaching. One of the most gripping myths is that of Medea, the key figure in the tale of the Argonauts who, under the command of Jason, sailed from Greece to Cholcis, a distant land on the Black Sea, in quest of the Golden Fleece.

According to legend, Jason did succeed in his mission, but only with the magic help of Medea, daughter of the King of Cholcis, who fell in love with Jason. After capturing the Golden Fleece, Jason and Medea fled to Greece. By then they were married and had two children. However, soon after returning to Greece, Jason deserted Medea and married a young princess. In revenge, Medea, through her powers of sorcery, murdered Jason's bride and, in a state of desperation and madness, killed her own two children in order to render Jason childless.

This myth has been interpreted in numerous ways over the centuries. It is often thought to speak of the humiliatingly inferior social state to which women have traditionally been subjected. More specifically, Medea is the image of the troubled soul in deep emotional conflict who, in her desperation and painful jealousy, destroys her rational being. Indeed, she epitomizes the tragic state to which intense jealousy can lead.

Both in ancient vase painting and in fresco, the tragic moment when Medea prepared to murder her own children appears frequently. That moment has been captured in a most compelling form in the monumental three-and-a-half-foot high bronze executed in 1980 by the eminent contemporary American artist Leonard Baskin.

Baskin's *Medea* stands boldly with her arms held firmly behind her as if bound together. Outwardly she is calm and seemingly in deep meditation. Yet in her right hand she fiercely clutches a dagger while the fingers of her left hand are outstretched and stiff as if paralyzed. The slight twist of her head, the tightly drawn lips and the deeply sunken eyes suggest conflict and inner torment. Anxiety is further suggested by the nervously trembling movement of drapery folds, most particularly along the sleeves that cover her strong arms and conceal the murder weapon she is about to use. Thus, this work is testimony to Baskin's command of technique and formal usage and, at the same time, a convincing visual statement of his depth of understanding of the human situation.

Leonard Baskin was born in 1922 in New Brunswick, New Jersey. He studied art at New York University, Yale University, the New School for Social Research in New York City and later in France and Italy. He has achieved international fame as a sculptor, painter and printmaker. Baskin currently lives in Leeds, Massachusetts.

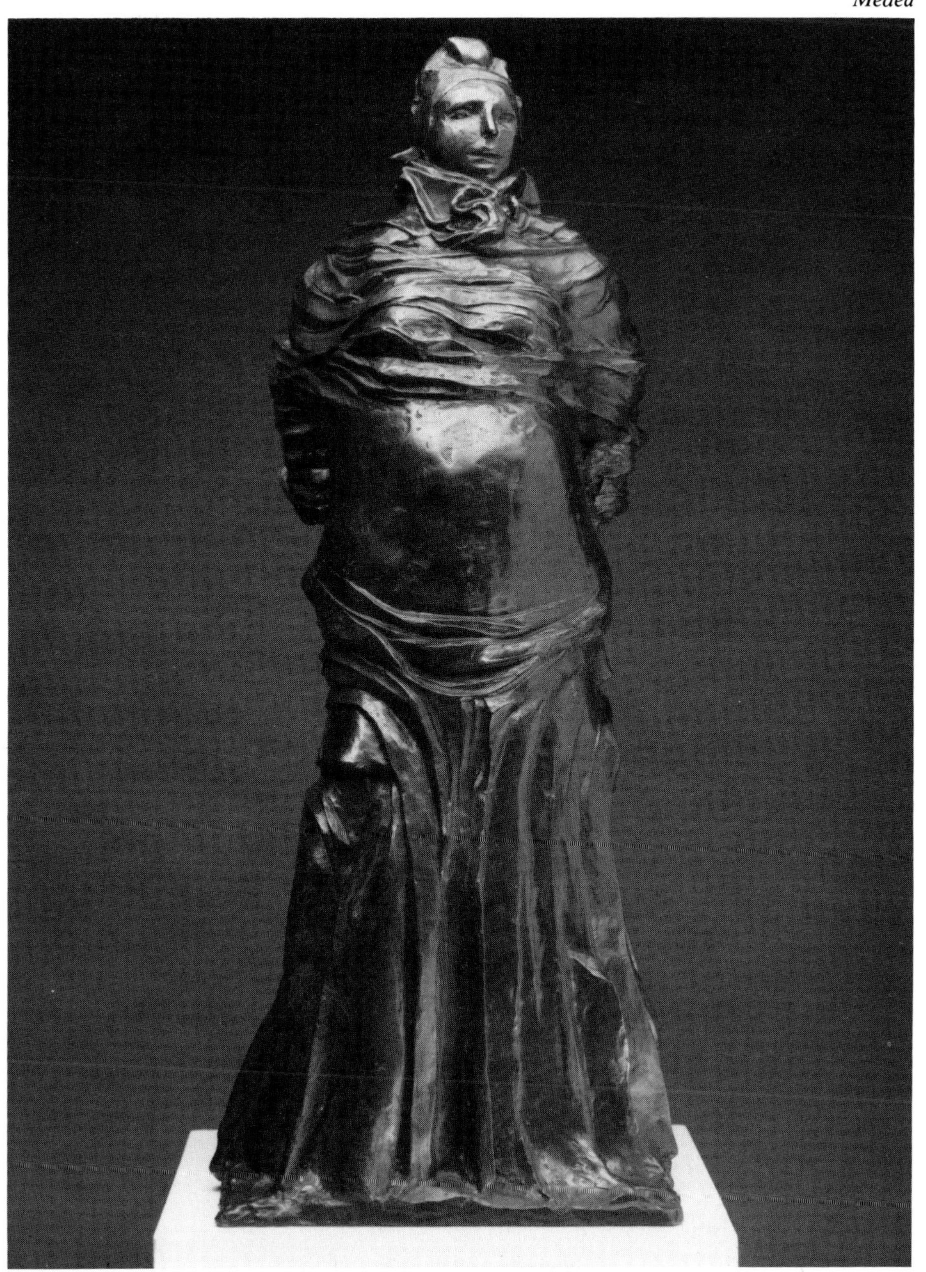

1987 Donation from Kennedy Galleries, Inc., New York City
(1987.55)

WILLIAM BAILEY (b.1930)

Still Life — Hotel Locarno
Oil on canvas, 1985
29⁷/₈" x 36"

This work titled *Still Life — Hotel Locarno* was painted in 1985 by the contemporary American artist William Bailey. Here the subject matter, rendered with impeccable clarity, consists simply of eight objects: two bowls, a pitcher, a goblet, a cup, a crock, a bottle and an egg. Differing shapes and sizes and marked variations in muted color tones and textures add visual interest to the composition and emphasize the individuality of each object represented. Yet all of the objects are assembled in an intimate relationship with one another on a shallow shelf against a flat tan background. And all are linked in an unbroken chain, for each touches an adjacent object either by direct physical contact or by connecting shadows. The result is an expression of the unity of diversity within the total assemblage.

Exacting technique in handling forms and textures imparts an intensity of realism that deceives the eye into believing the objects depicted are actual realities standing within a three-dimensional space. But Bailey should not be regarded as a traditional realist. For when we explore the work thoroughly, it becomes evident that this painting like every work of art is clearly an abstraction. Indeed the artist has reduced each form to its pure essence and his interest is focused more on orderly geometry and formal relationships of the parts than on actual imitation. And in the process of developing the composition, he has obviously allowed the play of light to vary in accord with his own interest rather than adhere to a strict observance of the operation of natural law as traditionally understood. In short, the composition is a world in itself, possessing its own laws which vary considerably from those that govern our everyday world of experience. It is this characteristic which makes a work of art different from a moment of living reality.

But there is yet another aspect of this work that ac-counts for the attention that it commands. For an almost surreal mood haunts the composition, an eerie mood of loneliness and silence that is much intensified by the wide expanse of empty space and by the shadows cast upon the wall and upon the objects in the assemblage. At the same time however, the gripping stillness is countered by the unexpected presence of the egg placed as if peeking from behind the crock near the right but charging the otherwise inert composition with a sense of potential life. For just as all of the elements shown are open vessels for drinking, eating or storing food, so the egg — certainly one of the most geometrically pure forms in nature — is a closed vessel. Symbolically it is the vessel of conception, of the germination of life and of immortality.

William Bailey was born in Council Bluffs, Iowa in 1930. During his youth he lived in various cities and towns including Chicago, Kansas City and once for a brief period during the early '50s in Wichita. For several years he attended the University of Kansas in Lawrence and subsequently served with the United States Army in Japan. Under Joseph Albers, Bailey studied painting at Yale University where he received his undergraduate degree and in 1957 his MFA. From 1962-69, he was professor of Fine Arts at Indiana University in Bloomington. Thereafter he returned to Yale where he was appointed professor of painting, a post which he continues to hold at present.

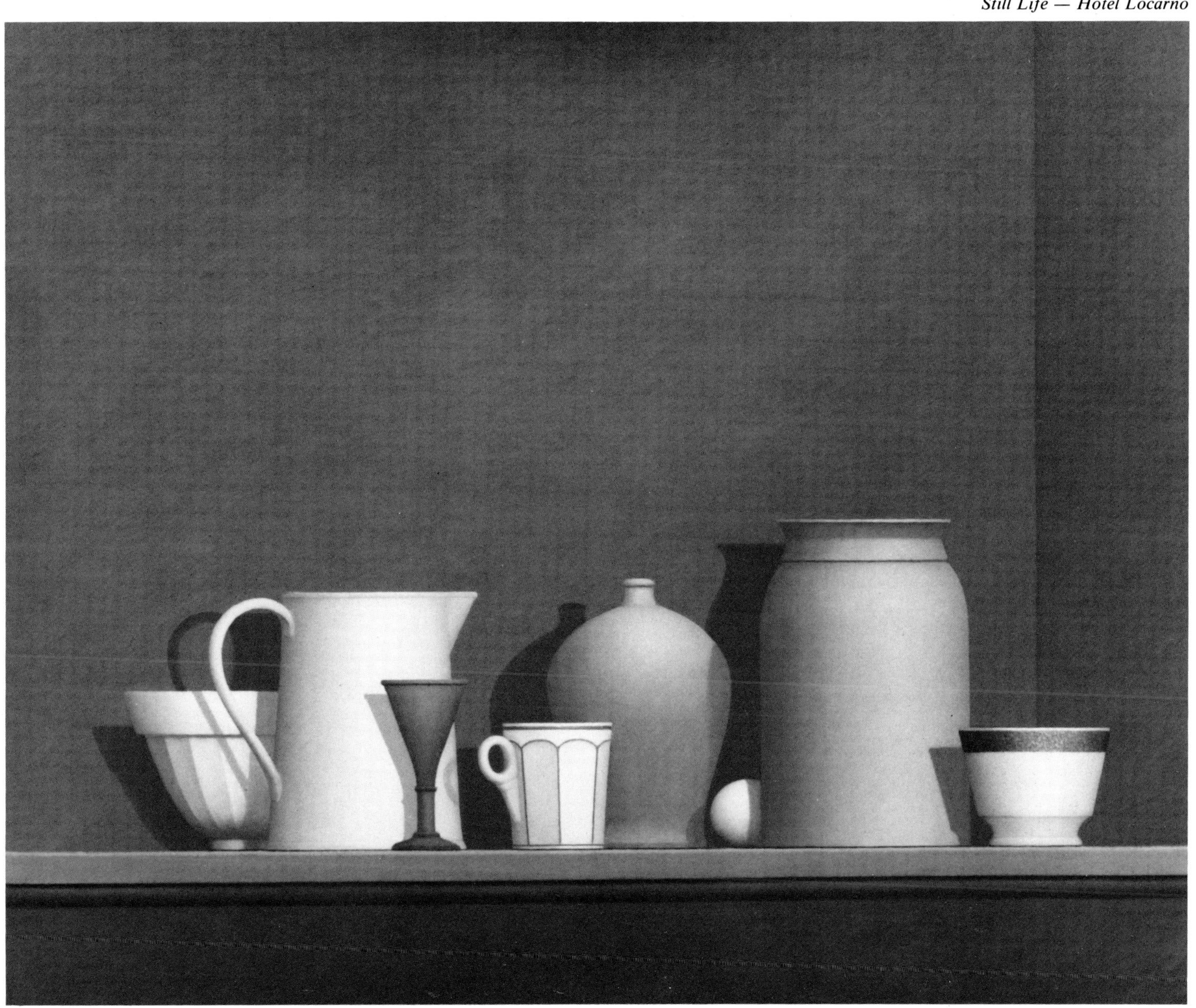

1986 Museum Purchase, Friends of Wichita Art Museum Art Fund
(1986.18)

GRANDMA MOSES (1860-1961)

The Block House
Oil on board, 1954
12$^1/_8$'' x 18$^1/_8$''

No words more fittingly describe the qualities of a painting by Grandma Moses than *honesty, freshness* and *childlike simplicity*. And one need only read her autobiography and then glance at her paintings to see how happily the two go hand-in-hand, how readily her paintings reflect her gentle personality, her joyous outlook and her affection for her world.

Grandma Moses began her career as a painter in 1937. She was 77 years old at the time and painted merely "...for pleasure, to keep busy and to pass the time away...". as she so amusingly informs us in her fascinating autobiography. She had no studio training or technical background and therefore painted in what is generally called a primitive or folk-art manner, emphasizing craftsmanship more than formal academic skills.

This particular work, titled *The Block House* and painted in 1954 when Grandma Moses was 94 years old, is rather typical of her style and of the folk-art manner in general. In its fresh conception, the entire composition brings to mind a child's garden of toys. Here the opening in the low white fence in the foreground emphasizes the wide path which, like an inviting welcome, draws us into the composition and then divides into two arms embracing the bold form of the block house where the eye momentarily halts and then moves on. Although the setting is peaceful, there is movement in the spirited gestures of figures, in the rhythmic interplay between small and large forms and in the harmonious relationship of color variations. The space of everyday experience is of course distorted and all parts are equally emphasized but clearly defined.

While this composition is in no sense an exact imitation of the visible world or of any object in the visible world, the stated facts which Grandma Moses presents are clear and one could never mistake what she intended to represent. Indeed, this work, like other primitive paintings, is a depiction of what the mind knows or imagines rather than what the eye sees. And, in this respect, a work by Grandma Moses stresses the universal rather than the particular. On the one hand, it is a truly popular art form in that it recalls the indigenous art which at one time or another has prevailed seemingly in all human cultures. On the other hand, in its magical simplicity it is fully reminiscent of the fantasy vision found in works by such contemporary masters as Chagall.

Grandma Moses was born Anna Mary Robertson in Greenwich, New York, in 1860. She married Thomas Moses and, many years later, became lovingly known by her grandchildren and by the world simply as Grandma Moses. She gained recognition as a painter when her works were exhibited in town and county fairs during the late 1930s. In October, 1940, she held her first exhibition at the Galerie St. Etienne in New York City and, soon thereafter, won international fame. She has exhibited throughout the nation and abroad and her works are included in major museum and private collections around the world. In 1948 she published her autobiography titled *My Life's History* and in 1950 she produced a film titled *Grandma Moses*. She died in 1961 at the age of 101 years.

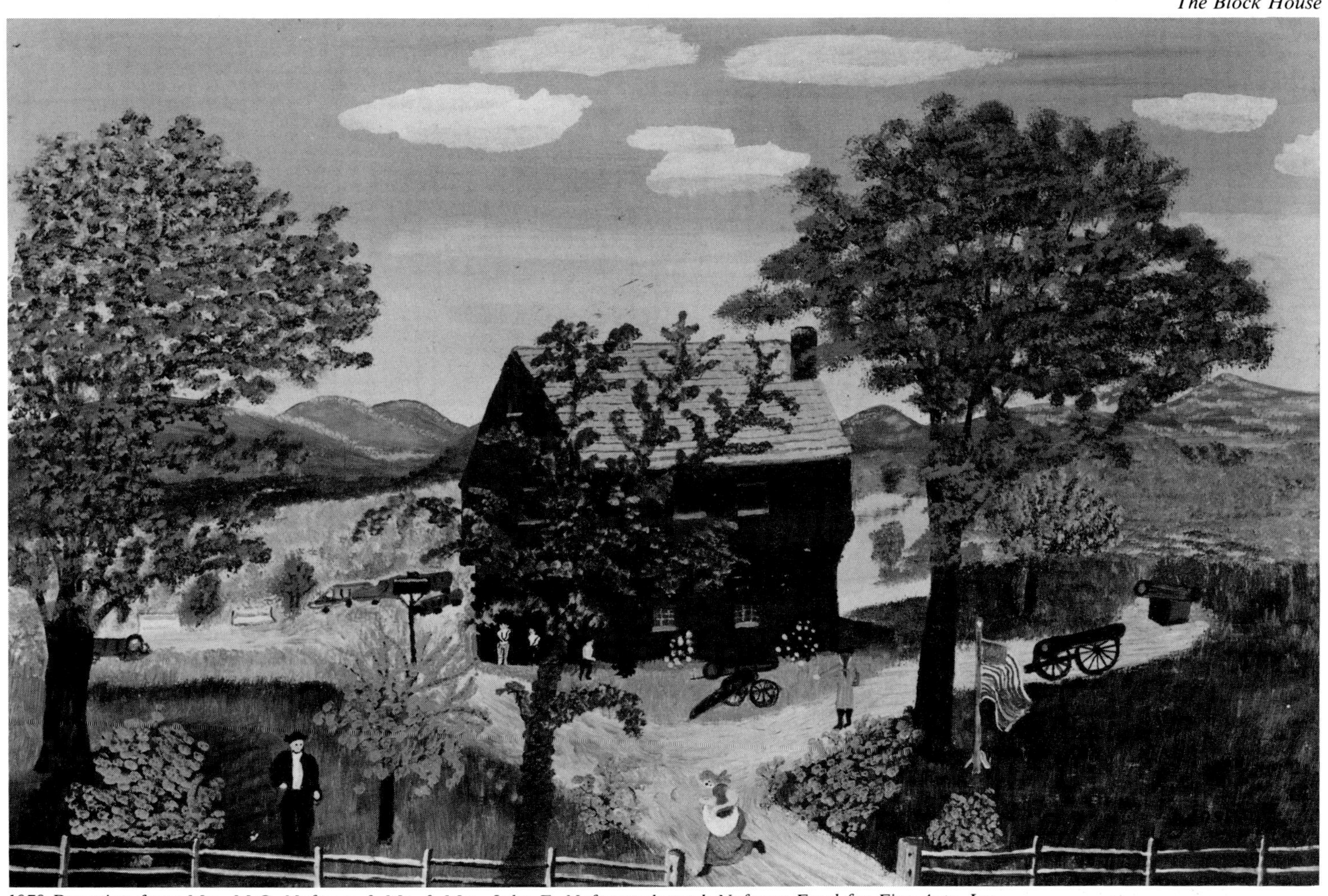

1979 Donation from Mrs. M.C. Naftzger & Mr. & Mrs. John E. Naftzger through Naftzger Fund for Fine Arts, Inc. (1979.30)

JACKSON POLLOCK (1912-1956)

Untitled
Brush, pen and ink on paper, 1945
17^1/$_8$" x 22^1/$_8$"

Probing into the sub-conscious levels of the human mind in search of new inspirational sources and of an expanded understanding of the nature of creativity commanded the attention not only of psychologists but also of artists during much of the early 20th century, especially in the period between the two wars. This attention led inevitably to a heightened interest in the strange relationships experienced in dreams as well as in a serious study of folk art, the art of the mentally disturbed and the art of children. All of these interests had far-reaching significance in the rise of surrealism which captivated the minds of many artists of the period both here and in Europe. And by the mid 1940s, aspects of surrealism became wedded with pure abstraction, often culminating in a movement known as abstract expressionism of which Jackson Pollock was one of the most noted exponents.

This untitled colored ink drawing by Jackson Pollock was executed in 1945 and precedes Pollock's first fully abstract expressionist painting by only a few years. What is important is that the seeds of Pollock's later and more mature method are clearly in evidence here. At the right, six small doodle-like sketches are vertically arranged. But the most interesting section of the drawing is perhaps the large mass at the left and center, densely filled with strange forms and ambiguous shapes which have been almost entirely obliterated by an overdrawn web of scribble lines and dark smudges. Interpreted psychologically, such a drawing may represent the artist's private associations with reality from which he withdraws by wiping-out the images of reality that disclose his fears and anxieties.

An especially interesting feature is the cubist-like space produced by the strong line dividing the central mass of the drawing and cutting through the lower half of a human figure. It is also of special interest that the forms which most frequently appear are, on the one hand, the sexually suggestive arrows and, on the other hand, the coiled snake and the snarling beast which as found in many cultures, are often regarded as archetypal images of evil and death.

That Pollock himself frequently suffered psychological illness is a well-known fact that might well explain many of the strange dislocations found in his paintings. But at another level of awareness, the withdrawal suggested here is in one sense very much an expression of alienation that characterizes the outlook of many creative minds of 20th century society where fears of destruction and the horrors of total annihilation inevitably find an outlet in works of art.

Jackson Pollock was born in 1912 in Cody, Wyoming and in 1930 began to study at the Art Students League in New York under Thomas Hart Benton. During the 1930s he suffered from extreme alcoholism and was under psychiatric care for extended periods throughout his career. In the mid '40s and early 1950s, he gained much notoriety as the first American Action Painter basing his approach on early experiments such as we find in this drawing. Tragically, Pollock was killed in an automobile accident in 1956 in East Hampton, New York.

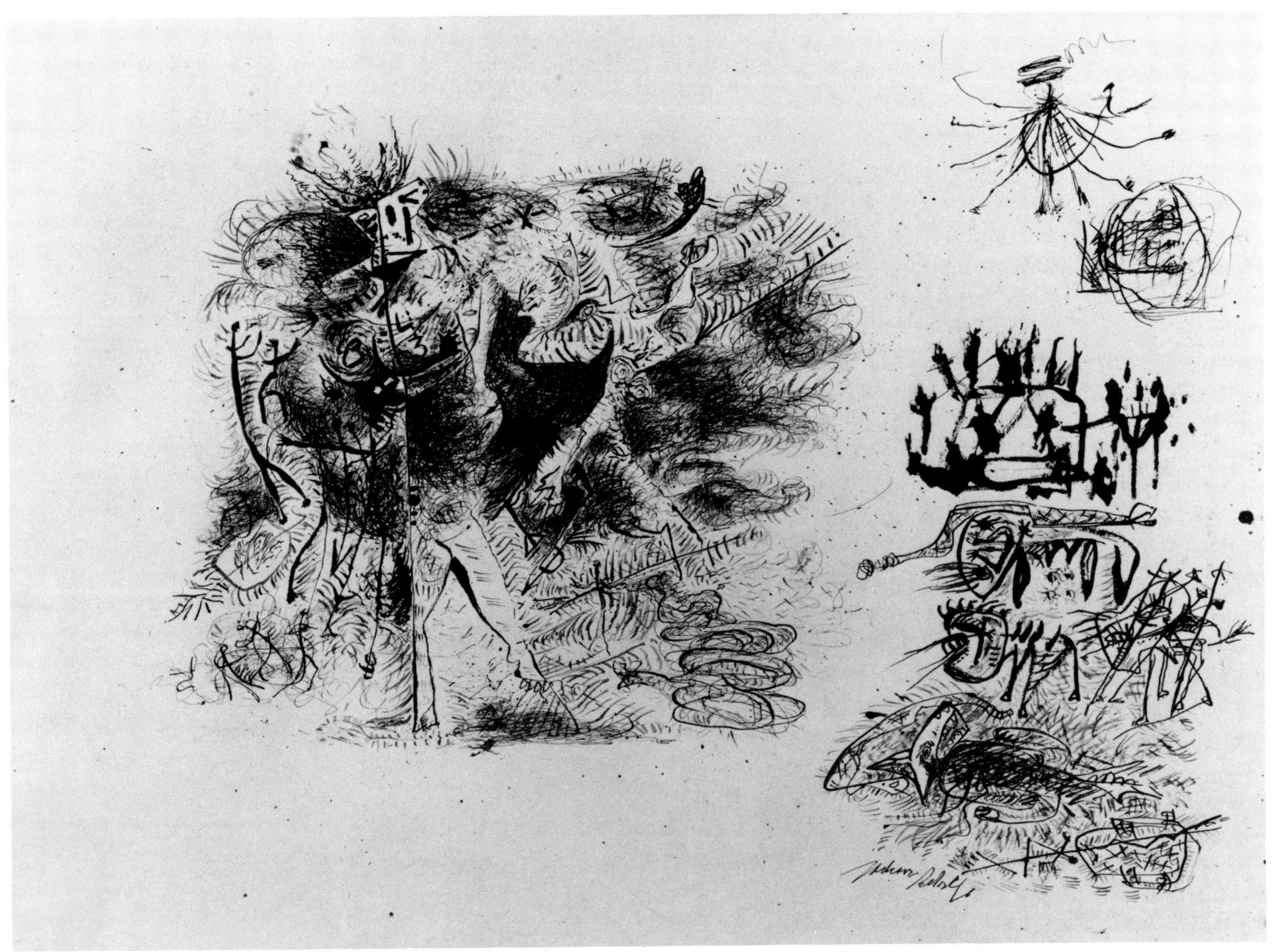

1983 Donation from Louise & S.O. Beren, Wichita, Kansas
(1983.67)

ADOLPH GOTTLIEB (1903-1975)

Ripple
Oil on linen, 1963
60^1/$_8$'' x 40^1/$_8$''

The noted American abstract expressionist Adolph Gottlieb executed this very handsome painting titled *Ripple* in 1963. In no sense is this work intended to be a literal imitation of anything existing in the world of visual reality. Instead it is a reality in itself — an invitation for us to enter psychologically the life of the painting and to discover meaning as it may relate to our own experience and feeling.

Compositionally this painting consists of a dark and unevenly painted background space against which a large magenta disc surrounded by swirling brushstrokes boldly stands out as a principal focal point. In the lower zone beneath the disc an irregularly shaped gray-black blob is visible which serves to accent the magenta disc and at the same time tends to lose its own identity as it merges with the dark background.

Such an organization of dissident yet complementary forms is essentially the signature of Gottlieb's later works, often referred to as "blasts". Actually, it was during the last two decades of his life that Gottlieb produced a long series of paintings in this manner all of which display strong inner tension between two opposing polarities, one a swirling and pulsating integrated whole, and the other, a disfigured and disintegrating blob.

It is purely by metaphor that we gain appreciation of the possible meaning introduced by the artist. Here the magenta disc is reminiscent of a radiant sun while the dark and unevenly shaped blob by contrast may be likened to earth. But the most interesting feature is the balance felt between the two unlike forms, one suggesting a heavenly spiritual plane of existence and the other earthly matter and decay. Although charged with tension between the two opposing images, the work is nevertheless a dynamically balanced composition which

in purely abstract terms points up the compensatory relationship found in real life situations, as for example the interplay between growth and decay, order and disorder, wholeness and formlessness, light and dark, the conscious and unconscious and, by extension, heaven and earth. Moreover, the underlying meaning is but the symbolic expression of a concept that is universally embodied in myths of all cultures throughout the ages. Indeed, the painting is essentially a contemporary meditation upon an archetypal theme which so forcefully describes a fundamental law of existence.

Gottlieb's mature style developed in the period just before and during World War II — an era marked by upheaval and despair which led many artists, both American and European, to withdraw psychologically from the world they saw about them and to seek expression in abstract rather than imitational forms. Gottlieb was born in Brooklyn, New York in 1903 and studied at the Art Students League and in various centers in Europe. Between 1937 and 1939, a period of almost two years, he lived in Arizona and became much absorbed in American Indian mythological signs and symbols which led to his use of pictographic forms in his paintings of the 1940's and early 1950's. But by 1956 and for the remainder of his life his primary theme was the balance between complementary entities such as we see in this painting titled *Ripple.* Gottlieb died in New York in 1975.

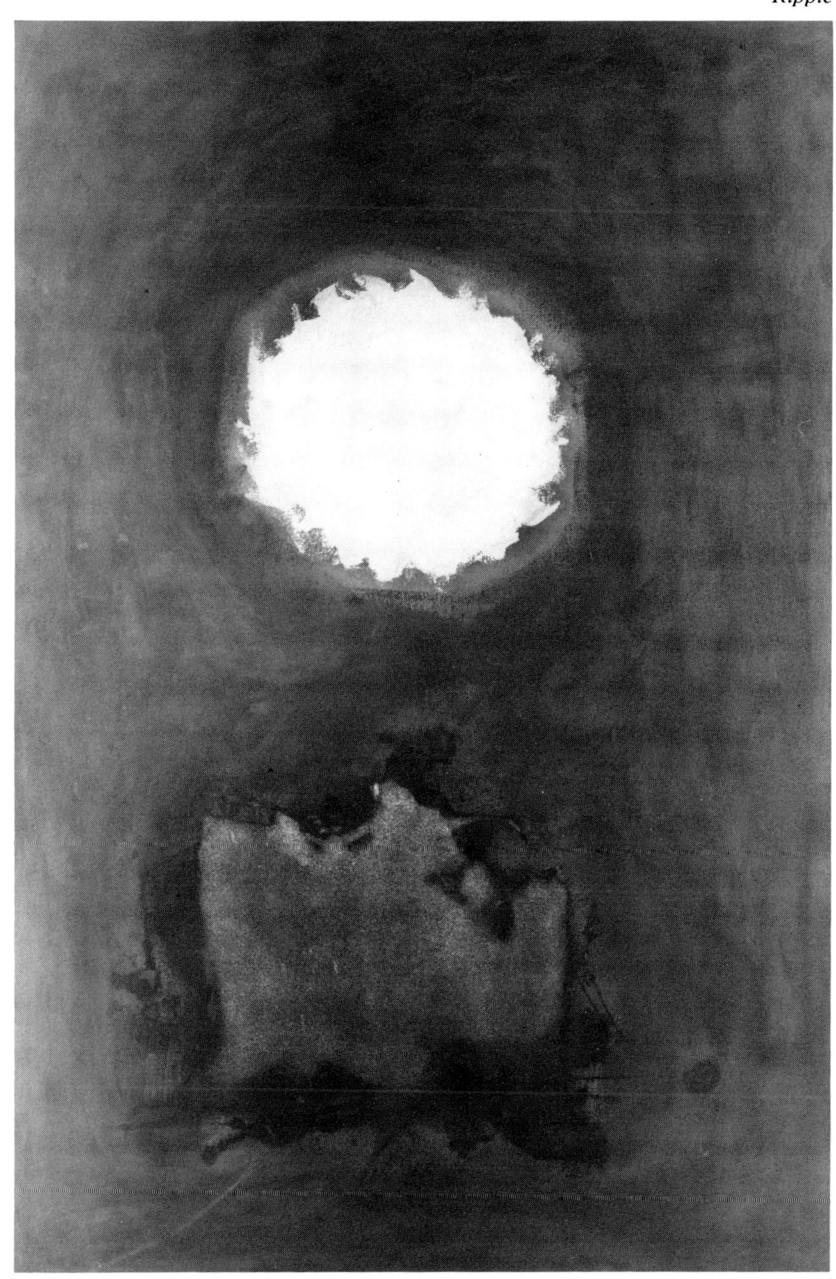

1980 Museum Purchase, Friends of the Wichita Art Museum Art Fund (1980.90)

SIDNEY GROSS (1921-1969)

Solar Rendezvous
Oil on canvas, 1966
84" x 66"

Abstract Expressionism was undoubtedly the dominant contemporary artistic idiom in American painting during the late 1940s and throughout the 1950s. The same general movement with variations was perpetuated into the ensuing two decades and to some extent has remained very much alive down to the present. One of the most accomplished and most promising exponents during the 1960s was Sidney Gross whose frequent New York exhibitions of his massive canvases were widely acclaimed until his untimely death at age 48 in 1969.

Stylistically, Gross added a new dimension by introducing a hard-edge quality to splintery and irregular multicolored forms. These characteristic tendencies are clearly evident in this work executed by Gross in 1966 and titled *Solar Rendezvous*. At the left in the painting is what seems to be a chaotically-organized cluster of small, brightly-colored interlocking shapes, some regular, others irregular. In sharp contrast is the more orderly arrangement of the structure at the right that appears to be energetically charged and, like a rocket, soars upwards, linking the massive black area in the lower register of the canvas with the pure white space above, unbroken but for the delicate orange and blue diagonal bars at the extreme upper right. What is especially interesting is that the entire compositon suggests how the space-age consciousness of the 1960s could find symbolic expression in a work of art in abstract form rather than in visually representational terms.

Most essentially, however, this composition constitutes a complex combination of free forms and color contrasts superimposed upon a highly controlled background of pure geometry. It illustrates that one of the most significant stylistic achievements of Sidney Gross as a second generation abstract expressionist was his extremely sensitive ability to harmonize the opposing romantic and classical poles of expression that for many centuries have dominated Western thought and the character of Western art, both in America and abroad.

Sidney Gross was born in New York City in 1921. He studied at the Art Students League, and during his career, was the recipient of numerous scholarships and painting awards. He was an instructor at the Parsons School of Design, the Art Students League and Columbia University. His works appeared in major exhibitions throughout the country, including the Carnegie Institute, the Pennsylvania Academy, the National Academy of Design and elsewhere. Gross died in New York in 1969.

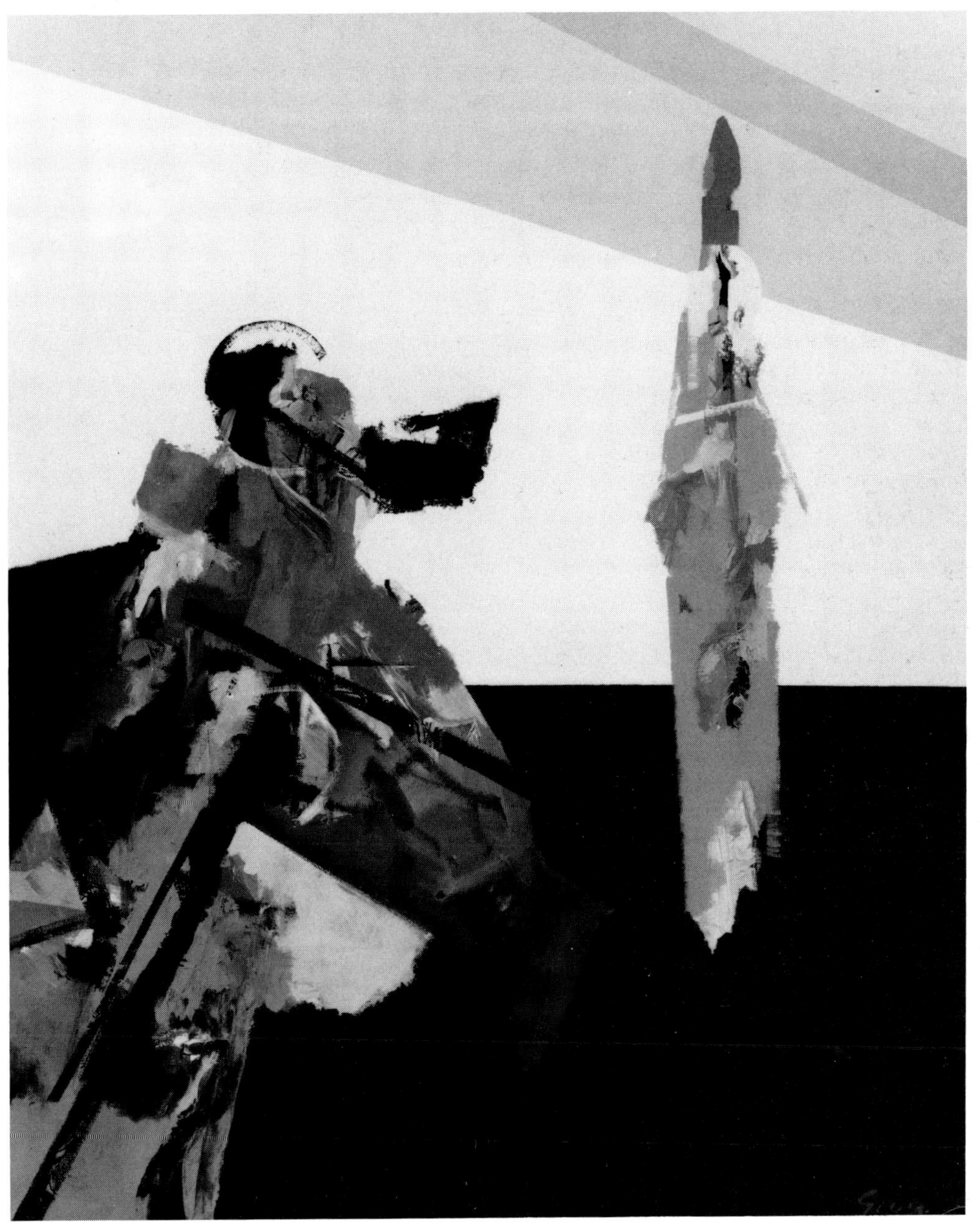

1987 Gift from Art Students League of New York City
(1987.27)

WILLIAM BAZIOTES (1912-1963)

Whirlpool
Oil on canvas, 1953
24^1/$_8$" x 20¼"

The eternal mysteries of time, of space and of the human mind and the ever presence of irrational forces in living existence are matters which have confronted mankind since the onset of human consciousness. These considerations are among the underlying realities on which much art of the 20th century, especially since World War II, has been based. Certainly, this is true of the work of the American artist William Baziotes who executed this painting titled *Whirlpool* in 1953. Here the imagery would seem to allude to the fundamental phenomena of organic creation and primal life and consists of a cluster of unevenly drawn ripple-like concentric semi-circles, a protozoan form with sinuous flagella and a crustaceous creature with open jaws edged by a zigzag line suggesting teeth... and therefore perhaps evil and pain.

Obviously, all of these references are but metaphors, for there is no intent whatever on the artist's part to offer a literal imitation of visual reality. Nor is there any clear and readily ascertainable interpretation of these forms. What *is* evident, however, is that the elements themselves are essentially free and imaginary forms, that the relationships seem non-logical and that the space is non-illusionistic, with the result that the painting possesses pictorial autonomy but in no sense conforms to conventional visual experiences or expectations.

Biomorphic imagery in a painting of this type is most closely akin to surrealism and seems to draw upon archetypal motifs that linger across the ages in the collective unconscious and can be recalled symbolically in dream and in myth, where natural objects take on properties that are strange in formal appearance and are otherwise unknown on a conscious level. But the evocative power here is matched by the poetic beauty experienced in the distinguishing painterly qualities, the balanced design and the subtle tonal nuances of the iridescent glow along the fringes of forms throughout the entire composition.

William Baziotes was born in Pittsburgh, Pennsylvania in 1912. In 1933 he settled in New York and studied at the National Academy of Design under Leon Kroll. Between 1926 and 1941, he worked under the WPA and during the war became deeply interested in surrealism and abstractionism. In 1948, with Mark Rothko, Robert Motherwell and Barnett Newman, he founded a school known as *Subjects of the Artist School* in New York. Baziotes was one of the principal painters of the post World War II abstract movement and the recipient of major exhibition awards and commissions during the late 1940s and 1950s. His works are represented in the permanent collection of major museums throughout the United States as well as abroad. From 1952 to 1962, he was associate professor of art at Hunter College, New York. Baziotes died in New York City in 1963 at the age of 52 years.

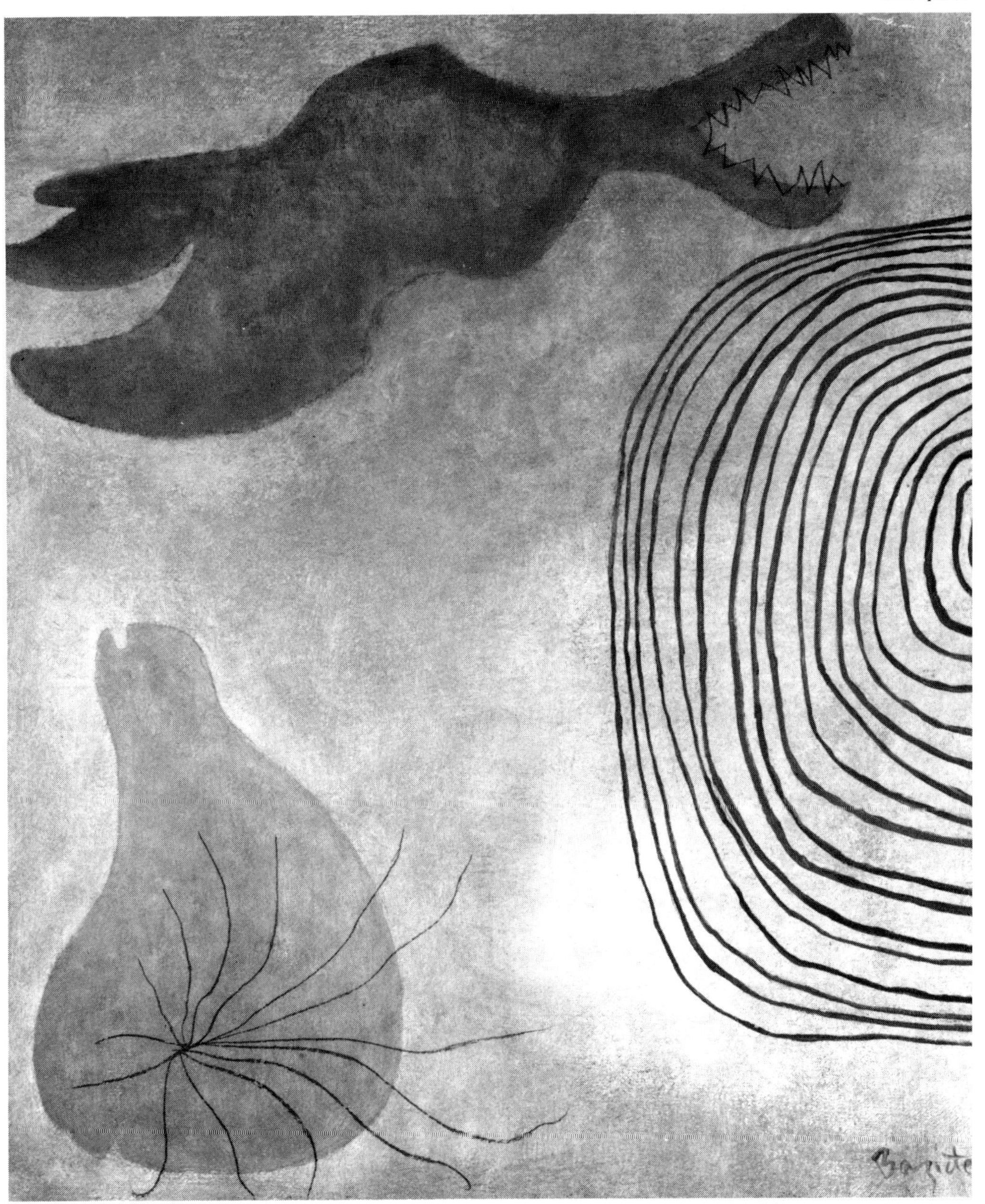

1982 Museum Purchase, Director's Discretionary Fund, Friends of the Wichita Art Museum (1982.11)

GYORGY KEPES (b.1906)

Alien Cyphers
Oil and sand on canvas, 1977
60'' x 60''

This stunning painting titled *Alien Cyphers* was executed in 1977 by Gyorgy Kepes, for more than four decades one of America's leading contemporary artists. The composition is a kind of landscape of contrasting forms and textures — darkness and light, density and airiness, opacity and clarity — and consists of strands and varied shaped granular patches of sand mixed with dark pigment and applied to an oil painted surface. Predominantly dark tones are balanced by the greenish-yellow luminescence at the left and by a faint glow issuing from the background and creating a vaporous aura along the edges of the darker masses.

In this work there are, of course, no recognizable images from everyday experience such as are found in so-called "realistic" painting. Instead, the focus of attention is on formal elements alone, rather than on any theme. But just as a familiar object or group of objects may have meaning in a representational painting, so in an abstract painting, line, color and form — the basic formal components of all art — may have meaning, even though all representational objects have been eliminated completely. What is different then is actually the distinguishing characteristic of all so-called pure abstract painting, namely that the meaning is simply disengaged from all conventional form, leaving us with the freedom to project ourselves into the work of art where we can derive new visual experience and discover new visual pleasure. In the process, we inevitably will introduce to some extent our own value judgments. But then, we do that in relating to any painting whether it be realist or abstract. Of course, it must be kept in mind that a representational painting can indeed be as much a source of aesthetic pleasure as can an abstract painting. However, the converse is also true: an abstract painting can be the source of as much aesthetic pleasure as can a representational painting.

In the case of this particular painting by Gyorgy Kepes, the pleasure which we experience would seem to derive quite simply from the harmonious interplay of complementary opposites of being: illumination and darkness, the conscious and the unconscious, the rational and the irrational. For as we view this painting, the rigid structure of what is metaphorically identified with dense primaeval matter appears to erode before our very eyes as a hidden light gently rises, producing a glowing resonance of exquisitely delicate tonal nuances and suggesting an all-embracing unity and a sense of renewal and the emergence of promising new possibilities.

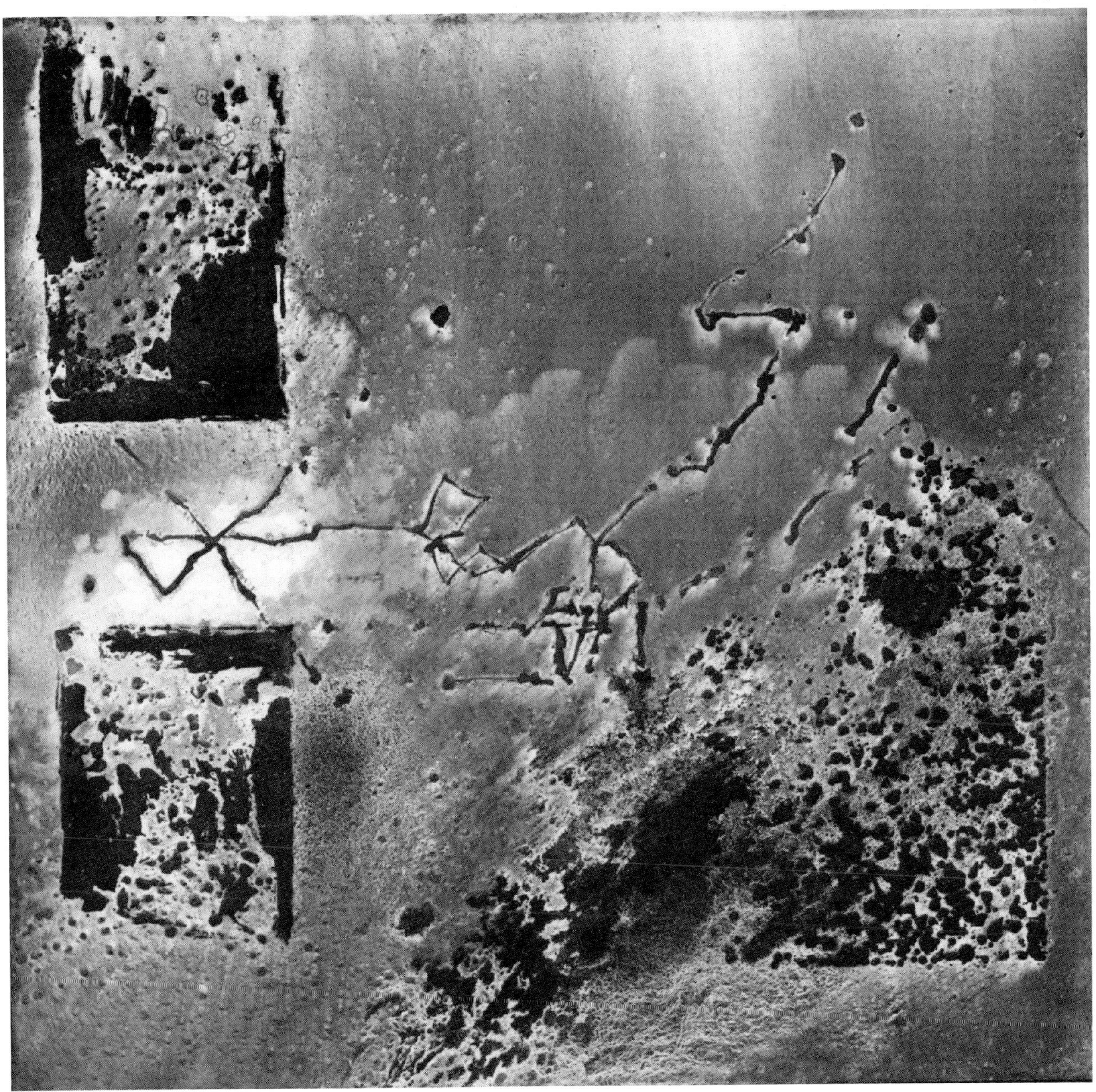

1980 Museum Purchase, Director's Discretionary Fund
(1980.32)

HELEN FRANKENTHALER (b.1928)

Sunday Green
Acrylic on canvas, 1976
49¾'' x 87¼''

This handsome work titled *Sunday Green* was painted in 1976 by the noted contemporary American artist Helen Frankenthaler. The composition consists of a masterfully subtle blending of blobs, streaks and patches of color, some strong and sharply vivid, others light and velvety soft. All interplay and overlap as if lyrically floating in an airy space filled with an all-pervasive and luminescent glow which seems to lift from beneath the pigment itself. For Frankenthaler's technique consists of painting certain areas of the canvas, staining others and leaving still others untouched. The result is that scattered parts of the white canvas background shine through, serving as the lighting agent which permeates the entire composition.

It is especially noteworthy that the energetic tensions built-up throughout are carefully resolved, thereby imparting both dynamic balance and a sense of structure to the composition, for the diverse forms clearly merge into one composite whole and at the same time maintain their distinct and individual identities. Indeed this quality is achieved with such skill and sophistication as to produce a purely abstract statement of unity derived from harmonious diversity — a statement at once both visually soothing and intellectually engaging.

Helen Frankenthaler was born in New York City in 1928. Rufino Tamayo and Hans Hofmann were among the illustrious masters under whom she studied. She has been the recipient of numerous coveted awards and has held many solo exhibitions in museums and galleries both in America and abroad, and her works are included in major museum collections throughout the world. In addition she has received commissions for large paintings and tapestries for permanent installation in public places such as hospitals and banks.

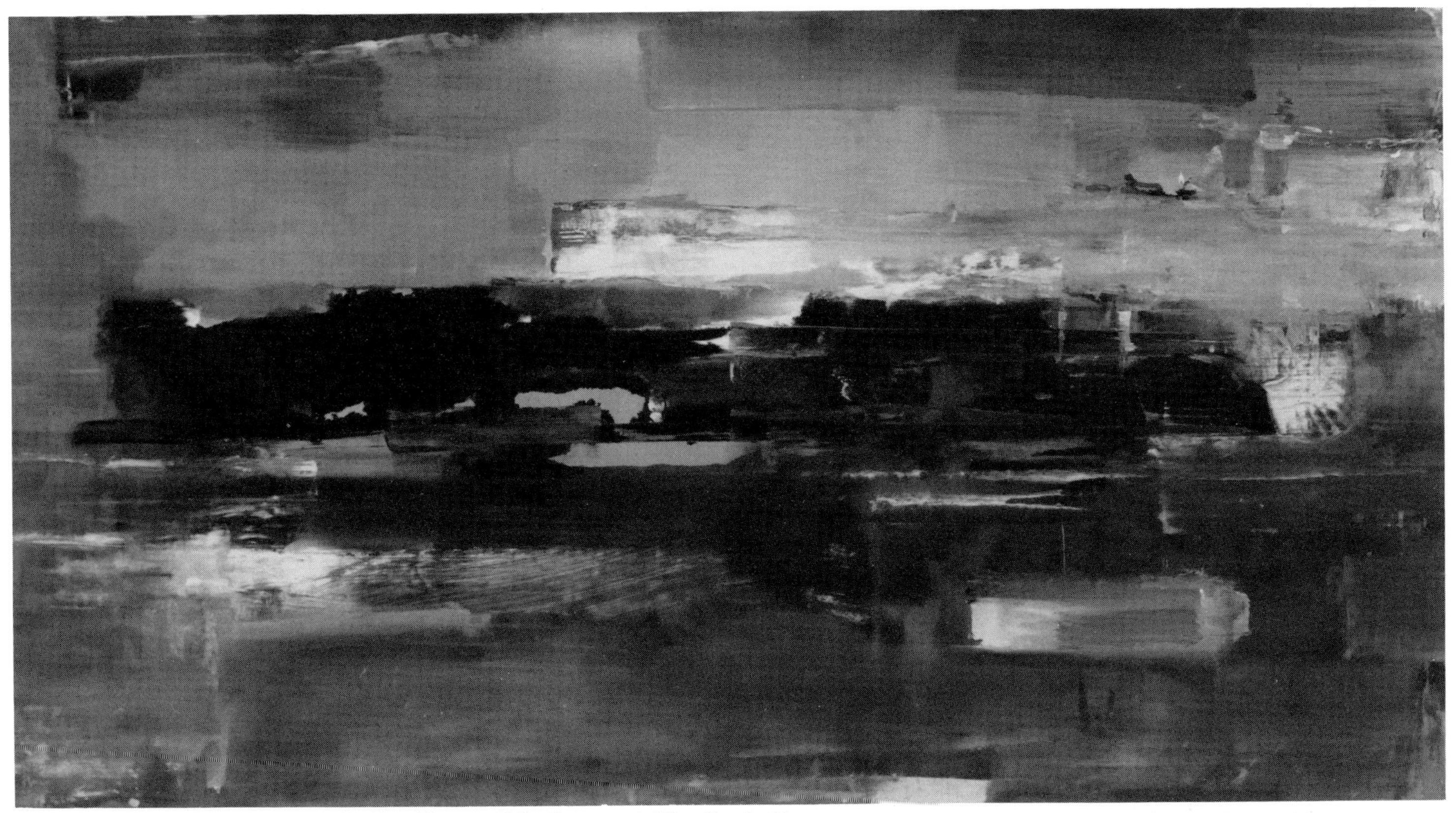

1978 Gift from Misco Industries, Wichita, Kansas: S.O. Beren and Allen Staub, Trustees (1978.39)

RICHARD ANUSZKIEWICZ (b.1930)

WAM '77
Acrylic on canvas, 1977
40¼" x 40¼"

WAM '77 is an acrylic on canvas executed by the American artist Richard Anuszkiewicz and commissioned by the Wichita Art Museum to commemorate the completion and public opening of the new Museum building in October, 1977. Hence the title of the work. In addition, the composition of the painting was adopted for a limited edition of 200 original serigraphs issued on the occasion of the public opening in 1977.

Stylistically, this work is pure color sensation intensified with the aid of a simple linear geometric grid. But the effects achieved quite obviously rest on a rigorous theoretical body of scientific fact. The painting itself and other stylistically related works by Anuszkiewicz exemplify a movement now known as retinal or optical art, or more simply as "op" art. That movement was practiced about 1960 and was soon recognized as a reaction against abstract expressionism which had largely dominated the art scene in the late 1940s and throughout the 1950s. Among the key aspects of "op" art are repetition of geometric pattern, hard-edge precision drawing, surface integrity and at the same time the production of an energetically charged surface that tends to pulsate as a result of color interaction or carefully controlled variation in the density of elements in the grid design.

In most instances, "op" paintings are entirely independent of traditional subject matter. In one sense however, this particular piece is an exception since the grid design here is based upon the simple geometric floor plan of the Museum building. Like the Museum architectural plan, WAM '77 as well as other works by Anuszkiewicz is symmetrically composed and is constructed of linear geometric forms that adhere tightly to the flat surface plane. Striking illusionistic effects are achieved by disciplined choices of colors — in this work red, blue and green — juxtaposed in a disciplined, orderly manner one against the other, as well as by variations in the density of precisely drawn hard-edge lines, and by the particular geometric patterns which make up the compositions. All of this comes about by virtue of the inability of the human eye to sort out fully the visual information contained in the painting. For when viewing a multicolor field the eye is unable to see any one color in complete isolation. Mutual interference, as for example between figure and ground colors, produces illusionistic distortion, sometimes in the form of surface movement, other times as an overall pulsating glow or in the form of flickering light emanations at points where a concentration of many narrow lines occur. The net result is a sophisticated statement on visual ambiguity whose presence can in no sense be ignored.

Richard Anuszkiewicz was born in Erie, Pennsylvania in 1930. He attended the Cleveland Institute of Art where he received the BFA in 1953 after which he studied at Yale and was awarded the MFA in 1955. It was during his several years at Yale that he worked closely with Josef Albers in color field investigations and it was through Albers that he was influenced by the Bauhaus doctrines on applied art, thus accounting for the many utilitarian adaptations of his paintings that he has willingly produced, including fabric designs, gift wrappings, rugs, etc. Anuszkiewicz's early works were traditional in technique and style. By 1955, after completing his work with Albers at Yale, he shifted to what eventually led him to become the leading figure in "op" art, a reputation which he maintains today after more than 30 years. Anuszkiewicz has served as visiting professor at various universities. His works are represented widely in major museums and private collections across the United States and abroad. He currently resides in Englewood, New Jersey where he also maintains his studio.

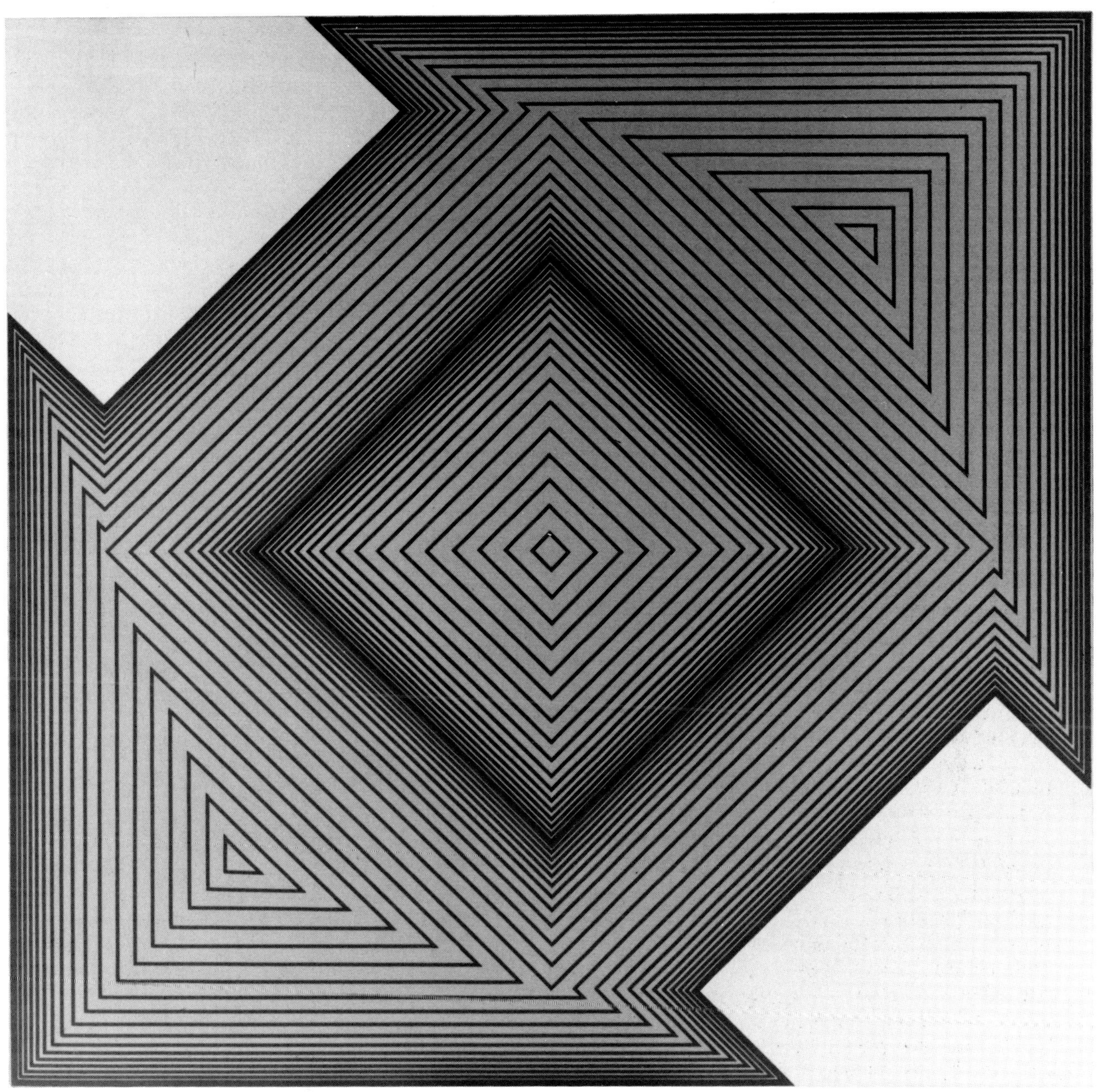

1977 Museum Purchase, Friends of the Wichita Art Museum Art Fund. Commissioned by Wichita Art Museum to commemorate the opening of the new museum
(1977.91)

NATVAR BHAVSAR (b.1934)

Kandariya III
Dry pigment & acrylic on paper, 1971-86
46" x 35"

In this forceful work titled *Kandariya III* by the American painter Natvar Bhavsar, subtle nuances in color relationships coupled with a tranquil but vital presence magically produce the impression of a vast outer space filled with a radiant burst of cool green light surrounded by a dusty glow of many speckled colors. Yet in no sense is this to be interpreted as a conscious objective on the artist's part for Bhavsar's work copies nothing and indeed is in every sense a genuine aesthetic expression. His works are entirely nonobjective and the effects which are so stirring and at the same time so tranquil are actually the outgrowth of a traditional folk painting technique which he learned as a youth in his homeland, in Gothava, Gujarat, India where he was born in 1934. That technique with which he became acquainted early in life is known as *Rangoli,* actually a kind of festive holiday ritual by which Hindus throw pure powdered color onto the ground to create decorative forms. And of course, it is this that is basically the background out of which derives the fascinating technique which Bhavsar currently employs in creating such lyrically expressive abstractions as *Kandariya III.*

Bhavsar settled in the United States in 1962. At that time he was 28 years of age and promptly became an active member of the New York School of Colorists and today must be recognized as one of the most innovative colorists in the world of American contemporary painting. In his youth, however, he was trained in the academic tradition and painted handsomely composed landscapes, portraits and figurative groups. But he abandoned such conventions early and his mature style became entirely non-objective. He uses no fiber brushes, no palette knife and no air brush, and neither pours, nor drips liquid pigment. Instead, he simply sifts dry powdered pigment through a fine screen strainer held above a horizontally stretched ground of canvas or, in this instance, of paper on which a wet acrylic binder has been applied. The process is, of course, not carried out haphazardly for as he moves the screen strainer about over the paper field, he must control the rhythm of his own body movements and is concerned at all times about speed and about the distance between the screen and the field in order to ensure both the desired distribution and the density of the color within any given area. And as the minute particles of pigment fall upon the field, they adhere firmly to the clear acrylic binder.

This procedure does indeed demand infinite care but it is a fascinating process, and, although the end result might well stimulate our imagination about what a visual experience of outer space would be, such is in no sense the deliberate intention of the artist himself. Indeed, in producing *Kandariya III,* what Bhavsar has done is to create an art work which has a life of its own, entirely independent of any reference to any sentiment or any material reality other than the reality of the work of art itself. He has simply given form and psychic meaning to color and color relationships. Admittedly, to the viewer Bhavsar furnishes the sensation for what seems like a vaguely familiar reality, whether intended or not, that is perceived as though through a diaphanous veil — a reality slightly blurred in its outlines and one not quite within our grasp but which perhaps corresponds best to what we sometimes experience in the subliminal state just below the threshold of consciousness, a state which may at once be tranquil and liberating and out of which we emerge refreshed and revitalized.

1986 Museum Purchase, Director's Discretionary Fund, Friends of the Wichita Art Museum (1986.48)

RICHARD HUNT (b.1935)

Extended Land Form
Welded cor-ten steel, 1975
67½" h. x 144" l. x 62" d.

Extended Land Form is a large-scale structurally stable cor-ten steel sculpture, executed in 1975 by the American sculptor Richard Hunt. The work consists of rather bulky interpenetrating forms with relatively sharp edges and, as is so often incorporated in Hunt's works of this period, a short but pointed spike that darts directly from a flat surface into the encompassing space. But while the physical monumentality of this piece would seem to depend largely upon the heavy interlocking features of design, the work itself in no sense relates conceptually to the formal constructionist tradition. Instead it is clearly the intrinsic moving vitality of this composition for it seems endowed with an inner spirit that refers back directly to ominous feelings evoked by so many of the precariously composed works that Hunt produced a decade or more earlier in his career.

Hunt has performed a wide range of experiments in the production of his sculptures generally using direct metal-techniques. His materials in this work as in most of his works are discarded machine parts or cor-ten steel plate, and the tools employed are the oxyacetylene torch and the arc welder which he uses with enviable precision and highly commendable technical skill.

An aspect of this work and of all of Hunt's sculptures is the fact that banal imagery so common to much of the contemporary art of the past 25 or so years is completely absent. There is no ridicule, no evident protest, no apathy. Instead we seem to perceive in this abstraction a kind of archetypal image of intentionality. For Hunt's work does indeed speak of expansion, of growth, of movement, of the potential for emergence and change. His message, conscious or unconscious, proclaims the capacity to move forward, to achieve new possibilities. And that message of course is merely the life instinct.

Richard Hunt was born in Chicago in 1935. He attended the Art Institute of Chicago and received the BAE in 1957. Upon graduation, he won the James Nelson Raymond Travel Fellowship award, enabling him to travel and study in Europe. Early in his career he earned an enviable reputation as a sculptor, for in 1956, while he was still a student, the Museum of Modern Art purchased one of his important early works. In 1968 he was appointed by President Lyndon B. Johnson to membership on the National Council for the Arts. He has frequently exhibited at museums and galleries throughout the nation and today is represented in most important museum collections. In the nearly two decades since 1970, he has received numerous major commissions for large-scale works installed in public places both in the United States and abroad. Hunt currently maintains his studio and his residence in Chicago but exhibits widely across the country and especially in New York.

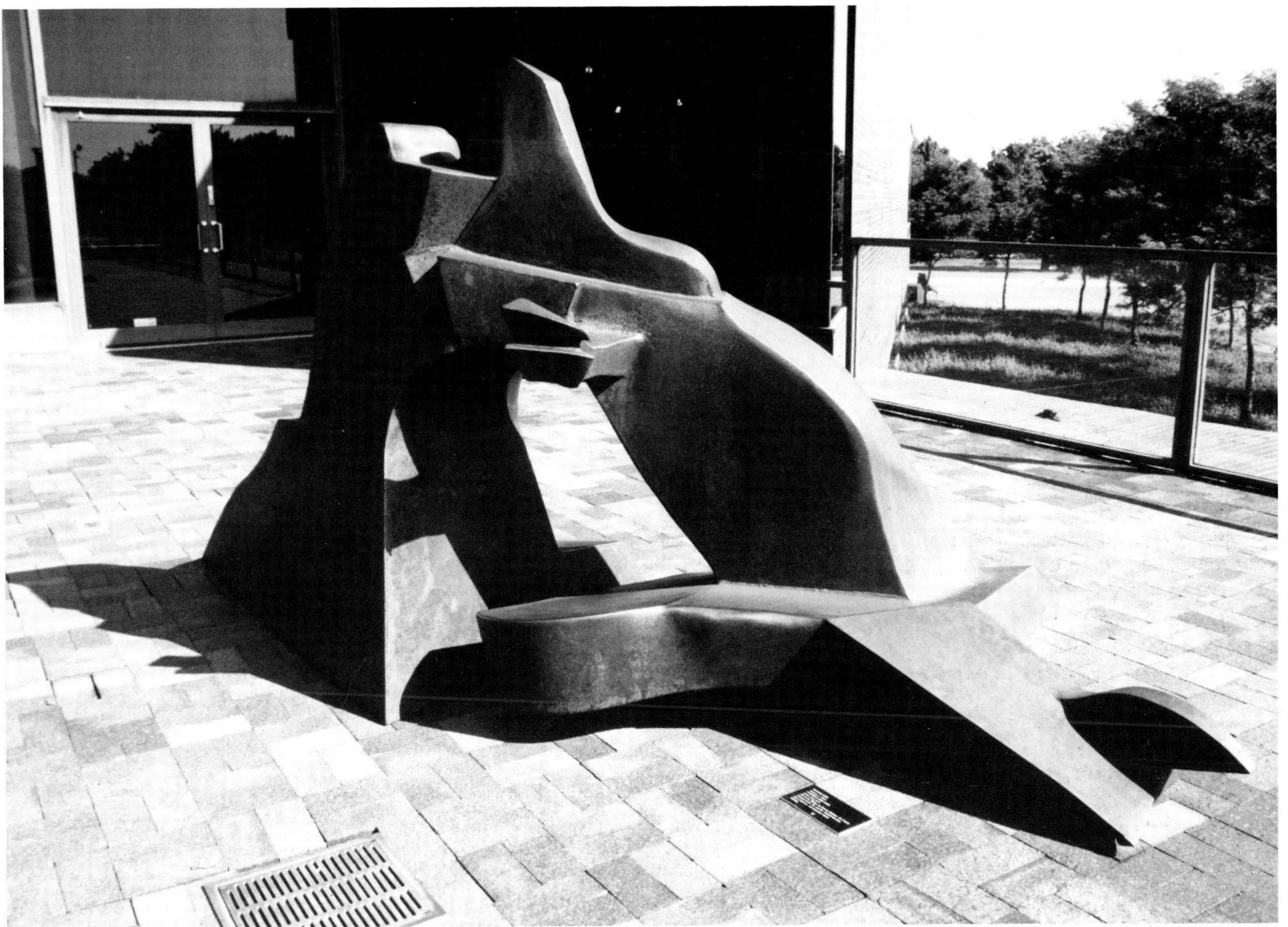

1976 Gift from the Wichita Art Museum Members Foundation, Inc.; Fourth National Financial Center; Mr. & Mrs. Kenneth Brasted; Mr. Harry Litwin; and Misco Charitable Trust, S.O. Beren and Allen Staub, Trustees
(1976.19)

ISAAC WITKIN (b.1936)

Yantra
Steel, 1977
60" h. x 236" l. x 145" d.

One of the most striking sculptures in the permanent collection of the Museum is this monumental brushed steel composition titled *Yantra* executed in 1977 by the American artist Isaac Witkin. The work is installed in a permanent location adjacent to a ramp leading to the main entrance to the Museum and is a rather massive piece, assuming appropriate scale in reference to the backdrop of the museum structure. Like the building, the sculpture hugs the ground echoing the angles of the building and at the same time punctuates the gently rising terrain of the northeast side of the Museum campus. In addition, the rich warm tones of the brown steel blend quite harmoniously with the coloration of the architecture further linking the aesthetic character of the building with the sculpture and at the same time enhancing the physical relationship between that architecture and the surrounding environment.

This work is constructed of six separate units firmly bolted together to form an approximate eliptical configuration nearly twenty feet across. Here Witkin has used heavy steel plate, and the various constituent forms introduced include flat broad surfaces, vertical, inclined or horizontal, some rectangular and others trapezoidal. From one point on the periphery of the complex appears a 3" thick protruding slab, gently twisted to create a hyperbolic-like surface. And in the center of the entire composition is an open hemispherical shape resembling a shell-like bowl. All of these shapes are artfully assembled in such a manner as to invite visual exploration and discovery, involving a spatial interchange between interior and exterior of the object and leading to a fuller understanding of the total constructional aspects of the work. What is especially relevant here is that these unrelated metal components, some perhaps accidentally shaped, have been placed in the hands of an artist who has converted them from an essentially meaningless miscellany into an orderly system of relationships.

A significant dimension of this work derives from the fact that the composition is quite literally a highly personal statement on the part of the artist himself and stimulates varied and perhaps conflicting interpretation by viewers. One compelling and provocative but often acknowledged aspect of the work is the sinister quality it evokes. Seemingly, this characteristic arises out of the skeletal structure and the silent stillness of the overall composition as well as from such particular features as the ruptured walls of the hemisphere where the seemingly impenetrable metal is virtually stripped open. The result is that in the mind's eye the total composition associates with destruction framed as if within what might be thought of as a post-cataclysmic time-continuum. But yet another and perhaps equally fitting interpretation is that this work, unlike anything normally encountered in our everyday existence, constitutes an entirely new and coherent language of artistic form as envisioned by the artist and one which, although we do not yet fully comprehend, nevertheless furnishes us a glimpse into a new configuration of world reality.

Isaac Witkin was born in Johannesburg, South Africa in 1936. He studied in England with Anthony Caro and for three years worked as an assistant to Henry Moore. His works are included in collections throughout much of the world and most especially in the Hirshhorn Museum, the Tate Gallery and the Storm King Art Center in Mountainville, New York. He has exhibited extensively throughout England and America and in 1984 served as visiting artist in the Skowhegan School, Maine. As early as 1965, Witkin was co-winner of First Prize at The Paris Bienale. Today he is recognized as one of America's leading contemporary sculptors, exhibiting actively in New York City and elsewhere.

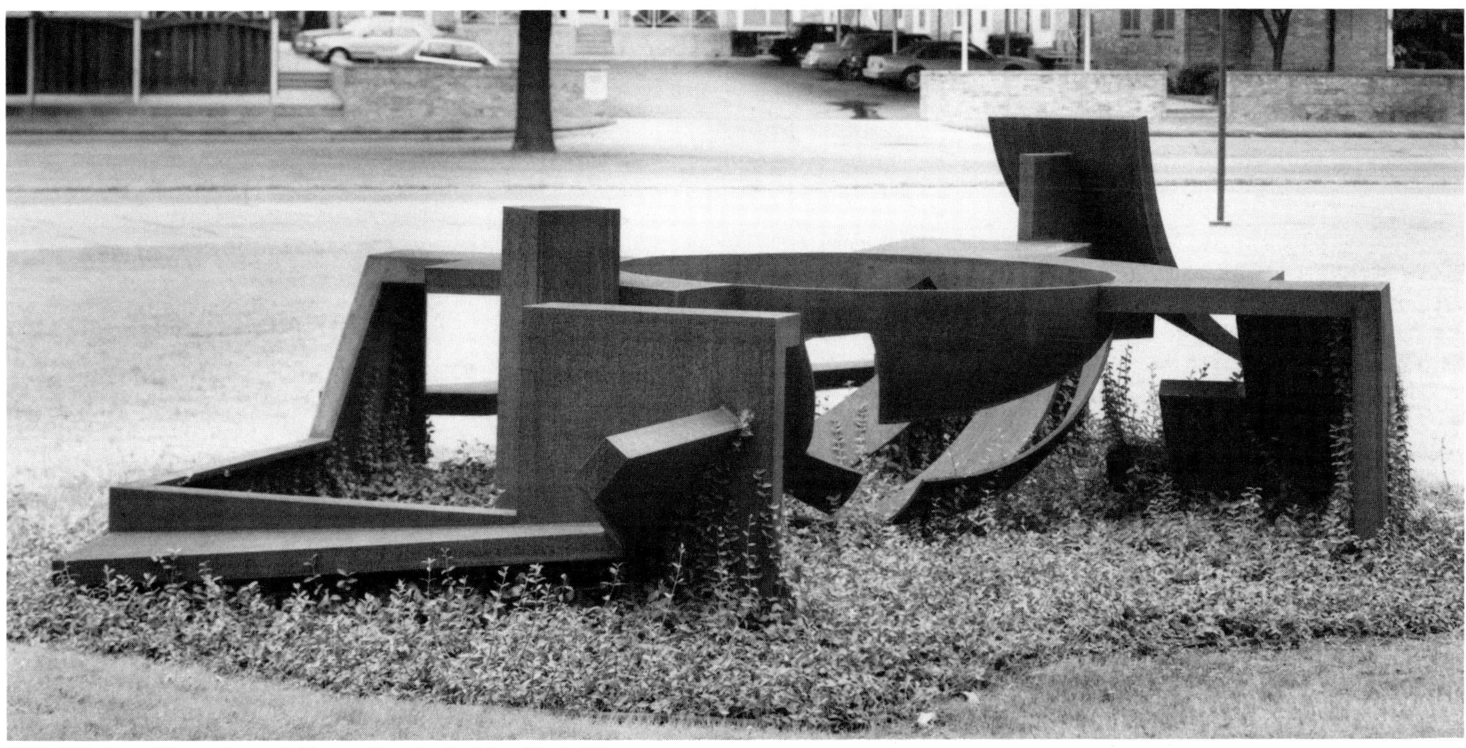

1983 Gift from Francoise and Harvey Rambach, New York City
(1983.41)

DOUGLAS ABDELL (b.1947)

Kaephae-Aekyad #2
Welded steel, painted black, 1979
96" x 112" x 22"

Permanently installed on the southwest lawn of the Museum campus and adjacent to the Sculpture Deck is this monumental abstract sculpture by the American artist Douglas Abdell and titled *Kaephae-Aekyad #2*. The work is constructed of welded hot rolled steel painted jet black and stands 8 feet high, 9 feet 4 inches long, and 22 inches thick.

Unlike traditional statuary, a work such as *Kaephae-Aekyad* must be considered in terms of what it does to the spaces around it and how it affects other objects nearby. As installed, the sculpture commands immediate attention for its presence is powerfully felt. Moreoever, the composition interrelates quite successfully with the Museum building. Indeed the tall and bold two dimensional black pattern of the sculpture harmonizes with the horizontal, black ribbon window in the background and, at the same time, presents effective contrast with the more delicate salmon tones of the building brick itself.

Although purity of form and relative simplicity of design such as characterize most minimalist sculptures are of course retained in this work, variety and diversity have also been effectively introduced, imparting a distinctive quality to what might otherwise be viewed merely as a flat, cut-out composition with identical faces, front and back. In this respect, Abdell's works are unique, and it is obvious that he discovers his forms through drawings, a fact which clearly accounts for the flat, two-dimensional qualities that inevitably result in an emphasis on surface treatment and surface awareness. And in the instance of this particular work, the broken outline of the composition and the large open area in the center are viewable only on the surface and are the specific elements by which the interplay of space and form functions to activate the space in which the sculpture itself stands. What is also of special interest here is the fact that the character of the broken outline with its pointed and projecting volumetric shapes presents an illusion of movement, directing the eye toward the building, thus again illustrating the mutual influence of the sculpture and the building.

Douglas Abdell was born in Boston in 1947. In 1968, he studied painting and sculpture in Florence, Italy, but received his B.F.A. degree with a major in sculpture from Syracuse University. Abdell has exhibited at major galleries in New York and has participated in numerous traveling exhibitions across the country. He currently resides in New York City.

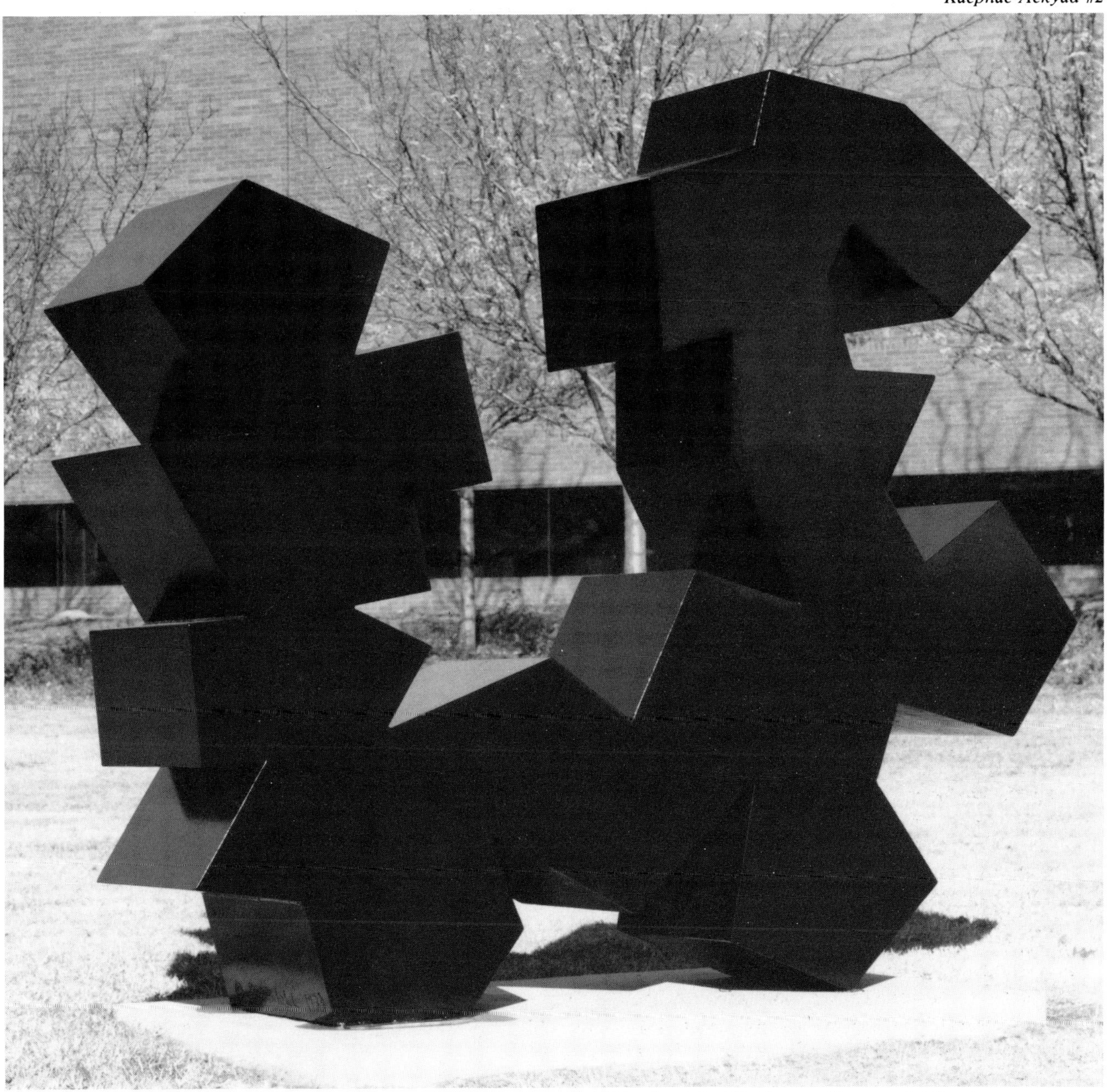

1985 Museum Purchase, Price R. & Flora A. Reid Foundation Fund and Friends of the Wichita Art Museum Art Fund (1985.58)

DOROTHY DEHNER (b.1901)

Watcher D
Cor-ten steel, 1985
108" h. x 28" w. x 28" d.

Dorothy Dehner is one of America's highly creative and most renowned contemporary sculptors. Over the years she has executed both large scale works as well as extremely small table pieces. She has never been concerned with depicting familiar objects but has preferred instead to create new realities which are emotionally charged and which project an iconic presence, commanding immediate and lasting attention. What is so fascinating about so many of Dehner's works is the sense of timelessness which they evoke, always reminding the viewer of the continuing links between the mythic past and the energy felt in tribal art on the one hand and of the dynamism of our own contemporary moment in time on the other hand.

This quite marvelous sense of temporal continuity is clearly suggested in this relatively recent work titled *Watcher D* executed early in 1985 and soon thereafter installed here at the Wichita Art Museum to commemorate the 50th anniversary of the founding of the Museum. Especially noteworthy are the structural relationships which Dehner has introduced in this work and the rich warm variegated color tones accomplished in her use of cor-ten steel.

Watcher D is actually a composition consisting of pure geometry in which the artist has effectively combined rectilinear with curvilinear forms. Moreover, *Watcher D* is a tall and erect assemblage with marked totemic character and as a result the work clearly makes anthropomorphic allusions, no doubt a debt to the teachings of her close friend John Graham and to the lingering influence of African sculpture which has fascinated her throughout her career.

As installed the work is intended to relate closely to its environment and stands in the exact center of the open key area at ground level immediately below the sculture deck where it adds a vertical accent to the horizontally oriented building as well as to the flat surrounding spaces. At the same time the rectilinear forms and color tones of the cor-ten blend with those of the building while the curvilinear forms echo those of the semicircular key itself thereby furnishing unity to the complex and concurrently activating what would otherwise be little more than a stretch of sterile space, open and empty.

Dorothy Dehner was born in Cleveland, Ohio in 1901 and has been active in the development of contemporary sculptural form in New York City for more than 60 years. She has produced important sculptures in bronze, wood and cor-ten and is widely represented in major collections, both private and public, throughout the United States and abroad. She has held more than sixty solo exhibitions in galleries and in American museums. Her studio is located in New York City where she actively continues to produce large scale sculptures and to prepare national exhibitions of her works.

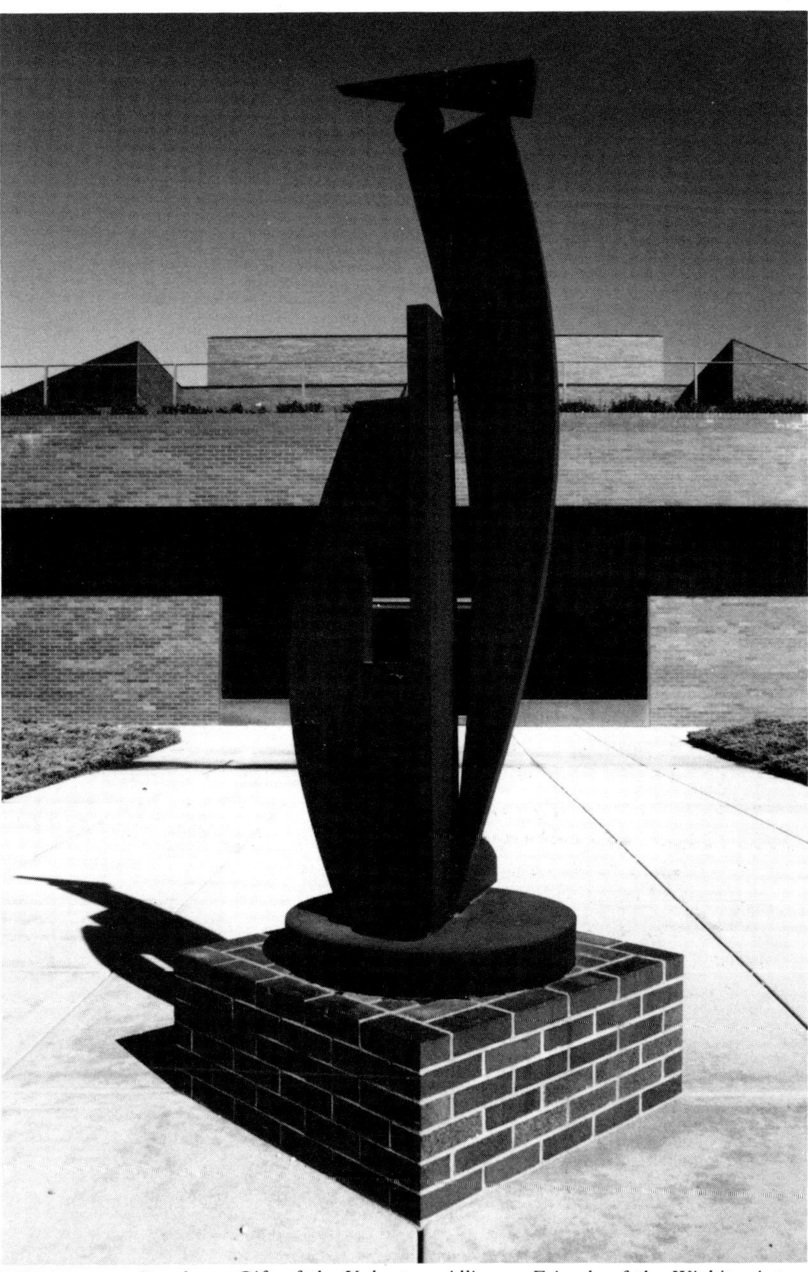

1985 Museum Purchase, Gift of the Volunteer Alliance, Friends of the Wichita Art Museum to commemorate the 50th anniversary of the Wichita Art Museum (1985.46)

BRITISH WATERCOLOR PAINTINGS

PAUL SANDBY (1725-1809)

In Hyde Park
Watercolor on wove paper, 1789
7¼" x 10⅞"

One of England's most versatile and certainly most highly respected 18th century watercolorists was Paul Sandby. Sandby is sometimes regarded as the father of British watercolor painting but such a classification is hardly valid, for certainly the British painted in watercolor for several centuries before Sandy's birth in 1725. Nevertheless, Sandby was indeed an innovator and, although he was not strictly a topographical painter himself, his experimental emphasis on landscape themes had long range influence on topographical painters in England throughout the late 18th and early 19th centuries.

This work, painted about 1789 and titled *In Hyde Park,* is a view with which Sandby was apparently well-acquainted, since his private residence was located immediately overlooking the park. Here the composition is clearly dominated by two ancient, massive trees which flank the dirt carriage path. On the one side, a low wooden fence gracefully winds along the edge of the path while, on the other, the path itself closely parallels the contours of a lake, quite probably the well-known Serpentine Lake artificially constructed in Hyde Park during the early 18th century. A single horse-drawn carriage passing between the two gigantic trees draws the eye into the distance where, just ahead of the carriage, is the tiny figure of a man on horseback.

Although Sandby may well have presented an accurate view of Hyde Park in this work, his interest actually would seem to have been more on the glorification of the natural setting than on topographical precision. Among the many characteristic features of Sandby's work is the gentle touch so evident in the fine fluid line used to define form. This is accomplished most effectively in the fresh handling of foliage where leaves are drawn as strings of short wavy squiggle curves. The same sense of refinement is found in the delicate treatment of cloud formations and of reflections and shadows, or again in the carefully controlled tonal gradations imparted to the forms receding into atmospheric distance.

Of particular interest here are the striking contrasts introduced such as the sharp shift in scale between the gigantic trees and the tiny horseman and carriage along the winding path, or the marked dissimilarity between the massive trees with their luxuriantly green foliage on the one hand and the pair of seemingly dead trees nearby bearing only scattered dry brown leaves. Above all is the mood of calm and tranquility which is so effectively achieved by the subtle variations of form and by the harmonious interplay of a wide range of soft color tones that pervade the composition.

Paul Sandby was born in Nottingham in 1725. Both he and his artist brother, Thomas, settled in London in 1760. Paul Sandby himself was a founding member of the Royal Academy in 1768 and was the first professional artist to use aquatint in England. He was primarily a landscapist who exercised an enormous influence both on his contemporaries and on many watercolorists throughout the early 19th century in England. Sandby died in London in 1809, leaving an extensive body of works that are today housed in major museums throughout Britain.

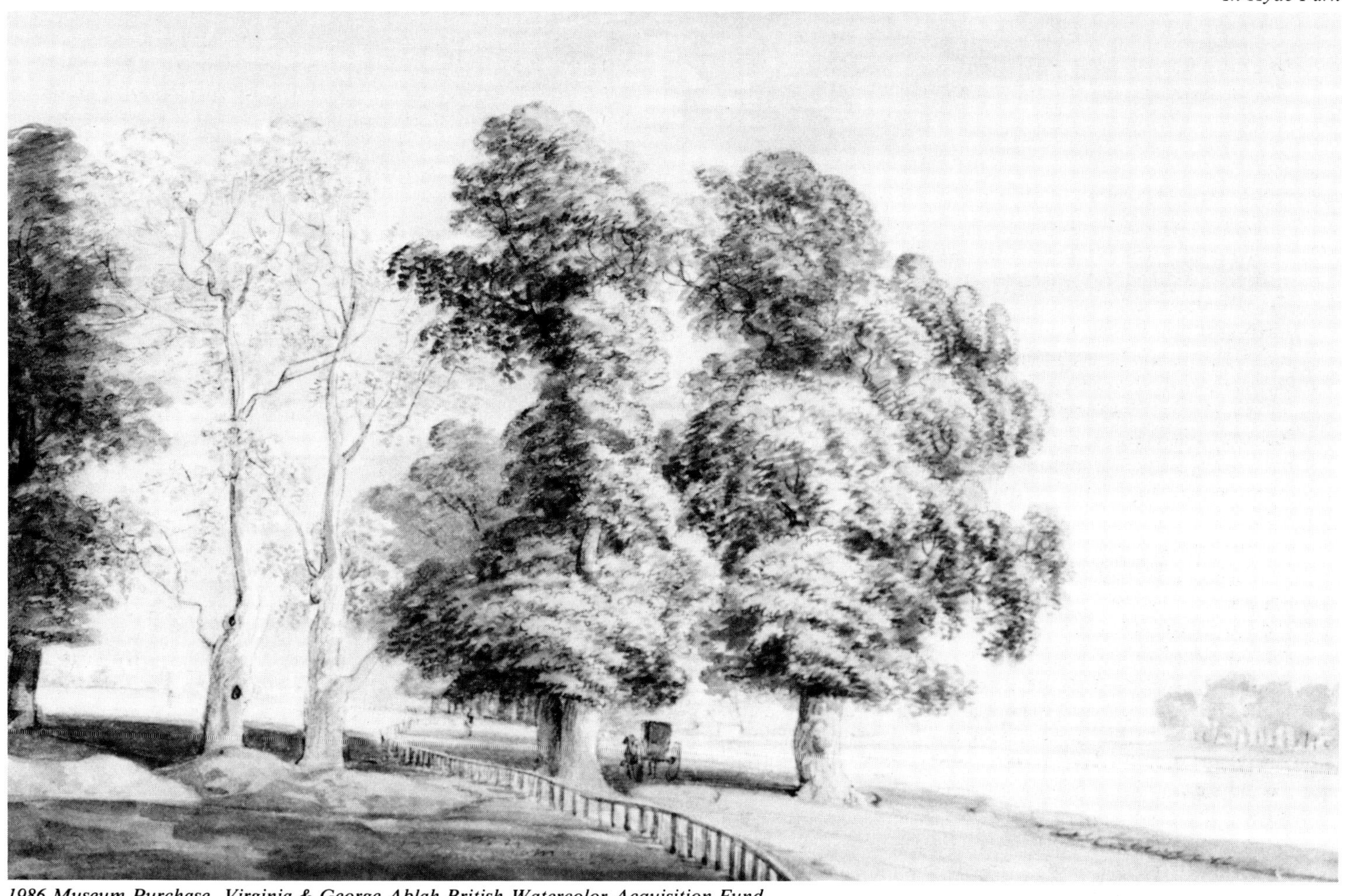

1986 Museum Purchase, Virginia & George Ablah British Watercolor Acquisition Fund
(1986.61)

FRANCIS WHEATLEY (1747-1801)

A Country Boy and Girl Returning Home with Firewood
Watercolor on wove paper, 1795
18¾" x 14"

This engaging watercolor painting titled *A Country Boy and Girl Returning Home with Firewood* was executed in 1795 by the British artist Francis Wheatley. Like many works of the period, this piece is most fundamentally a carefully delineated outline drawing with all areas neatly filled with pale color washes. Wheatley was widely recognized as an outstandingly competent draftsman and his skill is clearly evident in the crisp handling of all forms and especially of the figures of the young boy and girl who are given foreground prominence in the center of the composition.

The soft tones used here and the calm and idyllic rustic setting were qualities which theoreticians of the period associated with what they called "the beautiful". At the same time, the little cottage with its thatched roof, the irregular dirt path where the children walk, the old wooden bucket at the water well, and the loosely bundled firewood carried by the children were considered appropriate devices for a picturesque setting. What is so interesting is that here as in many of Wheatley's paintings, it is the primitive simplicity of rural life that the artist glorifies in his choice of theme, a theme flavored with extreme sentimentality, especially evident in the innocent expressions and the somewhat affected poses of the children and which is further accented by the delicate color tints used throughout the composition.

When seen through the eyes of today's viewers, such sentimentality is regarded as artificial, contrived and saccharine. Yet when this painting was executed, artists like Wheatley, perhaps unconsciously, were simply sensitively documenting their response to societal changes which they were quick to recognize and which were just beginning to take place as a result of industrial and technological changes then in progress. For ultimately the self-sufficiency of the traditional life style of many small villages would vanish as large factory towns began to rise. From that standpoint, both the theatrical effects and the expression of nostalgia suggested here would seem premonitory of the widespread changes that would eventually be experienced.

Francis Wheatley was born in 1747 in Covent Garden, London. He studied art about 1765 at Shipley's School, one of London's finest schools of drawing at the time. In 1769, he attended the Royal Academy. Throughout his career his works were highly admired and many were engraved for publication in widely circulated magazines. He was elected an associate member of the Royal Academy in 1790 and a full member in 1791. Yet the 18th century was a time when watercolor was considered appropriate primarily for producing preliminary sketches for oil paintings. As a result, Wheatley suffered serious financial hardships and in 1793 became bankrupt. He died in London in 1801.

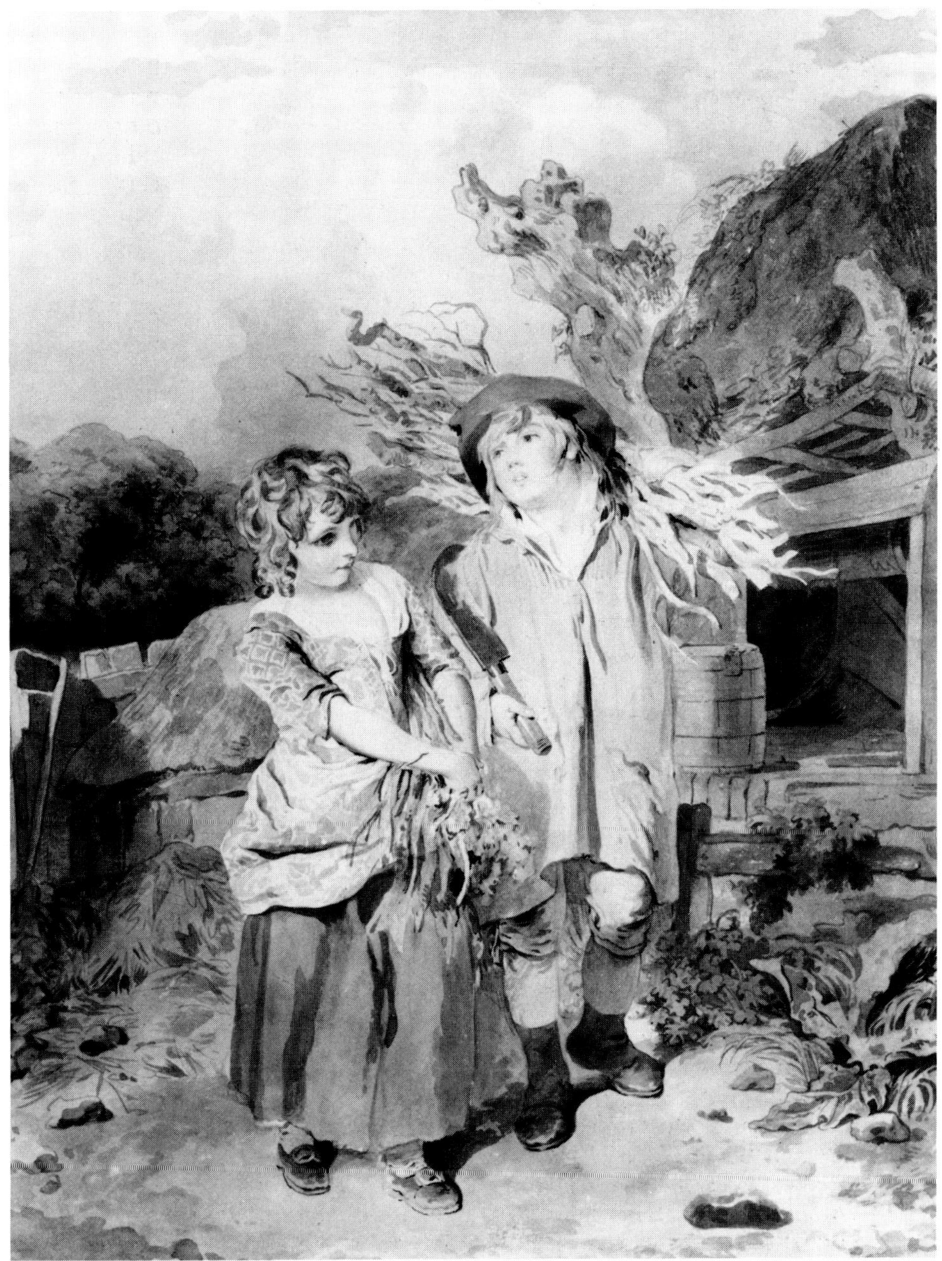

1986 Museum Purchase, Virginia & George Ablah British Watercolor Acquisition Fund (1986.21)

THOMAS GIRTIN (1775-1802)

Romantic Landscape
Watercolor on paper, c.1798
12½" x 19¹/₈"

This elegant watercolor painting titled *Romantic Landscape* was executed about 1798 by the eminent British watercolorist Thomas Girtin. Here a large cluster of trees at the extreme right and a high bluff topped by castle ruins at the left frame the composition and at the same time open a wide area which channels the eye into the deep space where in the distance steep and rugged hills and mountains can be seen. In the foreground a massive rock juts up in the middle of a rushing stream, and nearby a tiny figure of an angler is shown, almost lost in the vast but peaceful setting.

In this work Girtin has effectively caught the essential components of 18th century aesthetic theory. The precipitously overhanging cliff on which the castle is precariously perched and the wide expanse of infinite space were regarded as expressions of the "sublime," while the overall irregularity of the landscape itself, the abrupt variations in shapes, the knotted tree trunks and the presence of architectural ruins that add a nostalgic sense of the inevitable passage of time were together considered appropriate suggestions of the so-called "picturesque."

These aspects, so common in British landscape paintings at the end of the 18th century, exerted an enormous influence on American landscape painting early in the 19th century. What is most particularly significant however is the fact that this work by Girtin exemplifies a technical and stylistic revolution in watercolor painting, for during the 18th century, most British watercolors were essentially merely tinted drawings. In contrast Girtin's work is executed in pure watercolor, freely handled and applied directly to the paper rather than used simply to color outlined shapes. Moreover, Girtin has masterfully created atmospheric effects and at the same time his forms are suggested rather than painted in precise detail, with the result that the forms themselves seem loose and woolly yet are actually far more convincing in naturalistic appearance than those of any tinted drawings.

Indeed, this work demonstrates Girtin's tremendous precocity and accounts for the enviable reputation which he enjoyed during his productive if extremely short life. He was born in Southwark, then a suburb of London, in 1775. He was apprenticed to several prominent British artists of the time and later attended evening drawing classes at the residence of Dr. Thomas Monro who, although a physician, was instrumental in assisting numerous young artists.

It was in Dr. Monro's classes that Girtin first met J.M.W. Turner. The two young artists were exactly the same age and became close friends, often traveling together throughout England on sketching tours. By 1794, when he was only 19 years old, Girtin exhibited at the Royal Academy. In 1800 he was married but his poor health tragically culminated in his death in London in 1802 when he was only 27 years of age. For a young man, Girtin was highly prolific. Yet today, by virtue of his short life span, his watercolors are extremely rare.

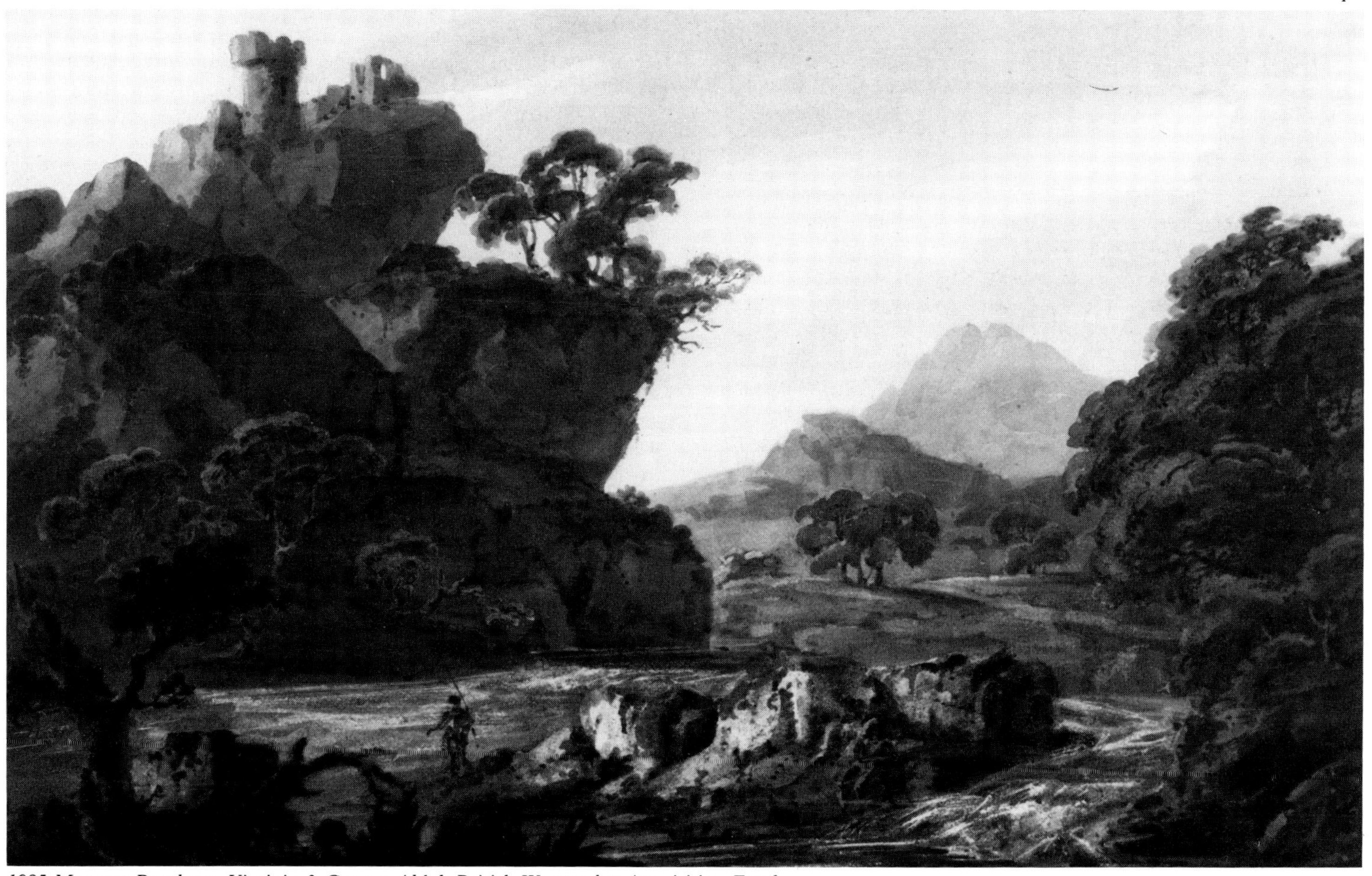

*1985 Museum Purchase, Virginia & George Ablah British Watercolor Acquisition Fund
(1985.45)*

FREDERICK NASH (1782-1856)

Inside of Westminster Abbey, with Funeral Procession
Watercolor, gouache on paper, 1811
40" x 30⁷/₈"

This large watercolor painting titled *Inside of Westminster Abbey, with Funeral Procession* was executed in 1811 by the British artist Frederick Nash (1782-1856). The tranquil and sombre mood appropriate for the subject is heightened by the vast space of the interior and the misty glow of light throughout the background and upper spaces of the composition.

Nash was widely recognized by many and by Turner in particular as the most outstanding architectural painter of his day, and certainly in the instance of this work he readily commands attention by virtue of his meticulous handling of the many bold and massive architectural forms and of the accoutrements of the Abbey interior. However, it is obvious here that he was as much concerned with the study of light and space as he was with either the architectural statement or the funeral procession theme. Indeed, what most imparts a masterful quality to this work is the exquisitely delicate and carefully controlled treatment of light as it floods the interior, dissolving forms in the distance and sharply defining shapes and textures in the foreground. And at the same time, of course, compositional interest is furnished by the lofty height and the sweeping diagonal spaces depicted and by the dramatic color contrasts of light and dark areas.

The Romantic spirit of the early 19th century with its mystical love of light and its reverence for the past — and most especially for the *mediaeval* past — is clearly expressed in this painting. And that turn of mind becomes understandable when we take into account that the period was one which experienced radical societal change due to the rapid development of industry and new technologies, and therefore often nostalgically looked back to what it regarded as a more secure and stable age. In this connection, architectural monuments of the past symbolically supplied a psychological need and thus frequently consumed the attention of many artists. But on the other hand, such artists as Nash were quite progressive and already at this early date were much concerned with the very aesthetic issues which later in the century were to become basic in investigating the impact of time on change or the powerful effect of light in defining reality. In that sense a painting such as this may be seen as a stage in the development of what would be the dominant impressionist manner of the last quarter of the century.

Frederick Nash was born in Lambeth in 1782 and spent his early years studying architectural drawing. Westminster Abbey was the setting that he chose for many of his most detailed works. But Nash also painted in open air, executing the same scene at various times of the day in order to explore the effects of varying light conditions on defining the changing character of the subject. He exhibited at the Royal Academy and was much admired by Benjamin West, the American-born president of the Royal Academy, for his "grand and pictorial sentiment". Nash was also a member of the well-known Old Watercolour Society. He died in Brighton, England in 1856.

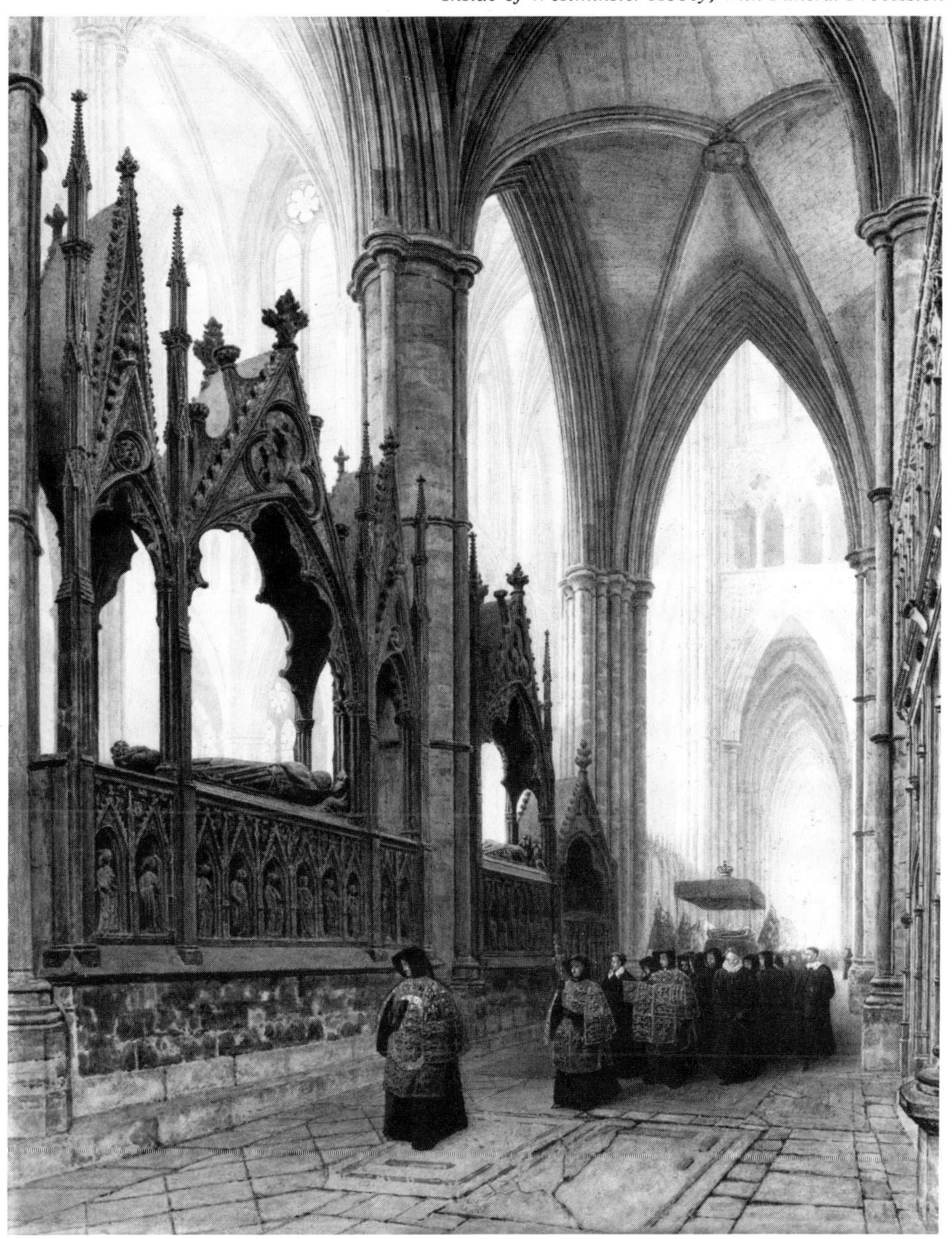

1984 Museum Purchase, Friends of the Wichita Art Museum Art Fund
(1984.4)

GEORGE BARRET, JR. (1767-1842)

Capriccio of a Mediterranean Sea Port at Sunset
Watercolor on paper, 1826
13⁷/₈" x 20³/₈"

The prolific watercolorist George Barret, Jr. executed this painting titled *Capriccio of a Mediterranean Sea Port at Sunset* in 1826. This is a most interesting work because, as the word *capriccio* in the title suggests, it is an imaginative fantasy consisting of views of a variety of architectural types juxtaposed in a single combination.

On the left is a small doric temple and on the right the ruins of a more massive Roman ionic structure standing on a high podium which bears a sculptural relief frieze depicting a scene of a sacrificial bull. In the far distance and partly dissolved in the rose-colored light of the sunset, are an Egyptian pyramid and a circular domed building recalling the Roman pantheon. Beyond is a low mountain ridge. Scattered across the immediate foreground are heavily sculpted coffer blocks from the ceiling of an antique building. In the extreme left foreground, nearly hidden by thickly overgrown vegetation, is seen a sphinx figure which rests atop a small open rectangular fountain house with flanking Corinthian pilasters and from which a jet of water gushes forward. The combination of forms, the compression of time, and the soft glow of fading light in the distant sky together evoke a mood of serenity, nostalgia, and the lingering presence of the past.

In his day Barret was distinguished as a colorist and a painter of poetic light. Moreover, in this work as in many paintings of the early 19th century, the graceful compositional balance and the idyllic quality imparted as well as the obvious interest in antique architecture reflect the inspiration of such earlier landscapists as Claude Lorrain whose works are known to have influenced Barret. But to the thought of the early 19th century, the sense of time — of desolation through the passage of time — is of particular significance and is much intensified here by the presence of the three Turkish soldiers in the foreground — two resting with their rifles and one standing with his left arm pointing outward, in the direction perhaps of the sphinx.

We cannot know fully what Barret's intentions were when he composed this fantasy. Yet it is enormously significant that the date of the painting coincides exactly with one of the most critical moments during the Greek Wars of Independence when the Greeks experienced near defeat at the combined hands of the Turkish Sultan and the Pasha of Egypt. British sympathy for the Greek cause ran high and it was in 1826 that the western powers including England, France and Russia entered the war on the side of the Greeks, helping to bring about the Turkish defeat and the ultimate liberation of Greece in 1829. That the painting might therefore be a propagandizing statement, couched in idyllic terms of a popular Claudian formula, seems more than a little possible. And indeed the three soldiers might well be a symbolic depiction of the Turks presiding over ancient Western Civilization. Moreover, the crescent moon — a symbol of the Ottoman Empire — together with the bird of prey hovering in the sky above and the sacrificial bull in the center of the relief frieze would further strengthen this interpretation.

For nearly 400 years, Western international diplomacy had been colored in varying degrees by the threat of Ottoman advances toward the West. And it was now in the Greek revolt against Turkey that such diplomacy was once again being put to the test. This little painting therefore presents an interesting example of the use of art in international politics.

George Barret, Jr. was one of the original members of the Old Watercolour Society. He was born in London in 1767 and the setting for most of his paintings was the area immediately around London for he rarely traveled. He died in London in 1842.

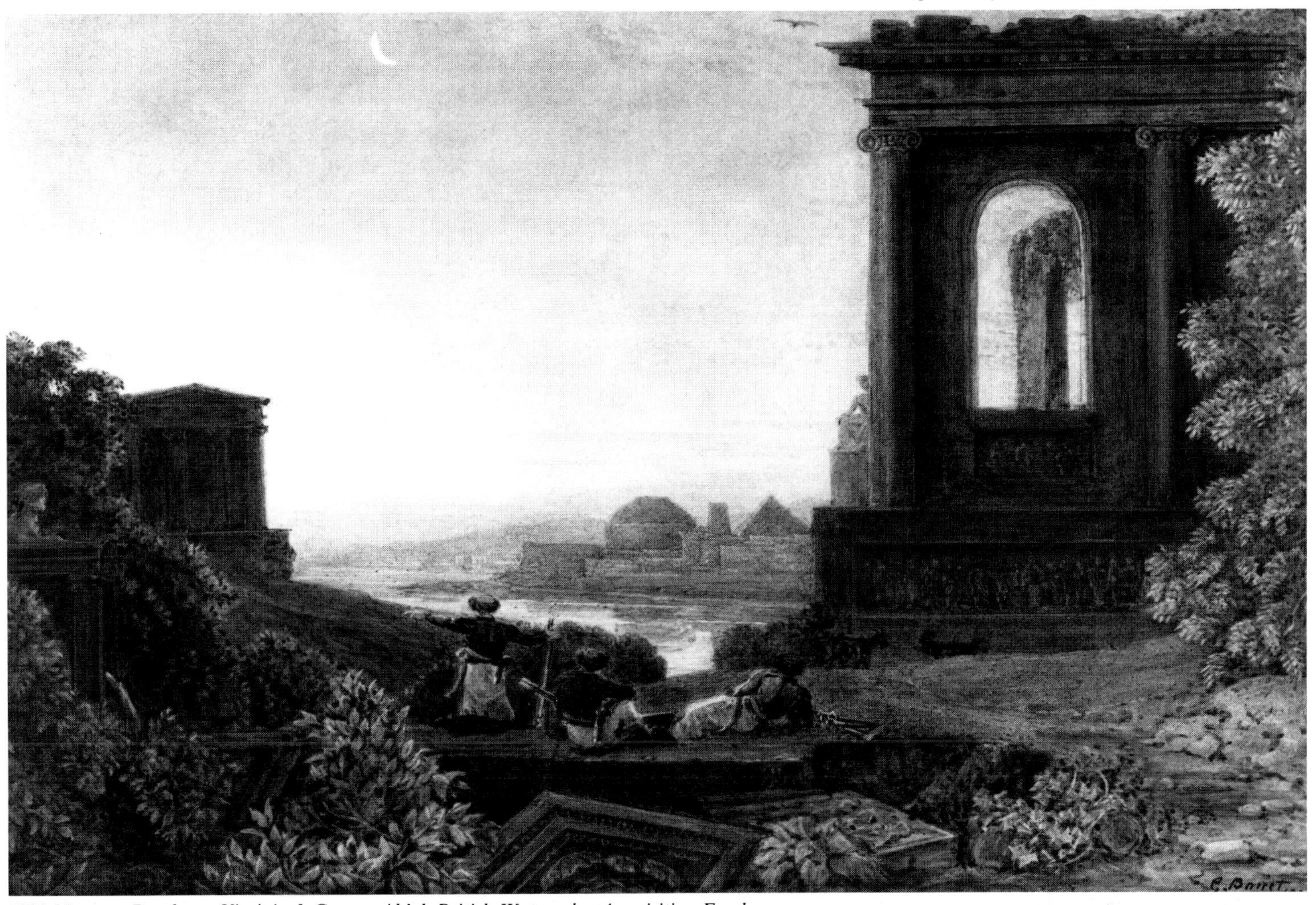

*1980 Museum Purchase, Virginia & George Ablah British Watercolor Acquisition Fund
(1980.82)*

ALFRED DOWNING FRIPP (1822-1895)

A Reverie
Watercolor on paper, 1850
$22^5/_{16}$'' x 20¾''

This charming Victorian watercolor painting titled *A Reverie* was executed in 1850 by the eminent British artist Alfred Downing Fripp and portrays a beautiful young Irish peasant woman rocking her infant asleep in a wicker cradle. Here, the setting is the interior of a small rough-hewn stone cottage with wooden rafters, a wooden door jamb and a stone slab floor.

Fripp's technique is quite remarkable. His drawing is meticulously refined yet spontaneous and the subtle chiaroscuro which he employs lends drama to his composition. Textural variations such as the flesh-like quality of the young woman's hands and face, the soft folds of her blue overskirt and the wicker of the cradle are skillfully and convincingly rendered.

Compositionally, the work is of much interest and quite typical of Fripp's fluid manner. Here the focus of attention is clearly on the mother and the child in the cradle, sharply illuminated by the light pouring into the cottage through the wide open door at the right. Touches of genre further enliven the work, as for example the spinning wheel and the toppled wooden stool with its three legs jutting outward toward us. But the surrounding space is treated with only just enough detail to establish an appropriate setting without competing with the intended central theme of mother and child. Moreover, the composition is largely saturated with rich warm tones which seem to rise to a climax in the red of the kerchief tied around the young mother's head, thereby emphasizing the focal theme again and at the same time imparting unity to the composition as a whole.

Threatened by the social changes that accompanied rapidly spreading industrialization during the 19th century, many British artists looking to the past through a golden haze resorted to sweet and tender sentiment as a vehicle for extolling the joys and virtues of the simple uncorrupted life such as that suggested here. At the same time it is interesting to note in this composition that while this painting portrays a mother and child, we are tempted at first glance to read the work as a nativity scene. And this throws light on another aspect of the period, namely the not infrequent tendency by the middle of the 19th century to secularize the traditional religious image in art, thereby pointing up a degree of ambiguity widely experienced in the Victorian period and recorded in many of the works of that period. Yet, even with the religious overtones suggested by the tiny rosary and cross dangling from the hood of the crib, when we investigate this work closely, we readily conclude that it was intended more as a secular than a religious scene. For the artist's care in describing the young mother's overskirt in a deep blue that is repeated in a segment of the nearby blue sea glimpsed through the open door at the right suggests some association between the woman and the sea itself. This suggestion is reinforced by the presence of what appears to be fine fishing nets bound and tied around the vertical wooden post at the left and lead us to speculate freely that this is a fishing cottage and that the mother is the young wife of a fisherman.

Alfred Downing Fripp was born in Bristol in 1822, and in 1840 settled in London where he studied at the British Museum and the Royal Academy. In 1844 he was elected an associate of the Royal Society of Painters in Watercolors and in 1846 a full member. Some of his most important works were executed during visits to Ireland and to Italy where he lived from 1850 to 1854. Fripp died in London in 1895.

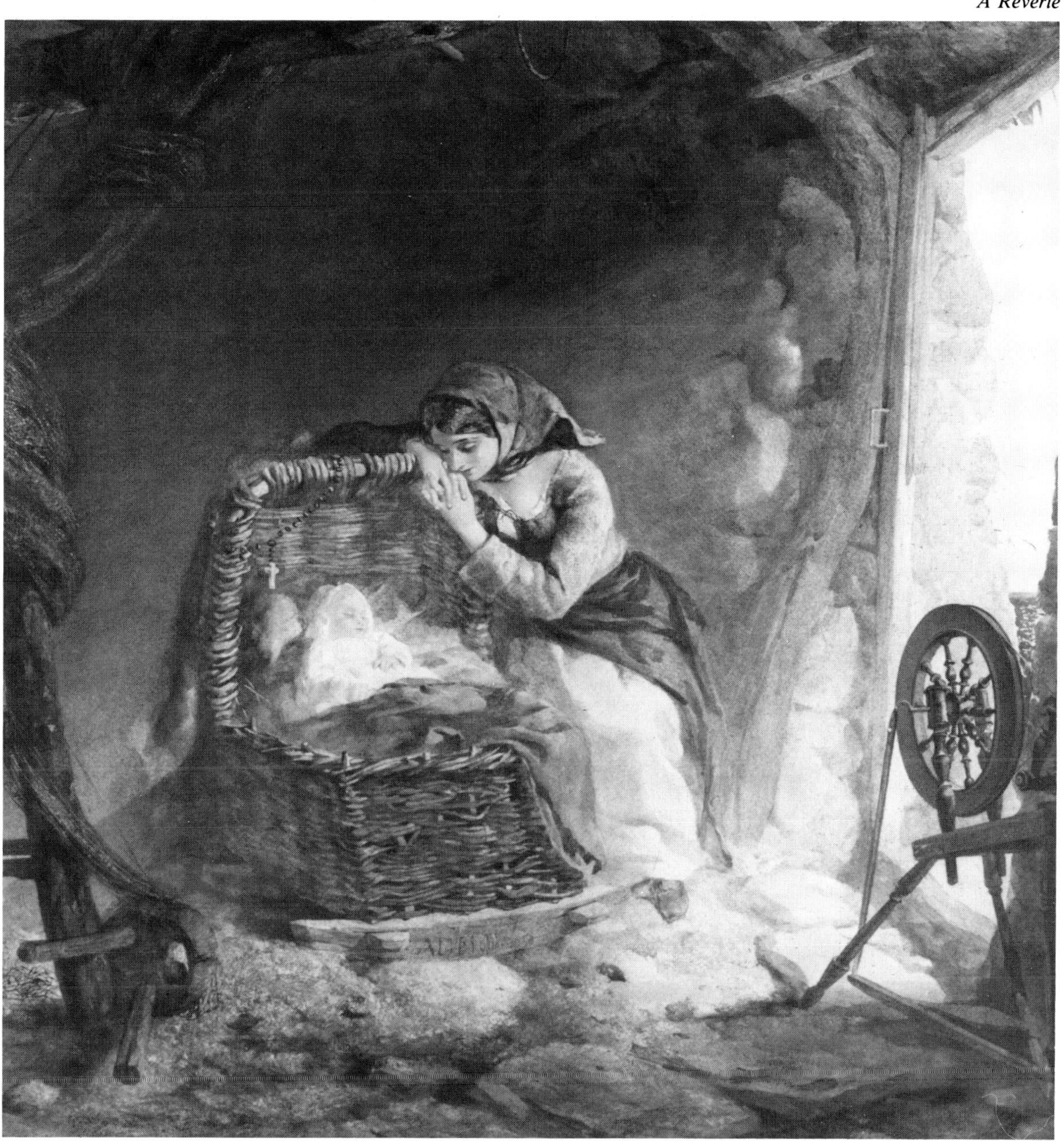

1979 Museum Purchase, Friends of the Wichita Art Museum Art Fund
(1979.34)

J. FREDERICK TAYLER (1802-1889)

Alms for the Blind
Watercolor on paper, c.1850
15⁵/₈" x 12½"

Industralized Victorian society generally preferred a realist art which depicted a commonplace incident rendered in literally understandable terms and one which at the same time often carried a hidden message with moralistic overtones. This striking painting titled *Alms for the Blind* and executed about 1850 by the English watercolorist John Frederick Tayler, illustrates that double tendency so well. Here beneath the arched gateway that opens onto the narrow lane of a town with its late mediaeval buildings shown in the background, a blind man carrying a long stick stands quietly with the assistance of a young barefooted girl dressed in tattered clothing. His long shadow falls heavily on the wall near which he stands and his empty hat is thrust forward by the little girl who stares directly into the spectator's eyes as she begs for alms, thus evoking sympathetic responses in us as we view the scene.

The drastically abrupt shift in scale between foreground and background and the rather theatrical manner in which the dominant foreground figures present themselves by looking directly toward us as spectators, as if about to intrude into our space, are quite typical characteristics of painting during much of the Victorian period. Indeed, it is through such compositional treatment that the artist captures and holds our attention and forces us to participate vicariously in the incident depicted.

As we view this work, we are thus reminded of the philanthropic appeals of Charles Dickens and of the general concern during the early and mid-Victorian period over social injustices, the impoverished and the handicapped. But the image of the blind also refers to man's spiritual blindness as described in Chapter 9 of the New Testament Book of John. And therein lies the other side of the moralistic message which could so easily escape notice except for those Victorian viewers well versed in scriptural teachings.

John Frederick Tayler was born in 1802 in Hertfordshire, England and studied at both Eton and Harrow. Although his family encouraged him to enter the Church, he chose painting as a career instead and worked with many of the major early 19th century artists both in England and in France including Bonington and Prout. He was elected to full membership in the Royal Watercolor Society in 1834 and became president of the Society in 1858. Tayler died in London in 1889.

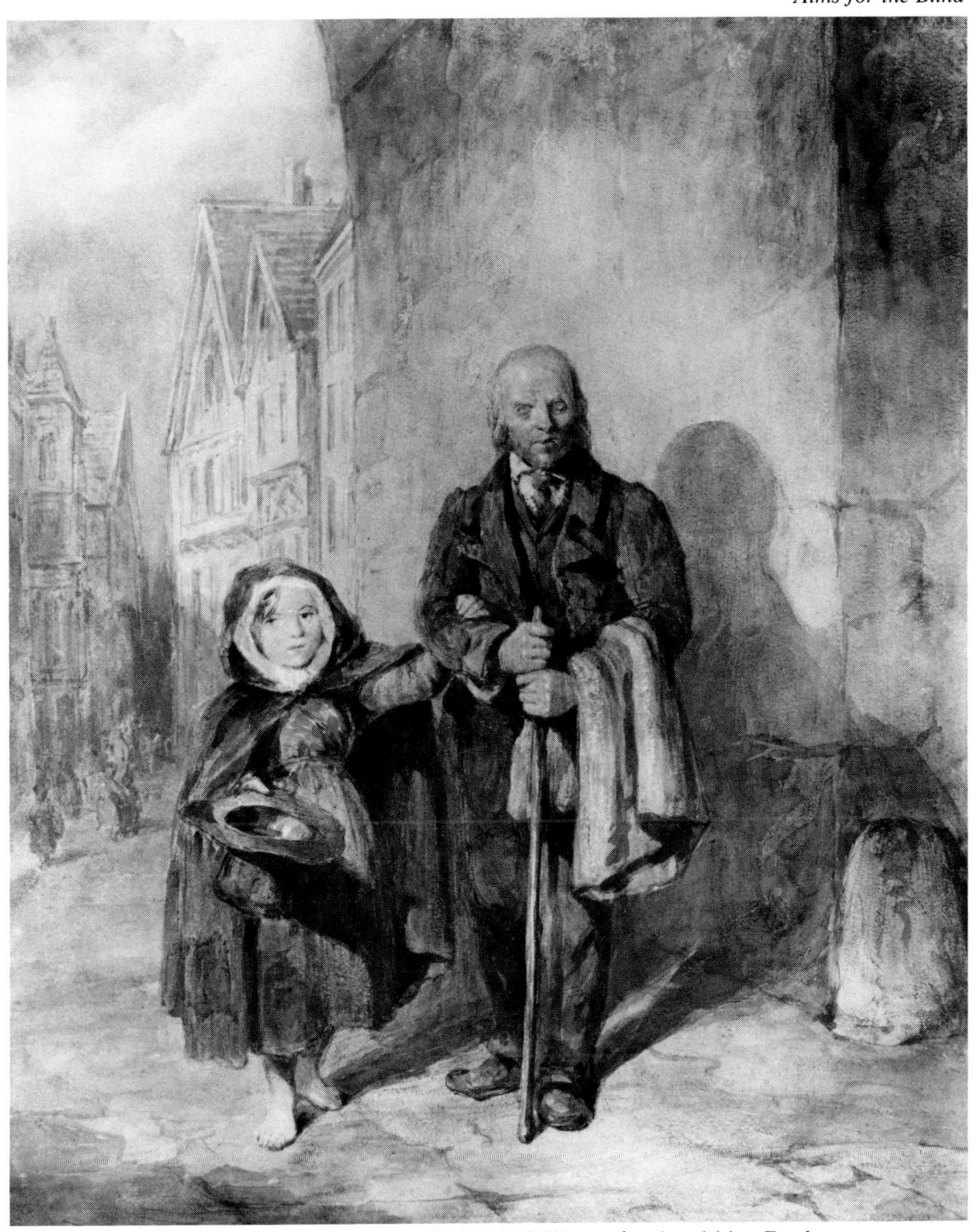

1980 Museum Purchase, Virginia & George Ablah British Watercolor Acquisition Fund
(1980.87)

DAVID COX, SR. (1783-1859)

Ludlow Castle, Shropshire
Watercolor on paper, 1852
$10^3/_8$" x $14^3/_8$"

One of Britain's most innovative artists of the nineteenth century was David Cox, Sr. (1783-1859). In this masterfully executed watercolor, Cox has painted the strong fortified walls of *Ludlow Castle, Shropshire,* which, with its tall square crenelated towers, commands the view of the Teme River valley along the border between England and Wales.

The castle was first built in 1086, but the architectural subject matter itself is only of incidental importance. Instead the significance of the work rests largely upon the stylistic elements that it embodies. Cox painted this watercolor in 1852, a late moment in his career by which time his treatment of light, wind and atmospheric effects together closely resembles some of the most distinguishing traits of what today we call Impressionism. And of course this work pre-dates the earliest French impressionists by more than two decades.

Of much interest is the fact that the paper on which this work was painted is actually a wrapping paper discovered by Cox in 1836 and used so extensively by him thereafter that it became known as *Cox Paper.* It was also known as Scotch paper since it was imported from Dundee, Scotland. Its rough texture seems to partially account for the shimmering effect found in works by Cox during the last several decades of his life. What is of comparable interest here is the fact that, although Cox the artist was surely innovative, he, like many others of his generation, was also extremely traditional in his outlook on life. And as we view this drawing of Ludlow Castle, we clearly witness the work of a man who was deeply responsive to the traditional notion of the sublime in nature, much as that notion had been formulated aesthetically by Edmund Burke nearly a century earlier. The sense of infinity, the steep cliff on which the castle seems so precariously to hang, and the overall all-inspiring mood of the setting together exhibit Burke's doctrine of the sublime. It is also this sense of the sublime which quite obviously carried the mind toward the idea of God during the era in which Burke wrote and even more so during the disruptive mid-nineteenth century age of religious uncertainty. Indeed Cox was a conservatively religious man and the concept of the sublime was effective reinforcement of his religious leanings and a fitting guide to the stylistic character of many of his works, especially those produced during his later years.

David Cox was born in 1783 in Birmingham, England, where he took drawing lessons during his early youth. In 1804 he went to London, studied under John Varley and worked as a scene painter in the theatre. He was married in 1808 and throughout his life he painted extensively in north and west England and in Wales as well as while on several visits to the Continent. In 1841 he returned to Birmingham where he settled permanently but continued to take extensive sketching trips each summer, often with his artist son, throughout England and especially north Wales. He died in Birmingham in 1859.

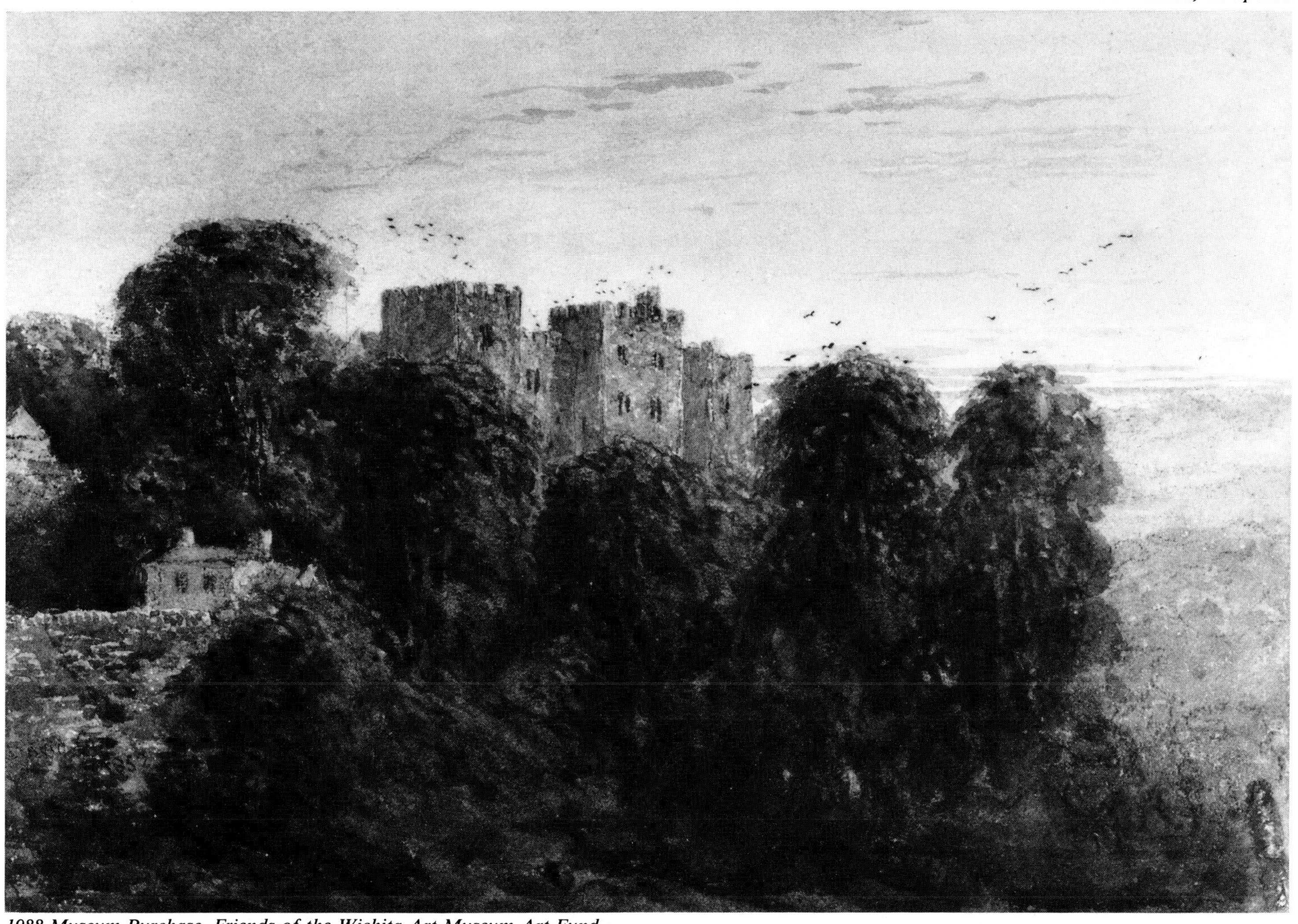

1988 Museum Purchase, Friends of the Wichita Art Museum Art Fund
(1988.7)

WILLIAM CALLOW (1812-1908)

A Market Square in a Flemish Town
Watercolor & gouache on wove paper, 1858
16¹/₈'' x 24⁷/₈''

Toward the middle of his long and highly prolific career, the noted British watercolorist William Callow executed an extensive number of large scale works which he composed for inclusion in major exhibitions where oils and watercolors were often in open competition.

This rather complex composition titled *A Market Square in a Flemish Town* was painted in 1858 by Callow following one of his many extended tours in Europe. The scene, organized somewhat in the manner of a symetrically-balanced stage set, depicts a broad picturesque open square where a typical European town market is held. Small groups of people are clustered at scattered locations throughout the site. Yet the tempo is less lively than one might expect, for the concentrated crowds that normally gather during market hours have dispersed and it would seem that the market is about to close down for the day.

As with many of Callow's fine watercolors of this period, an abundance of descriptive detail is introduced here, imparting an accurate character rendering of specific topographic features of the town as well as of the event itself including the partially enclosed stalls and the towering timbered mediaeval buildings at the left, the small stucco-surfaced houses with projecting wooden shop fronts at the right, the adjacent stone facade of a late Gothic church, and the stepped gables atop the row of narrow Flemish houses seen along the crooked and downward-sloping street in the central distance.

Callow's technique here is indeed typical of much of his work during this period, for the drawing is skillfully rendered in pencil and the forms thereafter are covered with clear transparent color washes. Throughout the composition the color tones employed are rich and warm with just an occasional dash of bright color added here and there to catch and momentarily halt eye movement and thus focus the viewer's attention on aspects of thematic detail.

William Callow was born in Greenwich near London in 1812. At an early age he left England for study in Paris where he came under the lingering influence of Richard Parkes Bonington and Thomas Shotter Boys. While still quite young, Callow was elected to membership in the Old Watercolour Society. Throughout his career, he was actively engaged as a drawing master, sometimes in France and at other times in England, always maintaining a thoroughly successful and lucrative practice. He traveled regularly and widely throughout England and in most of Western Europe and died at Great Missenden, England, in 1908 at the age of 96 years.

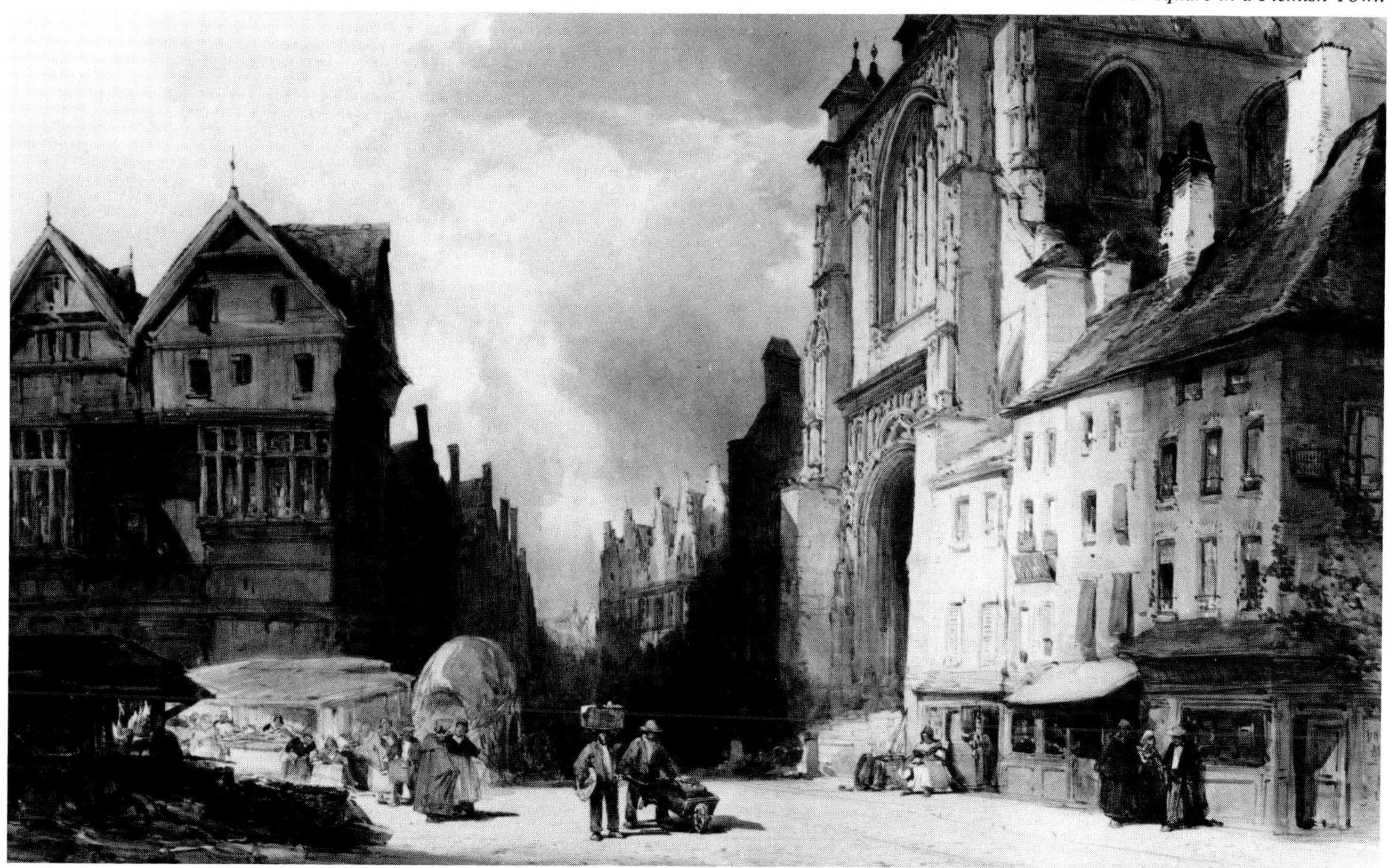

*1987 Museum Purchase, Virginia & George Ablah British Watercolor Acquisition Fund
(1987.19)*

JOHN HENRY MOLE (1814-1886)

The Beach at Hastings
Watercolor on paper, 1859
13⁷/₈'' x 21⁵/₈''

In 1859, the noted British watercolorist John Henry Mole executed this work depicting a scene on the beach at Hastings in Sussex, England. Here the treatment is quite literal with a massive rock, known as East Cliff, shown on the left overlooking a flat sandy beach that stretches into the distance toward the sea. In the foreground a fisherman is seen walking at a slight diagonal toward the viewer and carrying fishing nets over his shoulders and a boat hook pole in his right hand. At the extreme right, a second fisherman rests by the capstan. Particularly pleasing to the eye are the subdued but sensitively harmonized colors, the successfully rendered outdoor light and the convincing textural qualities of such forms as the wooden capstan, the marshy inlet at low tide, the scattered rocks along the beach and the soft golden brown sand.

Midway between the walking fisherman and the craggy cliff on the left, two barely visible figures are seated, and the contrasting scale here clearly discloses the vast spatial distance encompassed within this composition. Indeed, contrast is a key characteristic of this work — contrast between the gigantic and the tiny, between the eternal and the transient, between the brutal and the gentle. But certainly the most significant feature is the powerful opposition between the treacherously steep but awe-inspiring cliff on the one hand and the terrifying expanse of open space which stretches infinitely toward and beyond the horizon on the other. Yet, at the same time, these two opposing entities appear to unify the composition by virtue of their common characteristics of immensity and grandiosity. To the mid-Victorian mind these qualities stimulated an emotional state akin to the sublime and one which seemingly was regarded as more powerful than the beautiful itself. While this notion as employed here had considerable appeal during much of the nineteenth century, it was actually inherited from the philosophic outlook of nearly a century earlier as found in the theoretical teachings of such writers as Edmund Burke, William Gilpin and Uvedale Price.

John Henry Mole was born in Northumberland in 1814 and died in London in 1886. In 1848, he was elected to full membership in the New Watercolor Society, where he exhibited regularly. In 1884 he became vice president of the New Watercolor Society, by then known officially as the Royal Institute. His watercolors are in major museum collections throughout Britain, Europe and the United States.

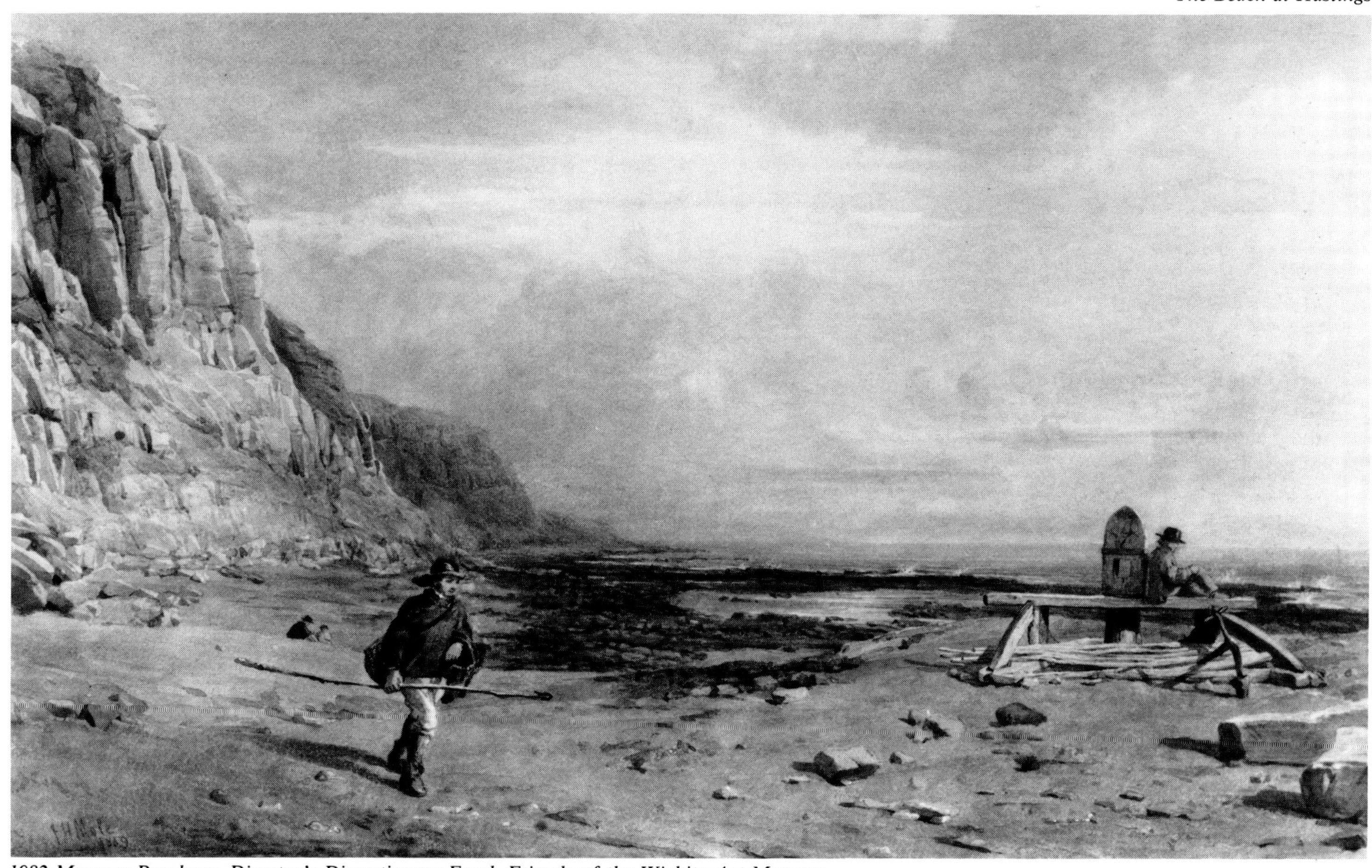

1982 Museum Purchase, Director's Discretionary Fund, Friends of the Wichita Art Museum
(1982.36)

NOTES

NOTES

NOTES